Rome versus Carthage

Rome versus Carthage

The War at Sea

Christa Steinby

Pen & Sword
MARITIME

First published in Great Britain in 2014 by
Pen & Sword Maritime
an imprint of
Pen & Sword Books Ltd
47 Church Street
Barnsley
South Yorkshire
S70 2AS

ISBN 978 1 84415 919 2

A CIP catalogue record for this book is available from the British
Library.

Typeset in Ehrhardt by
Mac Style Ltd, Bridlington, East Yorkshire
Printed and bound in the UK by CPI Group (UK) Ltd, Croydon,
CR0 4YY

Pen & Sword Books Ltd incorporates the imprints of Pen & Sword
Archaeology, Atlas, Aviation, Battleground, Discovery, Family
History, History, Maritime, Military, Naval, Politics, Railways, Select,
Transport, True Crime, and Fiction, Frontline Books, Leo Cooper,
Praetorian Press, Seaforth Publishing and Wharncliffe.

For a complete list of Pen & Sword titles please contact
PEN & SWORD BOOKS LIMITED
47 Church Street, Barnsley, South Yorkshire, S70 2AS, England
E-mail: enquiries@pen-and-sword.co.uk
Website: www.pen-and-sword.co.uk

Contents

Acknowledgements

My thanks to Pascal Arnaud, David Blackman, Paavo Castrén, William Harris, Chris Howgego, Jonathan Prag, Boris Rankov, Damian Robinson, Philip de Souza, Sebastiano Tusa and Johan Åhlfeldt for support and advice. Part of the work was conducted in the excellent research conditions provided by St Benets' Hall and the Faculty of Classics, at the University of Oxford. The writing of this book was funded by the Ella and Georg Ehrnrooth foundation and the editing process was supported by the Gerda Henkel Stiftung. I am grateful for their support. My thanks to Vincent Gabrielsen and the SAXO-institute at the University of Copenhagen.

Coins in the plate section are being printed by the permission of © Münzkabinett–Staatliche Museen zu Berlin and © The Trustees of the British Museum. My thanks to Sebastiano Tusa for the photo of the Egadi ram and the permission to use it.

My thanks to Rupert Harding and everyone at Pen and Sword. The manuscript was finished at the end of 2011; except for few exceptions no later publications have been added. Any omissions or mistakes are naturally mine.

Turku 16.7.2014
Christa Steinby

Illustrations and Maps

For a detailed view of the Ancient Mediterranean, see the digital map by © Johan Åhlfeldt http://imperium.ahlfeldt.se

Maps

Map 1. The Western Mediterranean during the Punic Wars.

Map 2. Fleets in the Second Punic War (previously published in *Ancient Society* 34 (2004) and Steinby, *The Roman Republican Navy*, *Commentationes Humanarum Litterarum* 123. Reprinted with the publishers' permission).

Plates

1. Carthaginian silver tetradrachm dated to 330–300 BC. Tanit/Horses's head. © Münzkabinett–Staatliche Museen zu Berlin, 18206042.
2. Roman *aes signatum*, or 'struck bronze' bar used in early Roman coinage. Anchor/Tripod. © Münzkabinett–Staatliche Museen zu Berlin, 18202537. Crawford, *Roman Republican Coinage* (RRC) 10,1.
3. Ram of a Roman warship (Egadi 1) This is the first of the rams discovered at the Egadi Islands. Photo Sebastiano Tusa.
4. Reproduction of Columna Rostrata C. Duilii for the victory at Mylae in 260 BC. Museo della civiltà romana, Rome. (Wikipedia Commons)
5. Roman bronze triens from 225–217 BC. Minerva/ Prow. © Münzkabinett– Staatliche Museen zu Berlin, 18200933. RRC 35,3.
6. Roman as, minted after 211 BC. Janus/Prow. © Münzkabinett–Staatliche Museen zu Berlin, 18201126. RRC 56,2.
7. Syracusan silver litra from 274–216 BC. Hiero II/Quadriga. © Münzkabinett– Staatliche Museen zu Berlin, 18203196.
8. Carthaginian Shekel from Spain, dated either to Hasdrubal's reign (228–221 BC) or generally to the period 237–209 BC. Barcid ruler/Prow. © The Trustees of the British Museum. Sylloge Nummorum Graecorum. SNGuk_0902_0091.
9. Silver denar from 125 BC. Roma/Elephants. © Münzkabinett–Staatliche Museen zu Berlin, 18201354. RRC 269,1.
10. Bronze coin minted in Etruria, 3rd centrury BC. Head of an African/ Elephant. © Münzkabinett–Staatliche Museen zu Berlin, 18220398.

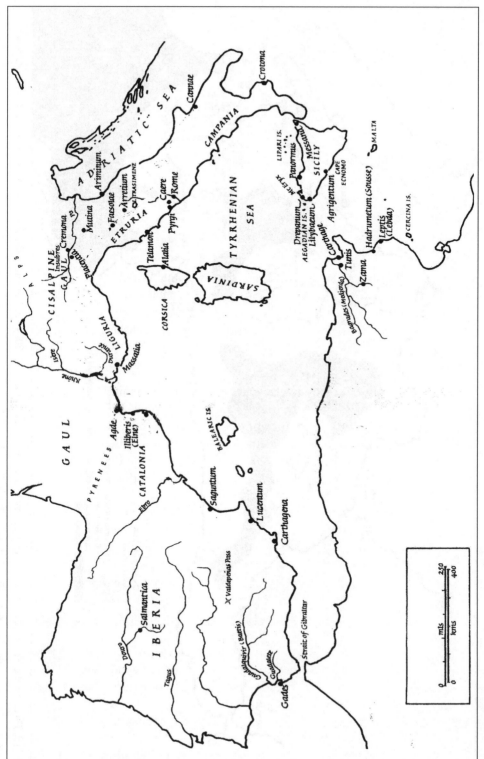

Map 1: The Western Mediterranean during the Punic Wars.

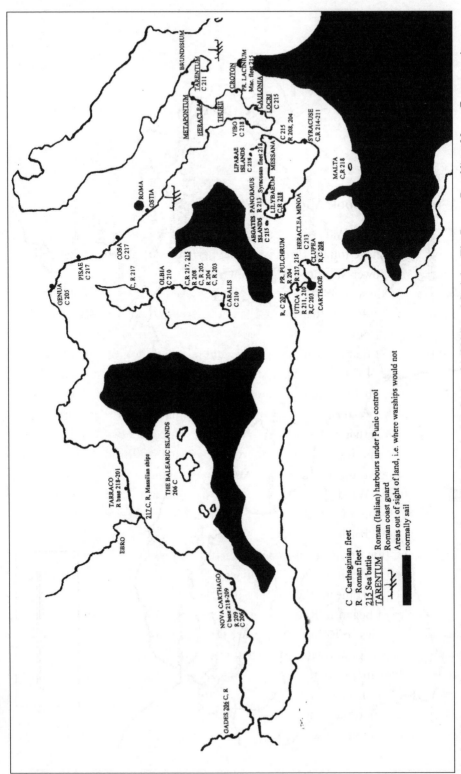

Map 2: Fleets in the Second Punic War (previously published in *Ancient Society* 34 (2004) and Steinby, *The Roman Republican Navy*, *Commentationes Humanarum Litterarum*, 123. Reprinted with the publishers' permission).

Chapter 1

Introduction

Why Another Book About the Punic Wars?

The Punic Wars are a crucial period of ancient history. Rome and Carthage fought three wars that permanently changed the balance of power in the Mediterranean. Everyone is familiar with the outcome of these wars: that Carthage was sacked at the end of the Third Punic War in 146 and that Rome became a world power with Pax Romana and Mare Nostrum.[1]

However, at that time, none of this could be taken for granted. The First Punic War (264–241) was the first armed conflict in which Rome operated outside Italy, challenging the Punic fleet for the control of Sicily and other islands in the western Mediterranean. The Romans had the initiative and forced the Carthaginians into an arms race by constantly building new fleets – a competition in which the Carthaginians could not keep up and thus had to give up Sicily. The contest for thalassocracy continued in the Second Punic War (218–201), which did develop into a serious maritime conflict and which Carthage actually lost at sea. It can be seen as the world war of its time: battles took place everywhere in the western Mediterranean, and during this war Rome also became irretrievably involved in the matters of the eastern Mediterranean. At the end of the war, Rome ruled over the western Mediterranean; the Carthaginian fleet was reduced to ten warships and a new era began in Roman–Carthaginian relations – the Carthaginians paid indemnities to Rome for the next fifty years and were also obliged to send ships and grain, thus participating in the Roman war effort against the Macedonian and Seleucid kingdoms. The Third Punic War (149–146) demonstrated the overwhelming power of the Romans and brings to an end a period in which the Romans had conquered all their enemies at sea, both in the west and in the east.

The year 146 thus marks the end of this story. It begins, however, many centuries before the Punic Wars. One of the objectives of this book is to demonstrate that it was not a case of the agrarian Rome vs. the seafaring Carthage, as has sometimes been presented, but the maritime history of both Rome and Carthage has its roots in the centuries preceding the wars, as do the causes that lead to the conflict. Rome and Carthage owe many of their characteristics to the Phoenician and Greek colonies founded from the ninth and eighth centuries onwards that brought trade, new wealth and new connections to the western Mediterranean. This is obviously the case with Carthage, which was founded by Tyrian settlers and gradually became the leading colony of the Phoenicians. Fifth-century Carthage was, alongside Syracuse and Athens, one of the largest states of its time in terms of wealth, power and maritime connections. Rome, on the other hand, was one of the cities on the Tyrrhenian coast where life was changed by the coming of the colonists – trade and interaction with the colonies made Rome an important and prosperous city. In the centuries before the Punic Wars, the Romans operated at sea as did any other nation in the Tyrrhenian. Consequently, in the Punic Wars, there were two seafaring nations competing for power over the western Mediterranean.

There is a vast amount of literature on the Punic Wars; the role of the fleets is obvious in the First Punic War through the great sea battles but the Second Punic War is usually seen as the great war on land, with Hannibal and the elephants crossing the Alps. This book concentrates on the fleets and warfare at sea and the role the fleets played in the Punic Wars and explains how land and sea warfare were interrelated, a fact that has often been underestimated.

Sources will also be discussed, including the question of why Polybius got it so wrong when he stated that the Romans were not seafarers – this has to do with the structure of his work, the integrity of his sources and also the fact that some of his ideas have been misunderstood. In previous research, the great Polybian idea that the Romans were novices has been readily accepted; it has influenced the way we see the Romans at sea in general as well as guided the way we use the sources. An image has been created whereby the Romans had not previously had a fleet, their brief interest in warfare at sea only lasted until the end of the First Punic War, and after that they, being 'landlubbers', practically discontinued the Roman navy and did not use it much in the subsequent wars against Carthage, Macedon and Syria. This idea has been used to explain every success and failure in the history of Roman republican seafaring. In this interpretation, any literary or numismatic evidence that seems to contradict the great Polybian idea has been played down. Consequently, researchers have not been able to use all the sources to the full and have treated the Roman navy as an anomaly, not seeing the great contribution it made to Roman expansion.[2]

This is quite wrong: there is other literature that gives evidence about the early Roman navy and evidence from archaeology that shows that Rome became a wealthy and important city because of its trade with the Greek and Phoenician colonies. Rome minted a substantial number of coins with naval images and built war memorials to commemorate victories at sea. Therefore, Rome was involved in seafaring and warfare at sea like any other state in the Mediterranean.

The Roman navy is nevertheless not the only one whose actions have been underestimated: the role of the Carthaginian navy in the Second Punic War needs to be given more attention, as it played a part in the total strategy directed from Carthage. This is also important from the point of view that, when we look at Rome's enemies at sea and its progress towards thalassocracy and world power in general, if anyone could have stopped Rome's success at sea it could have been the Carthaginians in the Second Punic War.

Sources

Our information is based on literary sources, inscriptions, coins and archaeological evidence. Archaeological evidence enables us to understand the development of the Greek and Phoenician colonization in the west and how Rome and Carthage developed as cities. We have information about some of the harbours the Romans and Carthaginians used. The Mediterranean is full of wrecks of cargo ships that are useful when studying ancient trade routes and the size and type of their cargo. No wrecks of ancient warships have been discovered yet, although we have interesting information on rams, including the Athlit ram discovered in Israel in 1980 and the rams found at the Egadi Islands in Sicily since 2004.[3] However, archaeology cannot be used to shed light on individual battles.

As for literary sources, our knowledge is mainly based on Polybius, Livy, Diodorus Siculus and Appian. The Greek historian Polybius (c. 200–c. 118) was closest to the events. He was one of the thousand prominent Achaeans deported to Rome after the Third Macedonian War in 167. In Rome, he established a friendship with Scipio Aemilianus, which made it possible for him to get to know Roman society and to travel extensively. Polybius was impressed by the process by which Rome conquered nearly the whole of the inhabited world as he knew it in less than fifty-three years and he explained to his readers the political institutions and the Roman character that made this possible. He thought that great lessons could be drawn from the study of history and that universal history should be preferred as it is only from that that one can make a proper notion of cause and effect and estimate the importance of events which took place contemporaneously in different parts of the Mediterranean.[4] As his sources Polybius used historians who wrote from the Roman and from the Carthaginian point of view. On the Roman side he used Quintus Fabius Pictor, Lucius Cincius Alimentus, Gaius Acilius and Aulus Postumius Albinus. On the Carthaginian side he read Philinus, Chaereas, Sosylus of Sparta and Silenus of Caleacte in Sicily – Greek-speaking writers who followed the events from the Carthaginian perspective. Only fragments of the works of these authors have survived. Polybius also questioned hundreds of eyewitnesses, used letters and published speeches and consulted official archives. He witnessed the destruction of Carthage in 146 but his account of it has been lost. Polybius' *Histories* originally comprised forty books, but only Books 1 to 5 are intact. They cover the First Punic War and the first years of the Second Punic War. The Roman historian Livy (59 BC–AD 17) wrote the history of Rome in 142 volumes. The volumes that have been preserved cover the period from early Roman history down to 293 and the period from 218 to 167; that is, to the aftermath of the Third Macedonian War. Livy based his work on literary sources. He used Valerius Antias, Quintus Claudius Quadrigarius, Gaius Licinius Macer, Quintus Aelius Tubero, Quintus Fabius Pictor, Lucius Calpurnius Piso, Lucius Coelius Antipater and Polybius. Livy is our main source for the Second Punic War. Of his accounts of the First and Third Punic Wars only short summaries exist.

Diodorus Siculus of Agyrium in Sicily (first century BC) wrote a universal history from mythological times to 60 BC, in which he discussed events in Egypt, Mesopotamia, Greece, Sicily and Rome.[5] He is an important source for the events in Sicily but his complete text comes to an end in 302 and the books in which he records the events of the Punic Wars are only preserved in fragments. He took his information from various sources, among them Philinus and Polybius. Appian (end of the first century AD–160s AD) was an Alexandrian historian who wrote Roman history covering the period from the time of kings to the emperor Trajan. As sources he used material from other authors, including Polybius. Our knowledge of the Third Punic War is mainly based on his account, for which it is likely he has used Polybius' lost narrative.

Information is also available from later sources: Velleius Paterculus (19 BC–c. AD 30), Valerius Maximus (first century AD), Florus (second century AD), Justin (second or third century AD), Eutropius (third century AD), Orosius (fourth century AD), Cassius Dio (AD 164–after 229) and Zonaras (twelfth century). These sources need to be used with great caution but they sometimes provide important details that are not recorded elsewhere. There are two limitations to the written material. First, most of the accounts were written a long time after the events, when Rome had already become a world power. Second, all of the accounts come from the Greco-Roman world; this means that we are reading the history of the winners. The Punic Wars were recognized as historic events even in their own time, yet no written history or archive has come down to us describing the conflict from the Carthaginian point of view; so, for example, we cannot fully understand the developments that led to the Second Punic War as the evidence from the Carthaginian side has been lost. As for Carthaginian society in general, we do have some genuine information; for instance, we know over 500 different men's and women's names from *stelae* and other documentary materials. Still, when it comes to our general knowledge of the city and its institutions, our information is derived from the Greek and Latin writers who were not completely familiar with life in Carthage and they may have been mistaken in their sources. In addition, they tended to use Greek or Latin concepts to describe Carthaginian institutions and society.

Inscriptions and coins give important first-hand information. These include Roman honorific and funerary inscriptions that concern action at sea in the First Punic War and coins with naval images minted by Rome and Carthage. Ship's prows are a common motif on coins and war memorials in the Hellenistic world and, in the Barcid coinage, there is a series of coins with a ship's prow. Starting from 225, the Romans minted great quantities of coins depicting a prow. However, there are also the *aes grave* coins, showing an anchor and tridents that belong to the period before the First Punic War. They cannot be dated to a particular event; they are generic images of power rather than a historical record.[6]

There is nothing comparable to the Athenian naval lists for Rome and Carthage. However, the Athenian practice of inscribing in stone a public record giving information about the annual number of ships, their rigging and what was done in terms of maintenance is exceptional in the ancient world. In Athens, as in any seafaring city, officials must have also kept a more detailed record that was updated regularly and was not written in stone. The Romans and the Carthaginians probably kept records written on perishable material such as parchment and papyrus. Their maritime system could not have worked without such record-keeping. Their fleets consisted of hundreds of ships and hundreds of thousands of people working on board as rowers and other crew members and on land building and maintaining the ships. In Rome, the census and enrolment records and copies of treaty obligations and tribute requirements were essential. Likewise, in Carthage records must have been kept, covering shipbuilding and the contracts made with mercenaries, including their pay. A few examples from the imperial period of extensive Roman military records have been preserved due to exceptional conditions: for example, the wooden Vindolanda tablets in Britain that were preserved in the anaerobic conditions in wet ground, and the *ostraka* (potsherds) used for writing found in the dry desert conditions at Mons Claudianus in Egypt. No first-hand evidence like this has yet been found for the Roman republican navy or the Carthaginian navy.[7]

As we read the ancient sources, there will be questions about ship numbers. We cannot do arithmetic with ancient figures but have to take them as they are. To mention a few examples, when Pyrrhus went from Italy to Syracuse, he took some of the ships that Agathocles, the tyrant of Syracuse, had prepared previously, and included them in his fleet. Nevertheless, we cannot say how many of the more than 200 ships that Pyrrhus used in the Sicilian operation came from his own fleet and how many from Syracuse. Likewise, if there are two sources discussing the same battle they often give different figures on how many ships each of the fleets had, and we cannot say which of the sources gives the correct figures: it would be wrong if we started correcting them. Numbers get easily corrupted in manuscripts. There are uncertainties about ship numbers in all the Punic Wars. I will return to these questions in the actual discussions of the wars.

Warships and Warfare at Sea in the Hellenistic Period

Ancient seafaring was largely dependent on weather conditions. Sailing was restricted to the annual sailing season and was only possible in good weather, and most voyages followed the coasts. This practice continued all over the world until steam engines became widely used in ships in the nineteenth century. The sailing season in the Mediterranean began in March and lasted until November; for the rest of the year the ships stayed in port unless an urgent voyage had to be made. Sailing in winter was avoided because cloud, fog and mist made navigation difficult and winter storms were dangerous. Seafarers preferred sailing close to the coast and used landmarks such as promontories and islands to locate their position. On longer voyages they would venture further out to sea but tried to ensure that the coast was always visible. They used the sun and night sky for navigation; the constellation of Ursa Minor was known in the ancient world as Stella Fenicia. The sailors were familiar with the winds and sea and land breezes and took advantage of them. Currents and tides did not generally play a significant role in Mediterranean seafaring except in narrow channels such as the Chian Strait, the Strait of Messina and the area of Syrtis Minor. Coastal routes were preferred, not only because of the protection they offered in bad weather but also because most of the ships, and especially the warships, had little room to store water and food, so easy access to the coast was essential to obtain supplies. This necessity became one of the basic elements in dictating strategy in ancient warfare at sea: warships could only operate in areas where they could reach the coast in order to take on water and food and rest their crews. As a result, the control of harbours and landing places was most important and this can be seen in the strategies adopted by Rome and Carthage during the conflicts.[8]

Warships worked in cooperation with the army, to transport troops to attack and ravage enemy territory. Raids were intended to put political, economic and psychological pressure on the enemy. The rowers had multiple tasks to perform. As well as rowing and beaching the ships, they built siege engines when needed and fought on land. Fleets were used to escort transport vessels and to support or disrupt sieges. Sea battles resulted from situations where rival powers fought for control of territory that offered safe harbours and landing places; they were most likely to occur when one side was intent on taking over an area controlled by a rival.[9] For example, in 260 in Mylae the Romans defeated the Punic fleet and then started to operate on the north coast of Sicily, and in 217 a Roman victory at the Ebro allowed Rome to extend its influence on the Spanish coast. During the Punic Wars there were many sea battles; in contrast, the First and Second Macedonian Wars saw no sea battles when the Roman navy established itself in Greece. This was because during these wars, Rome, with its allies, possessed overwhelming power at sea, which Philip of Macedon's fleet was not strong enough to challenge.[10]

The main shipbuilding materials were fir and pine.[11] The types of warships used in the Punic Wars – the trireme, quadrireme, quinquereme and six, as well as the pentecontor and other smaller vessels – were the result of centuries of development in Mediterranean shipbuilding. Advances in naval design had been made in the eastern and western Mediterranean and they were quickly adopted by other states around the coast. There were significant differences between the fleets of the various cities as each city commissioned ships according to the fighting force it needed and could afford. Cities constructed their own versions of the main types of ships – for instance, there were several different types of trireme.

The earliest evidence that has come down to us about warships is in the *Iliad*. Homer describes how the Greeks used their oared warships – longships – to transport men and their equipment to the battlefield. In this period oarsmen sat on one level and each one pulled an oar. The ships were triacontors with thirty oars and pentecontors with fifty oars. At the end of the eighth century BC, however, as naval tactics changed and ramming became more important, a two-level arrangement of the oarsmen was introduced. By using the same number of oarsmen but on two levels, one above the other, the ships could be made shorter which increased the power, speed and agility that were needed when ramming. Pentecontors were used not only for war but for commerce and piracy as well. Specially constructed harbours were not needed for the ships of this period: they used natural landing places along the coasts, where they could be pulled onto shore to dry out after a voyage.

In these archaic societies, pentecontors were not built and maintained solely by the states, as was the case later on with the more expensive triremes. Aristocrats owned ships and used them for various purposes. There was a horizontal social mobility of aristocratic families and individuals throughout the Mediterranean world. The Greek nobility used ships in war and diplomacy, to visit religious festivals and games, and they travelled abroad to keep up personal contacts with the leading families in other states. Similarly, the Carthaginians used ships to maintain contact with influential families in the Punic colonies as well as in Greek Sicily and Etruria, and the Etruscans were involved in trade and piracy. At the time, this activity was not regarded as dishonourable. Plundering was seen as one way to acquire wealth and status and so ships were used for piracy when the opportunity arose. The label 'pirate' was applied to an enemy to discredit him. Perhaps this explains why Etruscan and Tyrrhenian pirates are a common motif in Greek archaic literature and art and yet the Greeks probably behaved in a similar way at sea.[12]

The next step in ship development was the trireme, in which oarsmen were located on three levels on each side of the ship. The new design was probably introduced at Sidon and Corinth at the end of the eighth century and the first part of the seventh century BC. The trireme was clearly a more powerful weapon than its predecessor but it was expensive to build and operate so only the wealthiest states could afford them. The pentecontor required fifty oarsmen and ten to twenty additional crew members and soldiers, while a trireme required a crew of about 210. As a result, triremes were adopted slowly and at different times by Mediterranean states. So, during the Persian Wars (490–479), while the trireme was the commonest type of ship, other types were still deployed – pentecontors continued to be operated in the sixth century BC and even later. However, by the beginning of the fifth century

BC, the trireme had become the principal tool for projecting power in the eastern Mediterranean. The Carthaginians probably adopted triremes soon after they were invented[13] and the Romans introduced them to their fleet in 311, when the offices of the *duoviri navales* – naval commissioners in charge of equipping and refitting the fleet – were introduced. While the wealthier states developed ever more sophisticated ships, triremes, pentecontors and triacontors continued to serve in the navies of the smaller states; for example, pentecontors were still deployed in the third century BC and triacontors in the second century BC.

The development of new types of ship had so far been concentrated in the eastern Mediterranean. In the fourth century BC, however, the focus shifted to the west, where the introduction of the quadrireme, the quinquereme and the six took place. This was the result of naval competition between Carthage and Syracuse that, together with Athens, were the major maritime cities of their time. Pliny states that, according to Aristotle, the Carthaginians invented the quadrireme. According to Diodorus, Dionysius invented the quinquereme. He probably also built sixes.[14] These innovations in ship design and construction should be seen against the background of how the Greek colonists sought to put themselves on the map of a history shared with the old homeland. The Sicilians and especially the Syracusans sought to gain influence in the Greek world by making it clear that they were sharing the burden of fighting the barbarians. This attitude is revealed in the tendency of Greek texts to represent the battles against the barbarians in the east and west as happening in a synchronized manner: for example, Himera and Salamis in Herodotus; Pindar mentioning the battles of Salamis, Plataea and Himera as the crowing glory of the Athenians, Spartans and Syracusans respectively; and Timaeus highlighting the connection between Himera and Thermopylae. In effect, these authors were seeking to show that the west is superior to the east when it comes to fighting the barbarians.[15] In this case, the leading role in shipbuilding and innovation in ship design had shifted to Syracuse, to the new Greek world, and these new vessels were used in their campaign against the barbarians, the Carthaginians. The new types of ship were quickly adopted by the navies in the east – quadriremes were in use at Sidon in 351 BC, and the Cypriot kings who came to support Alexander after the Battle of Issus in 333 had quinqueremes. In the fleet of the city of Tyre, which Alexander besieged, there were quadriremes and quinqueremes, and Alexander's own fleet had both these types of ship. In Athens, quadriremes and quinqueremes are recorded in the naval lists starting from 330. According to Polybius, the Romans first introduced quadriremes, quinqueremes and sixes at the beginning of the First Punic War.

A quinquereme needed a crew of around 350. The aim with the new types of ship was to target the increasing problem of finding skilful oarsmen. In a trireme only one man sat to an oar, whereas in the ships of the higher denominations more than one man sat to an oar, thus only one skilled rower was needed for each oar-gang, the rest of the rowers being there for power. In a quadrireme, the oarsmen were probably located on two levels, with two men pulling each oar. In a quinquereme, the oarsmen were arranged on three levels, with the top and middle levels manned by two men pulling an oar.

All these warships were designed to operate using the same tactics as had been devised for triremes. They could be used to ram, in which case the agility and speed of the ship were important as the aim was to stop the enemy ship or to damage its oars so that it was immobilized and could easily be put out of action. Warships could also be used as platforms for hand-to-hand fighting and launching missiles, and soldiers, archers and javelin-throwers were included in the crews. Warships that were intended to be employed in this fashion required a more solid superstructure to accommodate the large number of fighting men and the hulls were modified to ensure greater stability. In consequence, such ships tended to be slow and less manoeuvrable.

Various ramming tactics were used. The *diekplous* or breakthrough was an operation in which ships were arranged in a column in front of the enemy. They then tried to break through the enemy line and, by using the ram, damage the hulls and oars of the enemy ships. The defensive tactic against a *diekplous* attack was to keep the ships close together, side by side, so that it was difficult for the attackers to find space between them. Alternatively, ships could be arranged in a two-line formation; the ships in the second line were positioned in order to stop any enemy ships that penetrated the first line. This method was used at the Battle of Ebro in 217 when the Romans, together with the Massilians, defeated a Punic fleet. Obviously, this tactic put the attackers at great risk as their ships might be rammed or lose their oars and become immobile, which would make them easy targets. In the manoeuvre known as *periplous*, attackers attempted to sail around the flank of the enemy ships so as to come at them from the rear. *Diekplous* and *periplous* tactics could only be carried out by well-trained and well-organized fleets and both types of tactic can be seen in operation in the battles of the First and Second Punic Wars.

Sails were used when possible, although rowing was considered to be faster – the average speed of a ship under oar was 7 or 8 knots. There are no surviving representations of how a trireme under sail appeared. Naval inventories, however, indicate that there were two masts on a ship. The main mast was probably located in the middle of the ship and another smaller mast at the front of the ship was probably raked and stepped forward. The sails were almost certainly rectangular. Battles always took place near a coast and, before the fighting started, all unnecessary weight, including the main mast and rigging, was removed and left on the coast so that the ships were as light and easy to manoeuvre as possible. During a battle, only oars were used. When breaking off a battle, the small sail at the front of the ship was raised on the second mast. As with battles on land, one side could refuse to engage. However, if the commanders chose to fight – or if they could not avoid it – they had to consider the speed of their fleet compared to that of the enemy and to decide whether they should adopt offensive or defensive tactics. If a slow fleet found itself in an unfavourable tactical situation, it might be forced to attack in order to avoid a certain defeat.

Several factors affected the speed of the ships. They had to be regularly hauled onto the shore or put into ship-sheds so they could dry out; if this was not done, their wooden hulls became waterlogged and they became heavy and slow. Newly-built ships were likely to be faster than the old and, of course, their speed depended on their design. The speed of the ships also depended on the strength of the oarsmen; rowing was exhausting work and rowers could be expected to do it for only a few hours a day. Sometimes actions were interrupted so that the crews could rest and the fighting then resumed the following day.

Standardized shipbuilding was used. The rival states of the Mediterranean borrowed shipbuilding designs and innovations from each other. For example, Polybius records that at the beginning of the First Punic War the Romans used as their model a Carthaginian ship that they had captured when it ran aground. The Romans were not completely unaware of how to build such a ship – Polybius exaggerates their ignorance – but they were keen to see the latest development in Carthaginian shipbuilding. The main Roman contribution to warfare at sea in this period was the *corvus*, the boarding-bridge, which they used to attack enemy ships in the First Punic War. This innovation is characteristic of the Hellenistic period in which the armies and navies knew their opponents well and were evenly matched. In these circumstances they were eager to come up with a new weapon or tactic that would give them an advantage. This kind of development is particularly visible in the armies and navies operated by the successors of Alexander the Great.

Alexander's successors competed for supremacy in the eastern Mediterranean and, in the arms race that followed, built ships of even greater denomination.[16] The names of these ships are puzzling. In the literature they are described as the 'seven', the 'eight', the 'nine' and so on – all the way up to the 'forty'. We do not know how they were constructed or how the oarsmen in them were arranged but big ships were a fleet phenomenon: they were used for ramming and needed the support of smaller vessels in the navy, which protected the larger ships. A large number of armed soldiers would have been aboard. Ships of these types were not used in the Punic Wars, except for a Carthaginian seven which had been captured from Pyrrhus.[17]

The Phoenician and Greek Colonies in the West

To understand what was at stake in the Punic Wars we need to take a look at the early history of the western Mediterranean. It begins with the Greek and Phoenician colonization and the simultaneous development in Etruria where cities grew from Villanovan settlements. Rome and Carthage emerged and gradually became the leading states of the region.

Phoenician and Greek colonization was a wide-ranging and complex process that brought about many changes in the Mediterranean[18] and I will concentrate on developments in the west. The colonization started in the ninth and eighth centuries BC and was driven by economic causes. A number of intertwined factors played a role – a hunger for land, a push to expand trade, including exports (for instance, wine and pottery) and imports (for instance, grain and metals), and a desire to develop craft industries. Strategic concerns and the pressure on resources caused by increasing populations were also significant.[19]

The Phoenicians were in the region first. Navigators from Tyre and Sidon established colonies all over in the Mediterranean. In the east, the Phoenician presence is attested in Cyprus, in the Aegean, in Rhodes and in Egypt in the Nile delta. In Spain, the process started around 800 BC, when small settlements were established from Gadir (mod. Cadiz, *gdr*, meaning wall or fortified citadel in Phoenician) all the way along the south and east coast including the Balearic island of Ibiza. The sites were located at the mouths of rivers and in places that provided good ports and agricultural land. The rivers led to the rich metal resources inland from which silver, gold, copper, tin, lead and iron were obtained. These colonies took part in the Phoenician trans-Mediterranean metal trade; they also imported materials from the eastern Mediterranean and produced products such as wine for export. They also traded with the neighbouring native societies. In Africa, several colonies were established in areas that are now parts of modern Tunisia and Algeria and on the Mediterranean and Atlantic coasts of what is now Morocco. There is evidence of a Phoenician presence from the eighth century BC in Malta. In western Sicily there were colonies at Motya founded in the eighth century BC and at Solus (Solunto) and Panormus (Palermo), both of which were founded in the seventh century BC. In Sardinia, colonies were set up at Sulcis and Tharros in the eighth century BC and at Carales, Nora and Bithia in the seventh century BC. These colonies controlled the important sailing route that ran along the Sardinian and Corsican coasts to Liguria. The colonies were more than modest trading posts; the gold and silver jewellery dated to seventh and sixth centuries BC found in Tharros is superior to that of Carthage in the same era.[20]

The most important of the Phoenician colonies was Carthage (*qart-hadasht* or 'new town' in Phoenician), founded in 814 BC by Tyre.[21] It was located on the coast of north-east Tunisia on a large peninsula that stretched eastwards from lagoons into the Gulf of Tunis. Carthage originally functioned as a trading station used by seafarers on their route from Gadir to Tyre. Timber for houses and shipbuilding was available in the forested mountains of Libya and the forests of Numidia. Yet Carthage was not a typical colony. Archaeological discoveries make it clear that while other Tyrian foundations in the west continued to operate as ports of call or trading posts, exceptional demographic, economic and urban growth took place in Carthage between the years 730 and 600. It has been estimated that Carthage in this period could shelter about 200,000 inhabitants. The city had its own dynamic and it developed features such as militarism and the 'tophet', a sacred precinct intended for human sacrifice, which cannot be found in the east. Even the early pottery of Carthage has unique features. As Aubet puts it, after the founding of the city, there must have been 'a strong determination to create a genuine "new capital" in the west'.[22]

As with the Greek colonies, which maintained close contacts with their mother-cities, the Carthaginians retained their links with Tyre. Language and religion played an important role in Carthaginian cultural identity as well as in private life. In every colony or commercial enclave a temple was built in honour of the chief divinity, Melqart (*melek-qart* or 'king of the city'). The figure of Melqart was linked with complex political and economic interests. A tenth part of the public treasury was sent as an offering every year when embassies from Carthage went to honour Melqart at Tyre – the profits from the western enterprise, as Aubet puts it. This link between Carthage and Tyre still existed in the Hellenistic period.[23]

Unlike the Romans, and like the Greeks, the Carthaginians bore only single names. The worship of the main gods of the old Phoenician divinities honoured in Tyre – namely Melqart, Baal Hammon, Astarte and Eshmoun – is visible in the make-up of many Carthaginian names. In Greek and Roman narratives the Punic names were modified, so, for example, Hamilcar is actually Abdmilqart, 'pledged to the service of Melqart' and Bomilcar is reduced from Bodmilqart, 'in Melqart's service'. Other names remained very much the same: Hannibal being 'he who enjoys Baal's favour', Hasdrubal being 'he who has Baal's help' and Mago being a shortened form of Magonbaal, 'may Baal grant', to mention just a few. Although, as already mentioned, we know of several hundred Carthaginian names, in the written historical records the leading Carthaginians only bear a narrow range of these. There are many leaders in Punic history named Hannibal, Hasdrubal or Mago but – except for the city's leader Mago in the sixth century BC and his descendants and the Barcids – it is practically impossible to tell how they were related.[24]

The Greeks were just as eager as the Phoenicians to gain access to raw materials, especially metals, and to exchange products. The location of their first colonies confirms this as they are at the focal points of the maritime routes of that period. The Greeks were obviously competing with the Phoenicians. Greek colonization began in the eighth century BC, when colonies were established in the Aegean and on the borders of the Black Sea. Around the Tyrrhenian Sea, the first Greek colony was set up at Pithecusae (Ischia) (c. 770); this was followed by Cumae (c. 740) on the coast of Campania, Zancle and Rhegium on the Strait of Messina, and Naxos on the eastern coast of Sicily. These colonies were founded by Chalcis and Eretria. From Cumae, the Euboeans could control the Bay of Naples and the sea route that led to the mouth of the Tiber, to Elba and the Bay of Populonia, while the colonies on both sides of the Strait of Messina controlled access to the eastern Tyrrhenian.[25]

In the eighth and early seventh centuries BC, other settlements were founded by Megara (Megara Hyblaea, c. 750), Corinth (Syracuse, c. 733), Achaea (Sybaris, c. 720, Croton, Metapontum), Sparta (Tarentum, c. 706), Rhodes and Crete (Gela), and Locris (Locri Epitzephyrii). Later on, new settlements were created by the original colonies: for instance, Mylae and Himera were started by Zancle, Selinus (c. 650) by Megara Hyblaea, Camarina (598) by Syracuse, Agrigentum (580) by Gela and Metauros, Medma and Hipponium were settled from Locris. In the sixth century BC a second wave of colonists moved west: the Phocaeans founded Massilia (Marseille, c. 600) and Alalia (c. 560) in Corsica. Immigrants from Cnidos and Rhodes moved into Lipara and the Samians into Dicaearchia in the Bay of Naples and Zancle-Messana.[26] These settlements had more than one purpose – for example, Pithecusae was not only a trading colony but was also involved in the processing of metals. The Euboean (mainly Chalcidian), Corinthian and Achaean colonial networks were the most important. In these networks, the various colonies had different functions; for instance, some colonies were mainly commercial or agrarian centres and others were ports or controlled maritime routes. This mixture of roles reflects the different motives that led to the founding of each colony. The area occupied by the Greeks on the southern coast of Italy and in Sicily later became known as Magna Graecia. It was not only an agricultural and manufacturing giant but also exported its products. Colonies developed at the same pace as their mother-cities, reaching the peak of the archaic civilization. Magna Graecia was the channel through which many important innovations came to Italy, including the potter's wheel, olive oil, ports, writing (Pithecusae), coinage, art and intellectual pursuits, probably also wine, large-scale cultivation and banking techniques. Rome benefited from these developments, directly or through the Etruscans.[27] The commercial and political balance of power in the archaic period was ultimately based on the supremacy of Sybaris, a sophisticated city with economic vitality and a fluid social structure, which enjoyed friendly relations with Miletus, the most advanced city in Ionia.[28]

The period between the ninth and seventh centuries BC saw a great change in Etruria as cities began to develop from Villanovan settlements. The new cities were large and impressive not only by Italian standards but also when compared with cities in the western Mediterranean world in general. They included Veii, Caere, Tarquinii, Vulci, Roselle, Vetulonia, Populonia, Volterra, Volsinii, Clusium, Perusia, Cortona, Arezzo and Fiesole. Etruria's economic prosperity was based on its mineral wealth. Ores of iron, copper, silver and lead were found, especially in the northern part of the Etrurian coast. International demand for these metals attracted entrepreneurs and their activities contributed to the complex network of exchange, which can be used to explain the large volume of foreign products that have been found in Etruria. The considerable purchasing power of the Etruscan economy from the late eighth century to the early sixth century BC can be seen from the gold, ivory and sophisticated works of craftsmanship that were imported from Greece and the Near East. During this period there was a lively traffic along the coast of Etruria and Italy in general, and merchants from Etruria, Greece and Phoenicia took part in it. The Etruscans established trading contacts as far south as the Gulf of Salerno, and their influence was felt in the plain of Campania. Etruscan goods were probably exported even more widely than this. They possibly projected their power beyond the

Tyrrhenian Sea: Etruscan artefacts, most of which date from between the late seventh and early sixth centuries BC, have been discovered on the coasts of Spain, France and Greece and at Carthage. However, it is also possible that these artefacts were moved to the places in which they have been found by a process of indirect transfer. The Etruscan thalassocracy peaked in the seventh century BC, before Greek colonization in the west was fully developed and before the network of Phoenician colonies became stronger under Carthage's leadership.[29]

National merchant fleets as we understand them in the modern world did not exist at this time. Within city-states or ethnic groups defence was organized and grain supplies were protected but otherwise little collective action was organized. Archaeological information gathered from shipwrecks and their cargo makes it clear that there was no such thing as a distinct Greek trade competing with the Etruscan trade. It is more likely that thousands of heterogeneous merchants from various cities sailed regularly back and forth along the coasts of the western Mediterranean, visiting colonial emporia and native ports, using small ships and carrying cargoes of mixed origin. Merchants took on cargo either little by little in several ports on their way or in a single consignment at ports that functioned as distribution centres for merchandise gathered from different regions. They traded goods according to demand and had to deal with a variety of local tastes, languages, cultural attitudes and social relations.[30]

Sanctuaries located outside the cities on or near the coast played a key role in the mechanism by which Greek and Phoenician goods, ideas and people came into contact with the societies in central Italy including Rome. Religious shrines in archaic Italy seem to have been open to foreigners but the purpose of these coastal sanctuaries seems to have been to attract outsiders and to encourage and supervise international trade. Many holy places had been centres of cult activity in earlier times but in the sixth century BC public communal sanctuaries started to develop and temples were constructed. Lavinium and the Forum Boarium in Rome are the most important examples in Latium. The remains of the temple found near the church of Sant' Omobono in the Forum Boarium, which date from before 550 BC, make it the earliest known example of this type of building in central Italy. Other extra-mural sanctuaries have been found in Gravisca – the port of Tarquinii – and at Pyrgi – the port of Caere – and major sanctuaries on the Tyrrhenian coast include a site at the mouth of the river Liris and sites at Antium and Ardea.[31]

Rome was, to begin with, just one of the Latin communities occupying the region from the Alban Hills to the Tiber. Latin was spoken there and the people attended the festival of Jupiter on the Alban Mountain. Despite a common ethnic and cultural background, disputes sometimes broke out between different sides of the community.

I summarize a long history that is attested in archaeology. Rome became an important city because of its location. It was situated between the Greeks and the Etruscans, the two most advanced and enterprising civilizations in Italy, and it controlled the main natural lines of communication in the region. Its position on the Tiber was ideal for monitoring the river traffic between the sea and the interior. It controlled the Via Salaria which ran along the Tiber valley and which was used to transport salt from the salt beds at the mouth of the river. It was also well placed to control the coastal route from Etruria to Campania, which crossed the Tiber at a natural ford downstream from the Tiber island. This was the site of the Forum Boarium, which was used as a cattle market, and the Portus Tiberinus, a river harbour. The arrival of the Greeks and Phoenicians and the commerce they brought with them changed life in the Tiber valley and in Rome in the same way as it had changed it across Etruria and this made Rome a prosperous city.[32]

Evidence indicating the influence of these trading contacts includes a substantial number of sherds in the style of late Greek geometric pottery of the middle and later eighth century BC that have been found at the Sant' Omobono sanctuary in Rome. Greek merchants from Pithecusae traded on the Tiber in the eighth century BC, as can be concluded from the fact that Greek potters started to make versions of Greek imports, probably in Veii or Rome. The spread of writing in Latium is first attested in the form of a graffito in a tomb at Gabii. A graffito on a Corinthian vase found at the Esquiline cemetery reveals that Greeks were living in Rome before the end of the seventh century BC. The Phoenician presence in the seventh century BC is shown by the Punic wine amphorae that can be found as grave goods in Latin cemeteries, and the Punic amphorae in Decima, Acqua Acetosa and Laurentina probably arrived through Rome. Around 600 BC, Rome became a part of the Etruscan sphere of influence and Etruscans visited the Omobono sanctuary.[33]

In the sixth century BC, the period of dynamic colonial expeditions was followed by a phase of equilibrium in Italy, especially in the Tyrrhenian region, between the Carthaginians, Etruscans and the Greeks. There was a truly international way of life in which various centres, irrespective of ethnic affiliation, reached very high levels of development. Direct contacts with the eastern Greek world, especially Ionia, increased, resulting in the infusion of eastern influences in art, religion and intellectual thought. This equilibrium was complex and unstable, however, and it gave way to a period of bloc politics in which each of these states tried to secure its own area of ascendancy.[34]

Chapter 2

Carthaginian and Roman Seafaring
Before the First Punic War

Enterprise at sea played an important role in the development of Carthage and Rome. Carthaginian–Roman relations were initially peaceful but grew increasingly strained as Rome became more powerful at sea in the fourth century BC. This rising tension is visible in changes in the wording of clauses in the four treaties negotiated before the First Punic War. The development in Magna Graecia and the struggle for dominance over Sicily between Carthage and Syracuse also need to be taken into account.

Carthage Extends its Power in the Western Mediterranean

The ties between the colony of Carthage and its mother-city of Tyre remained strong. However, Tyre's gradual decline, which ended when it fell to Nebuchadnezzar II in 573 after a thirteen-year siege, prompted Carthage to develop from a colony into a sovereign state. In the process it extended its influence across the western Mediterranean, in particular in the key areas of Spain, Sardinia and Sicily, and along the Gallic and Tyrrhenian coasts. Carthage gained hegemony over other Punic colonies because of the determination and energy of its people; it also benefited from the organizational weaknesses and division of other Punic city-states.[1]

Archaeological evidence shows increased Carthaginian influence in Ibiza from the beginning of the sixth century BC onwards.[2] However, in Spain the Phoenician colonies suffered a crisis at the same time. Several factors contributed to this setback: the siege and fall of Tyre, which had repercussions in the west; the crisis at Tartessos, north-west of Gadir, concerning mining activities; the formation of Iberian states in the hinterland of the colonies; and the fact that the growing power of Carthage caused a conflict of interests in the western Mediterranean.[3]

Carthage became involved in Sardinian affairs in the middle of the sixth century BC. The Punic colonies of Bithia, Carales, Nora, Sulcis and Tharros, which had previously been independent, were taken into the Carthaginian sphere of interest. The task of subjugating the island was not easy. During the period of Phoenician colonization, Semitic culture had affected only the coastal areas because of resistance from the indigenous communities living inland. It is not clear whether the Carthaginians fought the indigenous people as well as the Punic colonists; possibly they fought both as, at first, the colonists tried to remain independent and they may have been given support by their indigenous neighbours. By the end of the century, though, the Carthaginian takeover of Sardinia was complete. Sardinia is located 250 kilometres from Carthage; its position and the commercial possibilities it offered made it a very important asset for the Carthaginians. The island is mentioned in treaties between Rome and Carthage and restrictions were placed on Roman visits there. Sardinia remained a Carthaginian possession until 238, when the Romans conquered it in the aftermath of the First Punic War.[4]

Sicily during this period was a strategically-located rich and fertile island. The distance from Carthage to the western tip of the island is 140 kilometres, a convenient sailing distance for ancient ships, and whoever controlled it could also control the western Mediterranean. For these reasons the Carthaginians decided to take over the island. To begin with, they governed the western part through the old Punic colonies of Motya, Panormus and Solus, and this is the area referred to in the first Roman–Carthaginian treaty of 509. At that time the rest of the island was ruled by the Greeks. Between the sixth and third centuries BC there were frequent clashes between the Carthaginians and the Greeks; the leading Greek state was Syracuse. However, Rome then became involved, making an alliance with Syracuse. Rome eventually took over the whole island in 241 BC.

Competition between the Carthaginians and the Phocaeans resulted in war at sea. The Carthaginians tried to stop Massilia being transformed from a Phocaean staging post into a colony, and they lost a sea battle in front of the city in about 600 BC.[5] Another Phocaean colony was founded at Alalia on the eastern coast of Corsica in c. 560. It grew over the next twenty years, partly because, as the Persians threatened and finally took the Phocaeans' home-city in Ionia, refugees fled to the safety of the colony. The Phocaeans interfered with trade from the Etruscan cities to such an extent that the Etruscans joined forces with the Carthaginians and fought the Phocaeans in the sea battle of Alalia in c. 540. The Carthaginians and the Etruscans had sixty ships each and the Phocaeans also had sixty ships. The Phocaeans expelled the enemy fleet but Herodotus describes their success as a Cadmean victory: the Phocaeans lost forty ships and the remaining twenty were useless because their rams had been twisted. As a result, the colony was abandoned.[6] The battle was not fought over state concerns about trade but must be seen as a local conflict with very little effect on the activities of the merchants and their customers.[7] No evidence has come down to us of help being given to Alalia by Massilia or the other Phocaean colonies, evidently because the other Phocaean colonies were on good terms with the Carthaginians and Etruscans.[8] The Etruscans were probably led by Caere, one of the larger cities of southern Etruria. Since Roman interests coincided with those of Caere, it is plausible to suggest that Roman ships took part in the battle.[9]

After Alalia, the Carthaginians controlled the western Mediterranean and the Etruscans dominated the Tyrrhenian Sea. Corsica was influenced by Etruscan culture and the Carthaginians consolidated their control over southern and eastern Sardinia. The Carthaginians and Etruscans had commercial contacts and protected their mutual interests. Aristotle states that they reached 'agreements about imports and covenants as to abstaining from dishonesty and treaties of alliance for mutual defence'.[10] He does not refer to any of the cities concerned by name and we do not know the detailed contents of the treaties. However, according to Cornell, their purpose was 'to ensure rights of access to foreign trading ports and to protect the interests of merchants resident in them.'[11] They were not designed to exclude the Greeks or other traders; they were intended to set the limits to spheres of influence among partners.[12]

Archaeological discoveries confirm the Phoenician presence in Etruria; for example, the golden tablets found in one of Caere's ports, Pyrgi, are dated to c. 500 and contain a bilingual inscription in which Thefarie Velunas, the ruler of Caere, dedicated a sacred building to the Phoenician goddess Astarte as a sign of gratitude. This text indicates the wider context of Mediterranean communication and exchange as it was taking place at this time, for it was not written in Punic but rather in a Mediterranean dialect of Phoenician. As a dedication to Astarte, it can be grouped with other such dedications in the Mediterranean and the time-reckoning system used links it to Cyprus.[13] Moreover, the second port of Caere is called Punicum, making the presence of the Carthaginians clear. In Carthage itself discoveries have been made in the cemeteries that prove that imports came into the city from southern Etruria at the end of the sixth century BC.[14] While the examples given here concern Caere, it is possible that Carthage had treaties with other cities such as Populonia, Tarquinii, Vulci and Orvieto. It was no coincidence that the sanctuary of Pyrgi was built at about the same time as the first Roman–Carthaginian treaty was made.[15]

The First Roman–Carthaginian Treaty in 509 BC

Rome had, thanks to the trade with the colonies, become a large and powerful city-state by the standards of the archaic period. Both archaeological evidence and historical sources support the view that during the last decades of the sixth century BC, under Etruscan influence, Rome reached a level of development as high as that of the major centres of the south coast of Etruria.

The Forum Boarium, located beneath the Aventine, Palatine and Capitoline hills, was one of the most important coastal emporium-sanctuaries on the Tyrrhenian coast.[16] It had several advantages that made it a regular meeting place for foreign merchants, many of whom were residents – for instance, its Hellenized cults, its location outside the sacred boundary of the city and its association with the Portus Tiberinus, the river harbour. At the end of the sixth century BC Rome had a population of approximately 35,000[17], making it the largest city north of Tarentum.[18]

The treaties Carthage made with the Etruscans and the Romans gave it access to the central Italian coast. Previous agreements may have been reached between Rome and Carthage but the expulsion of Tarquinius Superbus meant the termination of previous agreements. The monarchy was replaced by the system of two annually-elected consuls. The end of the Roman monarchy was, according to Cornell, a revolution that took the form of 'an oligarchic coup against a populist tyranny'. Cultural and commercial links between Rome and Etruria continued as before.[19] The first treaty that we know of is recorded by Polybius who dated it to the first year of the republic, 509 BC, with the following text:

> The first treaty between Rome and Carthage dates from the consulship of Lucius Junius Brutus and Marcus Horatius, the first consuls after the expulsion of the kings, and the founders of the temple of Jupiter Capitolinus. This is twenty-eight years before the crossing of Xerxes to Greece. I give below as accurate a rendering as I can of this treaty, but the ancient Roman language differs so much from the modern that it can only be partially made out, and that after much application, by the most intelligent men. The treaty is more or less as follows: 'There is to be friendship between the Romans and their allies and the Carthaginians and their allies on these terms: the Romans and their allies are not to sail beyond the Fair Promontory unless forced by storm or by enemies; it is forbidden to anyone carried beyond it by force to buy or carry away anything beyond what is required for the repair of his ship or for sacrifice, and he must depart within five days. Men coming to trade may conclude no business except in the presence of a herald or town clerk, and the price of whatever is sold in the presence of such shall be secured to the vendor by the state, if the sale take place in Libya (Africa) or Sardinia. If any Roman come to the Carthaginian province in Sicily, he shall enjoy equal rights with others. The Carthaginians shall do no wrong to the peoples of Ardea, Antium, Laurentium, Circeii, Terracina, or any other city of the Latins who are subject to Rome. Touching those Latins who are not subjects, they shall keep their hands off their cities, and if they take any city shall deliver it up to the Romans undamaged. They shall build no fort in the Latin territory. If they enter the land in arms, they shall not pass a night therein.'[20]

According to Polybius, the treaty was preserved on bronze tablets in the treasury of the aediles beside the temple of Jupiter Capitolinus.[21] It is worth noting the difficulties Polybius had in reading the text. Ironically, this is the only record we have of the wording of the many treaties that Carthage presumably made with the cities in central Italy at that time, yet it was recorded by a native Greek speaker who was an outsider to both the Roman and Carthaginian cultures and who found it difficult to understand a text written in archaic Latin.

There is an extensive literature on the treaty and what it meant for Carthage and Rome respectively. Recent research generally accepts that it dates from 509 but the interpretation of it depends on how we see the positions of the two sides. Traditionally, the Carthaginian interests have been regarded as commercial and the Roman as political. Through the treaty Carthage sought to regulate its trading relations with Rome, while Rome – the new republic, with no navy and no interests at sea – received recognition of its claim to dominate Latium.[22] This is quite wrong. As Aubet puts it, the treaty in 509 sanctioned for the first time an allocation of areas of political influence in the west.[23] The treaty deals with the needs of a city-state, needs which at that time were restricted to matters such as civic security and the grain supply.

The treaty was concluded at a time when the previous equilibrium between the Carthaginians, Etruscans and Greeks had been replaced by bloc politics. The dynamics of power around the Tyrrhenian Sea were quickly changing. The Carthaginians fought hard to get Sardinia under their control. The Etruscans had made an unsuccessful attack on Cumae in 525,[24] aiming to eliminate the most northerly of the major Greek colonies on the Tyrrhenian coast so that they could continue their expansion southwards. Moreover, the destruction of Sybaris at the hands of Croton in 510 opened a new era in which Greek colonies experienced political turbulence and tyrannical regimes established themselves.[25]

The spheres of influence defined in the treaty reflect the situation at the time. The Carthaginian presence on the coast of Latium is confirmed but the Romans claimed Ardea, Antium, Laurentium, Circeii and Terracina. These cities were situated on the coast of Latium as far as 100 kilometres south of Rome and the Carthaginians were not supposed to interfere in their affairs.[26] This arrangement points to the nature of seafaring in the archaic age, when merchants acted not only as peaceful traders but as raiders and pirates when the opportunity arose.[27]

The restrictions the Carthaginians placed on where the Romans could sail were intended to protect areas that, as the archaeological evidence shows, Carthage had recently conquered. 'Fair Promontory' is the headland stretching from Carthage to the north, the modern Cape Bon, which forms the eastern side of the bay where the city is located. The Romans were not allowed to sail east of this point. Through this clause the Carthaginians presumably wanted to keep the Romans away from the Tunisian Sahel and the Emporia of Syrtis Minor so that they could safeguard their own trading links with the rich cities in the region.[28]

Despite the restrictions, Rome had access to an important market area: the city of Carthage itself and the territories west of it on the African coast, Spain, the Carthaginian part of Sicily and Sardinia. Many major ports were open to the Romans: for instance, Carales, Nora, Bithia, Sulcis and Tharros in Sardinia as well as Motya and Panormus in Punic Sicily. The treaty also takes into account the practical difficulties faced by seafarers, allowing them into the prohibited area if they were blown off course or if they needed to repair ships that were damaged.

We do not know to what extent the Romans took advantage of their access to this large market – no archaeological evidence of their exports is available from this time. However, we can say that Roman merchants, as any other merchants, using mixed crews, transported a variety of cargoes from port to port. In response to orders from the Roman senate, frequent shipments of grain to Rome are likely to have been made to compensate for the grain shortages experienced by the Romans between 508 and 384.

The Realignment of Power in the Tyrrhenian Sea

The following century and a half leading up to the second Roman–Carthaginian treaty in 348 BC saw great changes in the patterns of trade and sea power in the western Mediterranean. Carthaginian, Etruscan, Syracusan, Athenian and Roman shipping was involved in a wide range of enterprises.

A general economic decline took place between the late sixth century and the first decades of the fourth century BC. This downturn is visible in the quality and quantity of archaeological evidence – for instance, in finds from tombs in Etruria, Latium and the cities of Magna Graecia and Carthage. However, Sicily during this period seems to have done rather better. The reasons for the decline are complex and intertwined. Political instability in many of the Etruscan and Greek cities was one cause and changes in the balance of trade were another. The Greek-Tyrrhenian communities had formed a highly sophisticated consumer society, which now experienced great changes. The Etruscans' wealth and trade had been based on the extraction of metals but now, as the Phocaeans opened mines in Spain and the Athenians in Laurion in 483 BC, they lost their monopoly position. As a result, trading routes around the Tyrrhenian coast and the Strait of Messina were not as well used as before and the intermediate ports suffered. Yet, while some communities lost out, others profited from the changing situation. The seafaring cities of Etruria such as Caere and Vulci diminished in importance, while cities in northern Etruria benefited, as did the Etruscan centres in the Po valley and the Adriatic. Likewise, Cumae in Campania flourished and so did Posidonia and Velia. Sicily became the leader of the Hellenic colonies, with Syracuse as its most important state. In Rome, however, no new temples were dedicated between 484 and 433 and archaeologists have found less imported pottery dating from this period. One explanation for this is that Rome was involved at the time in wars against the Volsci and the Aequi and failed to capture sufficient war booty to finance the building of temples.[29]

Rome frequently suffered from grain shortages caused by wars, epidemics wiping out the workforce and climatic irregularities, and the Roman consuls had to import supplies from Campania, Etruria and Sicily. Such shortages were a common phenomenon throughout the Mediterranean. Attica, for example, always produced less grain than was required to feed the residents of Athens and the Athenians had to acquire additional supplies using a mixture of diplomacy, incentives, regulation and force. This meant maintaining trade networks, creating suitable conditions for merchants to do their business in Athens in general in order to make them willing to serve Athens with grain transports and protecting merchant shipping. Shipments were threatened by piracy and official acts of the enemy – though there was a thin line between these. Athenian warships were dispatched to rescue fleets of merchant ships carrying grain that were destined for the city. Food shortages are recorded in 386, 357 and 355 in Athens and again in the period from 338 to 322. Grain had to be shipped from the Black Sea area, especially around the Bosporus, and from Sicily and Egypt.[30] An inscription found in Cyrene dated to c. 330–326 shows that Cyrene on the coast of modern Libya provided grain to forty-one states in the Greek world.[31]

Stories of Roman grain imports between 508 and 384 can be regarded as reliable[32] and the information that has come down to us about how Roman requests for grain were met reflects the changing political situation in the Tyrrhenian. In 508, the senate purchased grain from the Volsci and Cumae.[33] Although Cumae was opposed to Etruscan expansion, it allowed the Romans to sail in to buy supplies. In 496 there was another shortage in Rome and consequently a temple was promised to Ceres, Liber and Libera and built in 493.[34] The main centres for the worship of Ceres were Cumae and Sicily and the establishment of this cult in Rome indicates the existence of not only cultural but also commercial relations with the Greek world of Italy and Sicily.[35] In 492, the consuls sent agents to buy grain from Etruria, Cumae and Sicily.[36] This is the first time Sicily is mentioned as a source of food for Rome. In the following centuries it is frequently named as a source but we do not know from which part of the island the grain was imported. The Romans had the treaty with Carthaginians, which may have facilitated the supply of grain from their part of the island; on the other hand, it is also possible that the supply of grain from Sicily was arranged by Gelon, the tyrant of Gela, who wanted to establish relations with Rome since the Romans could play a role in limiting the Etruscan hegemony of the Tyrrhenian.[37] The most fertile grain-producing areas of Sicily were in the east and in 486 grain was again imported from the island.[38]

In 477, during the First Veientine War (483–474), the Romans imported grain from Campania.[39] In 456 there was yet another case of famine in Rome and again in 453.[40] In 440 the Romans sent legates to neighbouring states *terra marique*, by land and sea, to obtain grain, and imports were made from Etruria.[41] In 433 grain was imported from the Etruscan coast, Cumae and Sicily,[42] and in 411 imports were made from Etruria and, again, from Sicily. Livy states that the Romans did not receive grain from the Samnites who ruled in Cumae, whereas the tyrant of Sicily gave them assistance.[43] The Samnites had taken over in Cumae in 421. The Etruscans did not want to lose the Roman market to Sicily and were keen to take advantage of the hostility between Rome and the Samnites. Dionysius I actually came to power in Syracuse in 407; anyway, it is plausible that Syracuse wanted to maintain friendly relations with Rome which would help Syracuse to resist pressure from both Athens and Carthage.[44] Other grain shortages in Rome followed in 399, 392, 390 and 384 but there is no information about the sources of the supplies that were imported.[45]

The balance of power at sea changed. The decline of the Etruscans opened new opportunities for the Carthaginians and, at first, they were able to extend their influence. The Greeks, however, confronted them; in 490 the Massilians, with help from Heracleides of Mylasa, defeated the Carthaginian fleet at Cape Artemision on the Spanish coast.[46] In 480, the combined armies and fleets of Theron of Agrigentum and Gelon of Syracuse defeated the Carthaginian army and navy at Himera in Sicily. The Carthaginian ships were destroyed in the camp at Himera, so no sea battle took place.[47]

After Himera, Syracuse became the leading Greek city in Sicily and Greek–Punic antagonism was replaced by rivalry between Syracuse and Agrigentum. The Carthaginians looked for other ways to expand and in Africa they occupied areas of northern and central Tunisia. Punic agronomy was renowned for its tree crops and wines, and its influence spread through the translation into Greek and Latin of Mago's now-lost book on agriculture. The Carthaginians exported agricultural products, carpets, rugs, hides, tapestry, purple dyes, jewellery, pottery, lamps and timber. They had paid a yearly fee to their Libyan neighbours for the site of Carthage and probably also for the territory outside but the payments ceased after 480.[48]

The Punic Sicily flourished but Carthage, after the thorough defeat that involved both its army and ships, was very much absent from the events of the island until the end of the fifth century BC. Consequently, Syracuse was able to extend its influence across the Tyrrhenian Sea and it was involved in inflicting the final defeat on Etruscan sea power at Cumae in 474. The Etruscans had probably attacked Cumae several times since 525. In 474, Syracuse sent at request of Cumae a fleet of triremes which together with the Cumaean fleet fought and defeated the Etruscans.[49] After the battle the Syracusan fleet took control of the southern Tyrrhenian Sea and, using Pithecusae in the Bay of Naples as a base, dominated the coast of Campania. Diodorus narrates that in 454–453 admiral Phayllus sailed to Elba and ravaged it but then took bribes from the Etruscans and sailed back to Sicily without having accomplished anything worth mentioning. The Syracusans exiled him and then sent Apelles north with a fleet of sixty triremes. He overran the coast of Etruria, sacked many places in Corsica, subdued Elba and returned to Syracuse with captives and spoil.[50]

The third big sea power in the Mediterranean during this period was Athens, which, like Syracuse and Carthage, was wealthy and had a strong maritime tradition.[51] After the Persian Wars, Athens turned its attention to the west, making connections with those centres that opposed Syracusan supremacy or had stayed on the margins of it. Among these were the Etruscans, the Latins and Apulians, Rhegium, Locri and probably also Carthage. The Roman embassy to Athens in 454 must be seen in this context.[52] Athens established a protectorate over Naples in 453, taking the naval base on Pithecusae under its control. In 427–425 three unsuccessful Athenian naval expeditions were mounted against Syracuse. The famous Sicilian campaign by Alcibiades of 415–413 also came to nothing, the Athenians abandoning most of their ships in the Syracusan harbour as they fled inland. This episode strengthened Syracusan power and enhanced its grip over mainland Italy.[53]

The Liparians, in particular, were put under great pressure by several rivals. Before the Battle of Cumae in 474, five Liparian triremes defeated a force of twenty Etruscan triremes, and in 427 the Athenians made an unsuccessful attempt to conquer the island. Then, in 396, the Carthaginians seized the island and exacted money from the inhabitants.[54]

The conquest of Veii in 396 made Rome the ruler of the Tiber valley. Veii was a match for Rome – a well-developed city with its prosperity based on trade and in command of a territory as large and fertile as that of Rome. The conflict had arisen from competition for control of the traffic in the Tiber valley. In military operations against Veii, Roman ships participated in the siege of Fidenae in 426. The city was sacked and the Roman dictator was awarded a triumph. Livy makes it clear that the cavalry won the victory for the Romans. He also refers to a battle in which Roman and Veientine ships clashed.[55] This was not a full-scale sea battle; ships were probably used to transport troops and booty. Fidenae was situated by the Tiber, only 9 kilometres north from Rome, and the river was the most direct route between the two cities – the Romans challenged the Veientine fleet.[56] Consequently, in 380–350 the Romans built a strongly-fortified colony at Ostia to protect the river traffic to and from Rome along the valley.[57]

During the Third Veientine War, Roman representatives made two trips to Delphi. In 398 they sent legates to ask for the oracle's advice and in 394, after having defeated Veii, they sent another embassy to donate a golden bowl to Apollo. The Roman legates travelled in a single warship and were stopped near the coast of Sicily by the Liparians. The Liparians let them continue their journey after hearing who they were and where they were sailing and some Liparian ships escorted them to Delphi, where the golden bowl was placed in the treasury of Massilia and Rome.[58]

Rome's relations with Massilia went back to the time when Massilia was founded and Rome made a formal alliance with it in 389.[59] The gesture of sending the bowl was probably taken on the initiative of Marcus Furius Camillus, who had contacts with Caere; this is likely to have been one of the political and religious innovations that he introduced.[60] In 399 the ceremony of lectisternium – a propitiatory banquet offered to gods and goddesses – had been introduced in Rome, in which Apollo, Latona, Hercules, Diana, Mercury and Neptune were honoured, the last two being the gods of trade and the sea.[61] The fact that the Romans sent a single ship to Delphi does not reveal anything about the total size of the Roman navy.[62] The Romans probably saw the voyage as a sacred embassy, *theoria*, for which a single vessel would be sufficient. Athens and other cities regularly sent sacred embassies, *theoriai*, to attend the great Panhellenic festivals overseas. Athens sent *theoriai* to Delos, Delphi, Isthmia, Olympia, Nemea, Sounion and to the sanctuary of Zeus Ammon. The sites of these festivals were accessible by ship. The crews consisted of religious officials as well as naval officers.[63] The cooperation of the Liparians meant that Rome could take advantage of a new friendly harbour in the south, close to Sicily.

Carthage became active in Sicily again at the end of the fifth century BC when hostilities with Syracuse resumed. In 409 Hannibal destroyed Selinus and took Himera. The Carthaginians also took Agrigentum and Gela.[64] In 405 Dionysius I of Syracuse made a treaty with them. According to Diodorus, the terms were as follows:

> To the Carthaginians shall belong, together with their original colonists, the Elymi and Sicani; the inhabitants of Selinus, Acragas Agrigentum, and Himera as well as those of Gela and Camarina may

dwell in their cities, which shall be unfortified, but shall pay tribute to the Carthaginians; the inhabitants of Leontini and Messana and the Siceli shall all live under laws of their own making, and the Syracusans shall be subject to Dionysius; and whatever captives and ships are held shall be returned to those who lost them.[65]

In 397, however, Dionysius took and destroyed Motya on the west coast of Sicily and in 396 the Carthaginians took Messana at the north-east corner of the island and destroyed it. Dionysius rebuilt the city in the following year. The unsuccessful Carthaginian campaign against Dionysius led to problems at home: the Libyans, joined by slaves, started one of the greatest rebellions in Carthaginian history.[66]

A Syracusan fleet of thirty warships seized ten Rhegian warships near the Lipari Islands in 389.[67] In 384 Syracuse sacked Pyrgi and attacked Corsica.[68] There is a brief reference in Diodorus' text indicating that the Romans sent 500 colonists to Sardinia in 386.[69] We cannot be sure about the exact dates and order of the events but the Romans might have tried to take advantage of this time of unrest to found a colony on the island. If the initiative had succeeded, they would have controlled the sailing route that ran along the Sardinian and Corsican coasts to Liguria. During this period the Romans were active on many fronts: they attacked Privernum in 357, the Aurunci in 345 and captured Sora in the same year.[70] They defeated Caere in 353 and Tarquinii in 351 and made a treaty with the Samnites in 354.[71]

We do not know if the Carthaginians took military action to defend their interests in Sardinia and Corsica and it was difficult for them to restore their position around the Tyrrhenian Sea. In their absence, Syracuse had put an end to Etruscan ambitions at sea and had attacked targets in Etruria and Corsica. It also attacked the west coast of Sicily, which had been safely under Carthaginian control. At the same time, the Romans had taken the place of the Etruscans at sea and had expanded their territory in Italy.

The Carthaginians sent an envoy to Rome seeking friendship and an alliance in 348.[72] Again, Polybius is our only source for the contents of the treaty:

> The Romans shall not maraud or trade or found a city on the farther side of Fair Promontury, Mastia and Tarseum … No Roman shall trade or found a city in Sardinia and Libya nor remain in a Sardinian or Libyan post longer than is required for taking in provisions or repairing his ship. If he be driven there by stress of weather, he shall depart within five days. In the Carthaginian province of Sicily and at Carthage, he may do and sell anything that is permitted to a citizen. A Carthaginian in Rome may do likewise.[73]

These clauses reflect the new era in Carthaginian control of overseas areas that had started in about 400. Trade along the North African coast, in southern Spain and Sardinia became a Carthaginian monopoly, while the older system continued to apply at Carthage and in Sicily, where foreign merchants could trade under supervision.[74] The ban on Rome founding cities in Sardinia and Africa must be seen in the light of its colonizing activities.[75] As to Mastia and Tarseum, there are opinions seeing these as two separate places; on the other hand, there are views that Polybius may have misunderstood an archaic genitive plural 'Mastian Tarseiom' which means Mastia of the Tartessians, which is probably the site where New Carthage was later founded in Spain.[76] Thus, the Romans were excluded from the area south of this point. This clause shows the Carthaginians' interest in southern Spain, which was especially important to them because of its Phoenician colonies, abundance of precious metals, fertile soil and plentiful supply of mercenaries. Carthage now had to defend its interests, not only against Syracuse but also against Rome.

The Romans Take the Italian Seaboard

As the Roman conquest of Italy progressed, wars became profitable enterprises that brought new land and wealth to the state and the soldiers involved. The Romans operated with a citizen army to which their allies contributed. Military pay was introduced in 406 and, from 394, the Romans imposed indemnities on their defeated enemies, often demanding clothing and food for their soldiers. Conquered communities were tied to Rome through bilateral treaties which defined their rights and obligations to the

Roman state. While the terms of these treaties varied, all of them stipulated that military aid should be given to Rome if requested. This requirement had an impact on cities inland and those on the coasts. The allies supplied heavy infantry and cavalry and also ships and crew. Thus, as the Romans conquered their enemies, they enhanced their own military strength; every war made them more powerful, increasing the amount of soldiers and ships in their use.

The societies with which Rome competed, including their first opponents the Latins and the Etruscans, were militaristic and aggressive. As diplomacy was primitive and there was no mechanism for the regular exchange of information between states to avoid possible disputes, crises were solved by making demands in public, often in situations in which disagreements had developed into a state of conflict. Therefore, there was nothing exceptional about Roman militarism – the Romans acted just as harshly as other states. Every state sought to expand its power, influence and resources and to limit those of others. However, the Romans were exceptional in that they managed to win even though they were fighting on several fronts, thanks to their superior military manpower.[77]

During the ninety years before the First Punic War Roman naval operations rapidly increased. The navy participated in Roman expansion in Italy, not only in support of the army but also functioning independently in a manner appropriate to a sea power. The coast under Roman control became the target of seaborne attacks and the Roman fleet was used to transport troops and raid enemy territories. In 348 (or 345–344) Rome's immediate coastline was targeted. Livy states:

> The sea was infested by fleets of Greeks, and so was the seaboard of Antium, the Laurentine district, and the mouth of the Tiber ... The campaign there seemed likely to be long drawn-out, for the Greeks were poltroons and refused to risk an engagement ... With the Greeks, [the consul] Camillus fought no memorable action; they were no warriors on land, nor were the Romans on the sea. In the end, being kept off shore, and their water giving out, as well as other necessaries, they abandoned Italy.[78]

The colony at Ostia probably played a role in defending the mouth of the Tiber, though we do not have information confirming this. Livy assumes that the hostile fleet was sent by the Syracusan tyrants,[79] and it has been suggested that Roman territory was the target because Rome had formed an alliance with Caere which was opposed to Syracuse.[80] However, by this time Etruscan naval power was very much diminished and Rome was now a force to be reckoned with on its own. Possibly the fleet came from Syracuse but it could also have been sent by Rhegium or Tarentum to warn the Romans that they should not expand southwards into the Greek sphere of interest.

Livy's comment that the Greeks were 'no warriors on land, nor were the Romans on the sea' has been used as a general justification for arguing that the Romans had no navy and that they were helpless at sea.[81] This is quite wrong. They sent troops to keep intruders away from their coast. A hostile fleet could not stay for long by a coast where it had no access to water and food. For example, Livy notes that in 302: 'a Greek fleet under the command of Cleonymus the Spartan arrived off the Italian coast and captured the city of Thuriae in the territory of the Sallentini. The consul Aemilius was dispatched against the Greeks, routed them in a single battle, and forced them back to their ships.'[82] Later on, Cleonymus landed in the territory of the Veneti in the Adriatic. The Patavini and the Veneti defeated his troops on land and then the Veneti attacked his ships. Cleonymus escaped with barely a fifth of his ships undamaged and, as Livy puts it, he failed in his attempts to take control of any part of the Adriatic coast.[83]

Victories over enemy armies and fleets were celebrated in a conspicuous manner all over the Mediterranean. Captured ships were evaluated: the victor kept the best ships, used those parts of the damaged ships that were serviceable and burned the rest. The beaks, the *rostra* of the captured ships, were the trophies that were put on display. The Romans mounted a display of this kind in 338 when they defeated the Latin–Volscian–Campanian coalition and built the *Rostra* in Rome to celebrate their victory over Antium. The consul Lucius Furius Camillus celebrated a triumph for victory over Pedum and Tibur and Gaius Maenius a triumph for victory over Antium, Lanuvium and Velitrae.[84] Livy states:

Some of the Antiate ships were laid up in the Roman dockyards [*navalia*], and some were burnt and a motion passed to employ their beaks for the adornment of a platform erected in the Forum. This place was given the name of *Rostra* ... Their warships were taken from them and they were forbidden the sea; they were granted citizenship.[85]

Triumphal processions started outside the sacred boundary of the city (*pomerium*) at Campus Martius where the returning commander and his troops waited for the senate's decision. The procession proceeded along the Forum Holitorium and the Forum Boarium, then through Circus Maximus, around the Palatine and then towards the Forum. It stopped at the crossroads of Sacra Via and Clivus Capitolinus, where the triumphator dismounted and ascended to the Jupiter temple. Inside, he performed the ritual act that completed the cycle of war. The setting of the beaks in the *Rostra* is the first known example we have of the dedication of spoils in Rome.

The memory of the Roman victory was also preserved in the *Columna Maenia*, located close to the Comitium, with an equestrian statue.[86] Anyone visiting Rome would get the message. The process of selecting the best ships of the enemy fleet and burning the rest was often repeated in later wars fought by Rome, including the Punic Wars.

Rome had now established its hegemony in central Italy; in combination with its allies, it was the strongest military power in the region.[87] We have no details of how Antium was taken but it is plausible that ships were used to transport troops and take home booty, to ravage enemy territory and perhaps besiege the port. It is also likely that the Romans confronted the Antiate navy, since one of the reasons for occupying Antium was to stop piracy. The Romans were not alone in their efforts to combat piracy. For example, Apulian pirates operated in the Adriatic and so Dionysius II of Syracuse established two cities in Apulia to act as safe havens for merchant ships. Dionysius' loss of power and the erosion of Syracuse's empire in south Italian waters by 344 created more opportunities for pirates based in Italy.[88] In 325/4 the Athenians founded a colony on the Adriatic coast partly to fight piracy.[89]

In 310 the Romans sent their fleet against Nuceria – at that time the strongest city in Campania – where the Samnites had installed themselves.

Livy states, 'a Roman fleet, commanded by Publius Cornelius, whom the senate had placed in charge of the coast, sailed for Campania and put out into Pompeii. From there the sailors and rowers set out to pillage the territory of Nuceria.'[90] The Romans went even further away to get more booty but, on the way back, they were attacked by the local people, who took away the plunder, killed some of them and drove the survivors back to their ships.[91] So started a campaign in which the Roman army captured Nuceria in 308 and took control of all the cities that had been dependent on it.[92]

Naples and Tarentum were in a class of their own and held positions comparable to those of the greatest independent political entities in the fourth-century Mediterranean.[93] Rome's alliance with Naples in 326 was its first success in the Second Samnite War (326–304),[94] and Naples was the first of the Greek communities to make such a treaty. It became a *socius navalis* – a supplier of ships, equipment and crew for the Roman navy – and the naval bases of Capreae and Pithecusae were incorporated into the Roman naval system.[95] Thus the alliance significantly augmented Roman naval strength. Naples had been one of the main naval powers to the north of Sicily at the time of Dionysius II of Syracuse (367–357), and both Syracuse and Athens had previously used the base on Pithecusae for naval operations. Now the Romans were free to use all these facilities.

Livy does not specifically mention the involvement of the Roman fleet but the circumstances indicate that it was there. The sources refer to the Neapolitan navy and to the promise given by Tarentum to send ships and troops to help to defend Naples against the Romans. While the Romans were besieging Naples, Nymphius, one of the leaders of the city, tried to convince the Samnite commander to take a fleet and sail past the Roman forces to the Roman seaboard, where he could ravage not only the coastal region but the vicinity of the city itself. In order to slip out without being noticed, the fleet would have had to sail at night and all the ships would have had to be launched at the same time.[96] This plan is comparable to the one used by the Carthaginians during the Roman siege of Lilybaeum in the First Punic War, when they succeeded in getting in and out of the city during the night.

In 313 the Romans planted colonies at Suessa on the Italian mainland and on the Pontiae Islands, where they acquired an additional base for their navy, but again, Livy does not mention the involvement of the fleet.[97]

It is likely that the Romans introduced the triremes into their navy in 311, at the same time as they created posts for two new officials, the *duoviri navales*. Livy writes, 'the people should likewise elect two naval commissioners to have charge of equipping and refitting the fleet.'[98] This is the only job description we have for these posts. Previously the Roman navy had probably used pentecontors, which were relatively cheap to construct and easy to operate compared to triremes. A fleet of triremes was expensive to build and maintain and needed state funding and organization. It required access to abundant sources of supplies, especially timber, permanent harbour and dockyard facilities with equipment, stock and personnel. An effective administration was important, in particular for the quick recruitment of skilled crews because triremes needed four times the number of men that were required for pentecontors. A steady stream of revenue was essential.[99] The *duoviri* had to supervise the whole system and they had to make sure that the transformation of the fleet was successfully carried out.[100]

The introduction of triremes in 311 was financed by the economic growth which Rome achieved in the second half of the fourth century BC. Archaeological evidence, especially from pottery, shows that Rome was an important manufacturing and trading centre in the years before and after 300. Morel speaks of a 'trade triangle' formed by Rome, Carthage and Massilia. The new wealth is visible in projects such as the building of the Via Appia between Rome and Campania and the Aqua Appia, the first Roman aqueduct – both started in 312. River routes along the Tiber, Anio, Arno and Po remained important for transport.[101]

There is no clear information about where the Romans obtained the timber for their ships. Timber was available in Latium, Etruria and Umbria and could be taken to Rome using the tributaries of the Tiber or Anio, as we assume that the dockyards were located somewhere in the area of the Campus Martius. There is a short passage in Theophrastus in which he discusses localities in which the best timber grows:

But largest of all, they say, are the trees of Corsica; for whereas silver-fir and fir grow in Latium to a very great size, and are taller and finer than the silver-firs and firs of South Italy, these are said to be nothing to the trees in Corsica. For it is told how the Romans once made an expedition to that island with twenty-five ships, wishing to found a city there; and so great was the size of the trees that, as they sailed into certain bays and creeks, they got into difficulties through breaking their masts ... wherefore the Romans gave up the idea of founding their city: however, some of them made an excursion into the island and cleared away a large quantity of trees from a small area, enough to make a raft with fifty sails; but this broke up in the open sea.[102]

There is no date to this text but the idea of fourth-century BC colonization on Sardinia and Corsica is plausible.[103] It probably took place after 348, because Corsica was not mentioned in the second treaty, which closed Sardinia to the Romans. We do not know what became of these two colonies in Sardinia and Corsica and, interestingly, the Roman writers are silent about them. The significance of these attempts is reflected, however, by the fact that Theophrastus, an author from the east, knew about the Roman expedition.

The Year 306 BC: An Important Year in International Politics

The Carthaginians continued to expand their territory in Africa. By 300, it rivalled the sum of the territory of Rome and all its allies combined. It included the rich agricultural land in the Medjerda valley, stretching for over 160 kilometres south-west of Carthage. The Carthaginians set up a system of garrison settlements that reached as far as 195 kilometres west and south-west of Carthage – using them, as Eckstein points out, as instruments of state power in very much the same way as the Romans and the Tarentines used their military colonies. They also collected annual tribute from Phoenician city-states in Libya, 400 kilometres to the east.[104]

Confrontations between Carthage and Syracuse continued. Agathocles had become tyrant of Syracuse in 316/15. His policy of extending Syracusan rule over other parts of Sicily met bitter opposition; consequently, exiles from Syracuse and other cities became the driving force in Sicilian history in 316/15–306, provoking both the Greek cities and the Carthaginians to take action against Agathocles and also fighting him themselves. In the subsequent war, Agathocles violated previous treaties and took many cities that had belonged to the Carthaginian *epikrateia* [domain]. The Carthaginians besieged the city of Syracuse, using their forces in a combined operation from land and sea. Then, in 310, Agathocles invaded the Carthaginian territory in Africa, the first time a European army had operated in North Africa. Eventually, however, the Syracusans were defeated on land and Agathocles fled secretly, leaving most of his troops. Ships were used to transport troops, grain and booty, and there were a few sea battles involving twenty to thirty ships on both sides. The Carthaginians generally controlled the sea but the situation changed when Agathocles broke the Carthaginian blockade of Syracuse, which they maintained with thirty triremes. Agathocles deployed a fleet of seventeen Syracusan ships and eighteen Etruscan ships and they defeated the Carthaginian fleet in front of the port. As Diodorus puts it, 'he [Agathocles] ruled the sea and gave security to his merchants.'[105] Storms damaged both sides: the Carthaginians lost a fleet that was on its way from Carthage to Sicily; some Syracusan cargo boats, which were filled with booty and were sailing from Africa to Syracuse, were driven so far off course that they ended up at the Pithecusae Islands, which were by then under Roman control.[106] The war ended with a treaty made on Agathocles' initiative in 306. The *status quo ante* was restored – Agathocles evacuated the towns he had taken in the Carthaginian *epikrateia* and the Carthaginians gave him 200,000 bushels of grain and gold worth 300 Greek silver talents.[107]

The third Roman–Carthaginian treaty, the so-called Philinus treaty, has caused much controversy. Ambassadors from Carthage came to Rome in 306 to arrange the treaty; it was renewed for the third time.[108] Our knowledge of the contents is again based on Polybius, who – unnecessarily in my opinion – denies its existence but refers to Philinus' description. Polybius writes:

The treaties being such, and preserved as they are on bronze tablets beside the temple of Jupiter Capitolinus in the treasury of the Aediles, who can fail to be surprised at Philinus the historian, not indeed for his ignorance of them, for that is by no means surprising, since still in my time, the most aged among the Romans and Carthaginians and those best versed in public affairs were ignorant of them; but how did he venture and on what authority to state just the opposite, to wit that there was a treaty between Rome and Carthage by which the Romans were obliged to keep away from the whole of Sicily and the

Carthaginians from the whole of Italy, and that the Romans broke the treaty and their oath by their first crossing to Sicily? There is as a fact, no such document at all, nor ever was there; yet in his second book he states thus in so many words.[109]

How we understand this treaty depends on how we see Rome's politics and position in general. Mitchell states that the Carthaginians were concerned with Roman expansion and did not want another power contesting control of Sicily. Carthage had two things to fear: first, that Rome and Agathocles could form an alliance and compromise Carthage's position and second, that there could be a war between Rome and Agathocles, in which case Rome might expand the conflict to Sicily. According to Meister, the treaty proves that Rome was at this point 'a significant factor in the power equation and was recognized as such by Carthage'. Russo and Harris also take the treaty as genuine, as does Thiel.[110] Walbank, on the other hand, does not believe the treaty is genuine since it would be impossible for the Romans at so early a date to claim Italy as their sphere of influence, with Tarentum untouched and the Samnites not yet finally defeated, and certainly it was not necessary at this stage to warn them off Sicily. Polybius could not find such a treaty in the archives at Rome and so Eckstein concluded that it had never existed. Hoyos argues that, since the Carthaginians enjoyed good long-term relations with many Italian communities, it would not have been wise for them to sacrifice these links in order to prevent Roman military or diplomatic intervention in Sicily when there was no sign of it occurring soon. He also makes the point that Philinus knew nothing of the other treaties.[111]

The Romans had visited all of these islands – for example, buying grain from Sicily since the beginning of the fifth century BC and trying to found colonies in Sardinia and Corsica. There are several reasons why, in my opinion, Polybius is wrong when he denies the existence of this treaty. He discusses the Roman–Carthaginian treaties in his third book when he describes the bitter argument that took place between the Roman ambassadors and the Carthaginians in the Carthaginian senate just before the outbreak of the Second Punic War. Although Polybius was writing a general history, he does not discuss the treaties in their context, explaining the situation in which they were created. This weakness in his approach follows from his decision to start the main part of his history from 220; he does not say anything about the treaty the Carthaginians made with Syracuse in the same year. He also tends to correct other historians if he thinks they were wrong; for instance, he criticizes Timaeus heavily in Book 12. Perhaps the passage above is a similar example; Polybius is attacking an error he thinks he has found in a fellow historian's work.

The Philinus treaty shows the unease with which the Carthaginians saw their situation in Sicily and in the Tyrrhenian area in general. They were concerned by Roman expansion and tried to limit their power at sea but there was nothing they could do to stop Roman expansion on land in Italy.

The year 306/5 is also the date of the first Roman contact with Rhodes, which, with its many harbours, functioned as a major *entrepôt* for trade from Egypt and the Levant. Polybius writes about the senate's reception of Pergamene and Rhodian envoys in the winter of 168/7 and states that 'although that state [Rhodes] had for nearly a hundred and forty years taken part in the most glorious and finest achievements of the Romans, they had never made an alliance with Rome.'[112] Scholars have been sceptical about the possibility of any kind of military collaboration starting from 306/5, however. As Schmitt has pointed out, this could be a question of an *amicitia* – a treaty of political friendship – which did not imply formal relations. Rome and Rhodes probably found common economic interests and collaborated in suppressing pirates. Since Schmitt came to this conclusion, new information has emerged from inscriptions supporting the idea of an *amicitia*.[113]

The term 'Tyrrhenian pirates', which is often used in the sources for the late fourth and early third centuries BC, should be interpreted broadly, since it refers not only to Etruscan pirates but to any pirates coming from the Italian peninsula. The activities of these pirates probably reflect the growth of maritime trade and the military expeditions which generated traffic between Italy and the eastern Mediterranean.[114] It is important to note that, in the Hellenistic world, policing the seas did not mean eliminating piracy altogether, as there are examples of states using piracy as a tactic to further their own interests.[115]

The Pyrrhic War, 282–272 BC, and its Aftermath

The Romans finally settled the Samnite question in the Battle of Sentinum in 296, in which they defeated the anti-Roman alliance of Samnites, Gauls, Etruscans and Umbrians. The last resistance against the Romans in their quest to conquer the peninsula came from the Greek cities in the south.

The only colony the Spartans had founded, Tarentum, had the best port in southern Italy. All the Greek colonies had been established by conquest and Tarentum was no exception. There was an unrelenting struggle between Tarentum and the warlike indigenous people, usually known as the Iapygians, who attacked the rich coastal plain of Tarentum. The militarism of Tarentum was a result of this difficult situation which, as Eckstein observes, was not unusual in Italy at the time. Tarentum was a ferocious and militarized culture in the same way as the Etruscans, the Samnites and Rome. Like Rome, Tarentum placed colonies at strategic defensive points in the indigenous territory it had seized. Tarentum also faced fierce competition from other Greek cities, first from Siris and Sybaris and then from Croton. Sybaris had founded Metapontum to block Tarentine expansion to the south-west.

Tarentum's influence grew gradually until it became the leading power in southern Italy. It seized the territory of Siris in the 430s and founded the colony of Heraclea. These actions intensified the enmity of Metapontum and Thurii. Dionysius I of Syracuse had created a significant empire in Italy in the 380s, destroying Rhegium, Caulonia and Hipponium and taking Croton and Locri. When the empire fell after Dionysius' death, the subsequent weakness of the Italiote cities was an important factor in the rise of Tarentum. In the 370s and 360s, Tarentine influence was visible in an area that reached from Rhegium to Illyria and to Naples. By the 360s, it had a powerful army, including infantry and a famous body of cavalry, as well as the largest fleet among the western Greeks.[116]

The Tarentines were active in the international politics of the time. They offered to send their troops and fleet to protect Naples against Rome in 326 and sent a fleet of twenty ships to support the war effort of Agrigentum and other Greek cities against Syracuse in 315/14.[117] They also made an attempt to mediate between the Romans and the Samnites at Luceria in 320.[118] In order to combat the increasing hostility of the indigenous people in the highlands, the Tarentines called in foreign commanders and their troops to defend their interests; nevertheless, the Tarentine army still played an important role in the second half of the fourth century BC and their reliance on mercenaries has been exaggerated. Archidamus of Sparta fought for Tarentum in 343–338 and Alexander of Epirus campaigned against the Lucanians and Bruttians in 334 but then the Tarentines dropped him. Cleonymus of Sparta arrived in 303 and held Metapontum for a while but the Tarentines turned against him and finally the Romans drove him out. Agathocles of Syracuse was likewise invited in by Tarentum and he supported the city in the same way that Dionysius I and Dionysius II of Syracuse had done. As well as helping the Tarentines in their struggle against the Lucanians and the Messapians in 298/7, he fought the Bruttians and Iapygians. Agathocles had interests of his own in southern Italy; his aim seems to have been the union of Sicilian and south Italian Greeks under his rule but he failed. As Purcell puts it, Cleonymus, Agathocles and finally Pyrrhus should not be seen as three unconnected *condottieri*; their story was part of a larger phenomenon, the near-birth of a Greek Successor state in the west. This was never achieved in Tarentum or in Hiero's Syracuse.[119] The term 'Successor state' refers to the development of large kingdoms in the Hellenistic world, when the kingdom of Alexander the Great was split between successors. Though his reign never covered the west, the idea of a large kindom was a possibility there.

The clash with Rome that led to the Pyrrhic War in 282–272 had its immediate cause in Roman provocation when Rome sent ten warships into the Gulf of Tarentum. Appian is our only source:

Cornelius went on a voyage of inspection along the coast of Magna Graecia with ten decked [kataphract] ships. At Tarentum a demagogue named Philocharis ... reminded the Tarentines of an old treaty by which the Romans had bound themselves not to sail beyond Cap Lacinium, and so stirred their passion that he persuaded them to put out to sea and attack Cornelius, of whose ships they sank four and captured one with all on board. They also accused the Thurini of preferring the Romans to the Tarentines although they were Greeks, and held them chiefly to blame for the Romans overpassing the limits. Then they expelled the noblest citizens of Thurii, sacked the city, and dismissed the Roman garrison under a flag of truce.[120]

No date is given for this treaty and we need to consider when the Tarentines first felt the need to set such limits which recognized their sphere of interest. Tarentum had enjoyed the mutually beneficial connection with Syracuse which made Tarentine power in the Gulf of Tarentum virtually unassailable,[121] so it is likely that the treaty was made in the 290s or 280s.[122] The death of Agathocles in 289/8 meant the end of Syracusan protection of the Greeks and created a power vacuum which the Romans sought to fill. In 285, the Romans liberated Thurii from a Lucanian siege and installed a garrison there to protect the city. Roman ships had probably already called at Thurii and, by doing so, they had entered the Tarentine sphere of interest. Thurii was Tarentum's rival in reputation and power and the Tarentines feared that Roman intervention would weaken their hegemonic position on the southern coast.

We do not know where the ships clashed. Franke suggests that the Romans sailed into the harbour of Tarentum[123] but such a provocative action would amount to a challenge to battle and it seems unlikely that the Romans would enter the base of the largest fleet of the western Greeks with only ten warships. The prohibition on the Romans sailing beyond Cape Lacinium had a military purpose and the events of 282 show the sharp Tarentine response to any infringement. Moreover, the Romans did not need to go into the Gulf of Tarentum to get access to their colonies in the Adriatic: Sena Gallica, founded in 295, could be reached by sailing along the coast, and Hadria and Castrum Novum, founded in 289, could be reached by land, over the mountains. When the Romans wished to enter the Adriatic, they could row across from Croton in a day, without going into the Gulf of Tarentum – there was no need for them to sail into the gulf unless they wanted trouble.[124]

When the Romans learned of these events, they sent an embassy to Tarentum with a list of demands: the prisoners should be released; the citizens of Thurii who had been expelled should be brought back to their homes; the property that had been plundered, or the value of what had been lost, should be restored; and the authors of these crimes should be surrendered to the Romans. The Tarentines declined Roman demands.[125]

They hired Pyrrhus of Epirus, whose involvement generated great interest across the Mediterranean, not least because he claimed he would conduct a Panhellenic campaign to free all the Greeks in southern Italy from the threat of the barbarian world. He won the support of the Hellenistic states, whose rulers were, as Franke puts it, 'glad to see this restless and dangerous man seek an arena for his activities elsewhere.' Pyrrhus received support in the form of Macedonian auxiliary troops and twenty Indian war elephants from Ptolemy Ceraunos. Antigonus II Gonatas provided the ships that were needed to transport troops and reinforcements. Antiochus I of Syria sent money to Pyrrhus and he probably also received financial support from Ptolemy I of Egypt.[126] Besides Macedonian ships, Tarentine ships were used to transport the elephants, cavalry, foot soldiers, archers and slingers to Italy.[127]

Southern Italy and Sicily became a war zone. Pyrrhus inflicted massive damage on the Romans, defeating them in the battles of Heraclea in 280, which brought him the support of the Samnites, Lucanians and Bruttians as well as Greek cities of the south, and again at Ausculum in 279. He then embarked on a short campaign in Sicily in 278. He intervened on the island at the request of Agrigentum, Leontini and Syracuse.

Before Pyrrhus set off for Sicily, Carthaginian envoys sailed to Ostia in 279/8 to make another treaty with Rome.[128] Polybius' account of the negotiations is very short and concentrates on military issues and how Rome and Carthage might assist each other against Pyrrhus:

A further and final treaty with Carthage was made by the Romans at the time of Pyrrhus' invasion, before the Carthaginians had begun the war for Sicily. In this they maintain all the previous agreements and add the following: 'If they make a written alliance with Pyrrhus, both shall make it an express condition that they may go to the help of each other in whichever country is attacked. No matter which require help, the Carthaginians are to provide the ships for transport there and back and hostilities, but each country shall provide the pay for its own men. The Carthaginians, if necessary, shall come to the help of the Romans by sea too, but no one shall compel the crews to land against their will.'[129]

The background to this treaty was extremely complex, as both Rome and Carthage had their own negotiations going on with Pyrrhus.[130] The Romans wanted to reduce the instability Pyrrhus' campaign was causing, especially as they faced the threat of renewed conflict with the Etruscans and the Samnites, whose sympathies were with Pyrrhus. Yet, despite their staggering losses, they followed the policy advocated by Appius Claudius Caecus not to make peace with Pyrrhus or Tarentum as long as the forces of the enemy remained on the soil of Italy. The Carthaginians, on the other hand, aimed to dominate the entire island themselves and did not want any competition. They needed to keep Pyrrhus out of Sicily while they continued their campaign against Syracuse. After the death of Agathocles, there had been a struggle for power in Syracuse. The new tyrant Hicetas had invaded Carthaginian Sicily but was defeated. The Carthaginians were still besieging Syracuse from land and sea when Pyrrhus arrived on the island. So, in Sicily, the Carthaginians were working on two fronts – they were fighting another war against Syracuse and they were using diplomacy to ensure Roman support for their efforts to maintain their position on the island.

This treaty needs to be seen in terms of an agreement to provide assistance with mobile warfare. There is no evidence in the sources of the involvement of the Roman fleet after 282. However, for this period the usual sources are absent: Livy's narrative breaks off at the end of Book 10 in 293 and Diodorus' complete text comes to an end in 302. Thiel argues that, after the treaty, the Romans gave up maintaining their own navy. Roth takes the treaty to imply that, before the First Punic War, Rome lacked the necessary logistical infrastructure to transport provisions and troops.[131] I disagree with both these interpretations. This undertaking was the biggest in Roman military history so far and the fleet was certainly used whenever possible. As the conquest of Italy proceeded, Rome had also built up a logistical infrastructure by capturing ports and it had used ships in various operations. At the time it is likely that the Romans already had maritime bases – for instance, in Locri and Brundisium.[132] It is reasonable to assume they were transporting troops in their own ships. Perhaps they also operated ships provided by their allies and the treaty allowed them to use additional ships from the Carthaginians. Presumably they helped to blockade harbours – for example, Tarentum – and even assisted in sea battles, as it was very much in the interest of both parties to make Pyrrhus leave.[133] They also agreed to uphold the clauses of the previous treaty. This must have been a reference to the Philinus treaty since there was no point in repeating the clauses of the treaty of 348 which forbade the Romans from sailing to Sardinia and the North African coast but kept open the Carthaginian province of Sicily.

An example of the treaty in action was the occasion in 278 when Carthaginian ships patrolled in the Strait of Messina in an attempt to prevent Pyrrhus from crossing to Sicily. Diodorus writes:

> The Carthaginians, having made an alliance with the Romans, took five hundred men on board their own ships and sailed across to Rhegium; they made assaults, and though they desisted from the siege, set fire to the timber that had been brought together for shipbuilding, and they continued to guard the Strait, watching against any attempt by Pyrrhus to cross.[134]

However, Pyrrhus evaded them and reached the island. The Carthaginians were besieging Syracuse with about 100 ships but thirty of them had been sent away to carry out other tasks when he arrived. Diodorus does not describe the type of Carthaginian ships that were present. Those ships that remained did not venture to give battle so Pyrrhus sailed unchallenged into Syracuse.

Pyrrhus took advantage of the city's military resources. Just before his death, Agathocles had put together for the invasion of Africa a fleet of 200 quadriremes and sixes. Diodorus states that Pyrrhus acquired 120 decked vessels, twenty without decks and the royal nine. The total number of ships in Pyrrhus' fleet, including those he had brought with him, came to more than 200.[135] This large fleet gave him great mobility to operate, with 30,000 foot soldiers and 25,000 cavalry. The campaign proved to be disastrous for the Carthaginians and by 277 they had lost all their cities in Sicily except for Lilybaeum. However, having lost the support of the Siceliots, Pyrrhus returned to Italy in 276. Appian describes how the Carthaginians attacked his fleet: 'He set sail for Rhegium with 110 decked ships, besides a much larger number of merchant vessels and ships of burthen. But the Carthaginians made a naval attack upon him, sunk seventy of his ships, and disabled all the rest except twelve.'[136] In the following year Pyrrhus was defeated by the Romans at Beneventum and returned to Epirus. Tarentum surrendered in 272 and became a *socius navalis*.[137]

The great loser in this war was Carthage. The treaties it made with Rome and Syracuse in 306 to stabilize the situation in Sicily had offered only a short-term solution to its problems. There had been another conflict with Syracuse, the Carthaginians had failed to keep Pyrrhus in Italy and the only state that could have helped them was Rome but they did not want to call on Roman help in Sicily. The military situation was quickly recovered after Pyrrhus' departure and, by the outbreak of the First Punic War, Carthage had taken back most of western Sicily, including Panormus and Agrigentum. Nevertheless, Pyrrhus' campaign had shown the vulnerability of Carthaginian rule in Sicily and what an enemy could do with a combined force of infantry and cavalry transported on ships that allowed them to operate all the way round the island.

Without doubt, Rome was the great winner in this conflict, gaining new international status. The Alexandrian poet and grammarian Lycophron describes Rome as having kingly power over earth and sea and becoming the avenger of Troy's destruction.[138] Ptolemy II Philadelphus sent an embassy to Rome in 273 and the Romans established relations with Ptolemaic Egypt. A treaty of friendship, *amicitia*, was made, and Rome sent an embassy to Egypt in the same year. This treaty was not the result of diplomatic convention, since neither Hellenistic nor Roman practice required such a thing.[139] Opinions about it are divided: Badian states that the treaty was not taken seriously by anyone. Harris argues that, if Philadelphus complied with the treaty in refusing to lend Carthage 2,000 talents in the First Punic War, the treaty was serious enough. Neatby points out common interests: both Rome and Egypt had reason to fear the aggrandizement of Carthage and both dreaded the dominance of a single power in Greece – a difficult situation that Rome had just experienced. Moreover, Egypt had extensive trading interests and it was to its advantage to ensure that Rome and not Carthage ruled over southern Italy. The Egyptians saw advantages in winning the friendship of the dominant power in Italy and securing a friendly reception for Egyptian traders in Tyrrhenian and Adriatic ports.[140] The influence from Egypt can be seen in the fact that the system of control marks in didrachms minted in Rome in 265–242 was developed from the system used on silver decadrachms of Arsinoe II of Egypt.[141]

The Romans continued their conquest of the Italian peninsula. The Latin colonies of Paestum and Cosa were founded in 273 and in 272 Rome expropriated from the defeated Bruttians half of the Sila forest. Dionysius of Halicarnassus, writing about the area, noted that the forest was packed with trees that were suitable both for house-building and shipbuilding, and Harris sees this Roman gain as one step in their preparations for war.[142] Indeed southern Italy offered ample resources: surplus grain, timber for shipbuilding and abundant manpower.

The issue of the role played by the *quaestores classici*, established in Rome in 267, needs to be considered in this context and it has been debated widely. Quaestors had mainly financial powers; they administered the public treasury (*aerarium*). The problem is that the late source Johannes Lydus is the only one that actually refers to the new quaestors as 'classici' and we cannot be sure what their task was and how many new quaestors were added at this time.[143] Thiel and Sage state that their task was to superintend new naval allies and to acquire ships and crew from them. According to Rankov, when Rome was just beginning to be monetized, it is much more likely that these officials were concerned with allocating citizens to their *classes* (five graded property classes) for the *comitia centuriata* – the assembly that enacted laws, elected senior magistrates and decided on declaration of war and peace. Staveley and Harris suggest that part of the new quaestors' job was to collect Italian revenues.[144] In my opinion, the new quaestors were not directly involved in acquiring ships or crew from the allies. It is likely that the newly-obtained naval resources were administered by the *praefecti socium*, who had overall command of allied units, including the heavy infantry and cavalry. These men were of senatorial background and three of them were assigned to each legion. The sailors and rowers were recruited by the local magistrates.

During the Pyrrhic War, a new conflict was developing in the north-east corner of Sicily. Messana was occupied by the Mamertines, a group of rebellious mercenaries. They had been recruited from the Campanians, the Oscan-speaking descendants of the hill tribesmen who had taken Campania at the end of the fifth century BC. Agathocles had hired them to help him fight the Carthaginians. After his death, they had been freely admitted to Messana. Soon, however, they took advantage of the confusion that prevailed in Sicily and seized the city, using it as a base to raid the Carthaginians and Syracusans in the neighbouring territories and levying tribute from many parts of Sicily. However, they did not join Pyrrhus in his campaign against Carthage.

The Mamertines found support in Rhegium, where the Romans had placed a garrison to protect the city.[145] The soldiers there were Roman citizens of Oscan-speaking Campanian origin. In the course of the Pyrrhic War they expelled or massacred the citizens and took possession of the city in the same way that the Mamertines had done at Messana. Thus, for a period, rebellious soldiers of Campanian origin occupied cities on both sides of the Strait. After the Pyrrhic War, the Romans sent an army to besiege Rhegium. Most of the garrison was killed at the assault but more than 300 were captured and taken to Rome, where they were beheaded in the Forum. Hiero, who had taken control of Syracuse, sent grain and soldiers to help in the siege.[146]

Chapter 3

The First Punic War, 264–241 BC: Arms Race at Sea

The First Punic War broke out in 264 over the question of Messana and the Mamertines who were occupying it. The Romans, in sending their legions first to Sicily and soon afterwards to Africa, did something they had never done before. However, their actions were consistent with the events of the previous decades, when southern Italy and Sicily had become a war zone and the battle for Sicily had extended beyond the island into Carthaginian territory in Africa.

As well as describing the main episodes of the war, this account looks at the key questions of how the Romans managed to take Sicily whereas the Syracusan tyrants and Pyrrhus had failed, and did the Carthaginians, who had fought both of these enemies, change their tactics now that they had to fight the Romans?

Polybius, our principal source for the history of the war, will also be discussed. He derived his narrative from two accounts written in Greek. The first was by Philinus, a Greek from Agrigentum, who probably lived at the same time as the First Punic War. He took a pro-Carthaginian stance because the Romans sacked his city and enslaved the population. The second account used by Polybius was by the Roman senator Quintus Fabius Pictor, who fought in the Second Punic War. By his time, the Romans had become aware of the importance of their image abroad and of the concern their actions in south Italy and Sicily caused in the Greek colonies and the Hellenistic world. Therefore, he had a mission to explain events to Greek readers and to show that the wars were justified.

Polybius portrayed the Romans as novices at sea and wrote: 'my readers should … not be kept in ignorance of the beginning – how, when, and for what reasons the Romans first took to the sea.'[1] This claim contradicts everything we know about Roman maritime interests during the centuries before the war, so his point of view needs to be explained. First, the structure of Polybius' work should be taken into account: the first two books are different from the rest of his work; they are introductory and give the background to the *Histories* proper, which begin from 220.[2] Polybius looks for reasons for the Roman success; he discusses the Roman innovation and determination in order to explain Rome's ability to conquer the world. His description of how the Romans began to build ships and went to sea serves as an example of the strength of Roman character – of how the republic got involved in new and difficult enterprises and was successful.

A partial explanation may also be found in the activities of Fabius Pictor. He had a mission to improve Rome's reputation abroad and there were political advantages in playing down Rome's naval capability – hence the idea of Romans as beginners which Polybius adopted. Moreover, claiming that something was being done for the first time is a standard Roman topos. In triumphal inscriptions and eulogies, Roman generals and statesmen often make this assertion even though it may not be true and perhaps Polybius believed their rhetoric.

The conclusions of research into the beginnings of the Greek navies are also useful in this context. As van Wees points out, evidence shows that trireme navies were widespread before the Persian Wars and their creation established the mechanisms and principles of state control and public funding that made the naval expansion of the 480s possible. However, this opinion has been hard to reconcile with the accounts given by Herodotus and Thucydides. They state that Athens and the other Greek cities had almost no triremes until a few years before the Persian invasion and so the evidence concerning the early fleets has not been taken seriously.[3] Perhaps a similar misconception has come from Polybius' account. In order to create an exciting starting point for his narrative of the war at sea, he wrote that the Roman navy was built up from nothing but his version of events should not be taken literally.

The notion that the Romans were novices in maritime warfare has distorted our interpretation of the sources and our understanding of their actions at sea. Thiel, for example, calls them landlubbers and says that 'the First Punic War in particular gives ample proof of their being clumsy beginners in naval warfare.' Their successes and failures have been evaluated against the false assumption that they were beginners. It has also led to misreadings of Polybius and of Livy on the Second Punic War. Their accounts contain authentic information about practical matters – for example, on how ships were beached after every voyage and how the crews operated on land. Every nation in the ancient Mediterranean practised a similar system, yet these passages have been connected to, and used to confirm, the idea that the Romans were inexperienced at sea.[4]

We cannot be sure about the exact numbers of warships in Roman and Punic fleets as there are too many uncertainties in the sources. While the figures for warships in a particular battle are usually known, we cannot say how many ships the states owned in a given year. Their location is also uncertain – we do not know how many were in Carthage and Rome or in the various Punic and Roman bases in Sicily. Likewise, it is not possible to calculate how many transport ships were used on a regular basis, as our sources only mention them on occasions when something went wrong. Attempts have been made to reduce the numbers of ships taking part in battles on the assumption that figures over 300, which are sometimes given in the ancient sources, must be too high. However, revising the figures can create even more difficulties, so it is perhaps best to take them as they are presented in the sources.[5]

The Outbreak of the War

Hiero helped the Romans defeat the rebels of Rhegium. As the axis of mutual support between Rhegium and Messana was cut, the Mamertines started to lose their positions in Sicily and, in the conflict that followed, they suffered a crushing defeat by the Syracusan army at the river Longanus.[6] Consequently, in 265, one group of Mamertines asked for assistance from the Carthaginians while another sent an embassy to the Romans, in both cases promising to surrender the city to them.[7]

The exact chronology of these events is unclear. We do not know if the two requests were made at the same time or whether the Mamertines first contacted the Carthaginians and later, being dissatisfied with the response, contacted the Romans. In the event, the Carthaginians acted first. According to Diodorus, after their severe defeat, the Mamertines decided to approach Hiero as suppliants. The Carthaginians interfered before they could go ahead with this plan. The Carthaginian general Hannibal was moored at the island of Lipara and went to Hiero, offering his congratulations. We do not know what was said but he somehow managed to forestall any further action on Hiero's part. Next, Hannibal persuaded the Mamertines to accept a Carthaginian garrison in Messana and Hiero withdrew to Syracuse.[8]

While the Carthaginians had quickly taken advantage of an opportunity to enhance their position in Sicily, the Mamertines' request for support was a controversial issue for the Romans. Sicily was well-known to the Romans because they had been buying grain from the island since 492 and they had long-established relations with Syracuse. Polybius' account, which probably follows that of Fabius Pictor, raises many questions. He records the moral concerns that were discussed in the senate. There the question was raised why Rome should help the Mamertines when the Romans had recently executed their own citizens for similar actions. The Romans also saw that the Carthaginians already controlled North Africa and a great part of Spain and possessed all the islands in the Sardinian and Tyrrhenian seas. The addition of Messana and then Syracuse to their empire would give them the control of Sicily as well. In consequence, they would hem Rome in from every side and threaten the whole of Italy.[9] Polybius' account probably exaggerates Carthaginian power and the danger it represented for Rome.[10] It does not seem a sufficient justification for Roman intervention at Messana, especially as Polybius describes elsewhere how Roman aims gradually changed following the success they made. He summarizes the decision-making as follows:

The senate did not sanction the proposal at all, considering that the objection on the score of inconsistency was equal in weight to the advantage to be derived from intervention. The commons, however, worn out as they were by the recent wars and in need of any and every kind of restorative, listened readily to the consuls, who, besides giving the reasons above stated for the general advantageousness of the war, pointed out the great benefit in the way of plunder which each and every one would evidently derive from it. They were therefore in favour of sending help; and, when the measure had been passed by the people, they appointed to the command one of the consuls, Appius Claudius, who was ordered to cross to Messana.[11]

Bleckmann points out that the resistance Claudius confronted in the senate was designed to make sure he would not gain a decisive advantage over his fellow aristocrats through taking excessive booty, hence he took the matter to the citizen assembly. Scholars have debated the role of the members of the senate who came from southern Italy – the Atilii from Calatia and the Otacilii from Beneventum. Thiel, Heurgon, Clemente and Lancel point out that these families, together with the Claudii, who had traditionally supported an aggressive policy towards southern Italy, must have contributed to the radical solution of the problem and members of these families frequently commanded troops during the war. Lazenby, on the other hand, maintains that, even if there were links between the Roman and Campanian noble families, we cannot take it for granted that they would promote the interests of the traders and manufacturers of Campania. The men in the senate who wanted a war in Sicily were eager to win military glory and to extend their influence and that of their families. Harris emphasizes the desire for glory. However, Bleckmann rejects the assumption that there were permanent groupings of families who supposedly worked together in Roman politics; he maintains that the only permanent type of political collaboration in this period was between immediate relatives.[12]

The decision was probably made in *comitia centuriata*. Roman assemblies heavily favoured the wealthiest citizens and this is especially true of the *comitia centuriata*. Voting was by groups and, for this motion to pass, the more prosperous citizens – including the equestrian order – must have supported it. The decision was made by men who would profit from state contracts to supply and equip the army and by arranging the sale of prisoners of war as slaves. The promise of booty might well have persuaded the less wealthy to back the decision and ordinary soldiers could expect to profit from plunder on the battlefield.[13] Appius Claudius Caudex probably presented the motion to the people as the other consul of 264, Marcus Fulvius Flaccus, was away campaigning against the Volsinii.[14]

The reasons for the positive Carthaginian response to the Mamertines' request must be found in the strategic situation in the area. The significance of Messana was the same as it had been in 396, when Himilco had seized the city. At the time Diodorus noted: 'it had an excellent harbour, capable of accommodating all his ships, which numbered more than six hundred, and

Himilco also hoped that by getting possession of the straits he would be able to bar any aid from the Italian Greeks and hold in check the fleets that might come from Peloponnesus.'[15]

After their experiences in the Pyrrhic War, the Carthaginians wanted Messana as a lookout post to deter Greek or the Roman fleets from landing. The Romans, on the other hand, needed to be free to pass through the Straits as they sailed around Italy; the presence of a Carthaginian fleet in Messana would threaten them, especially as the Carthaginians also controlled the Lipari Islands. Moreover, the Romans were well aware that the Greek cities in southern Italy and Sicily had always had close links and, although Rome had conquered southern Italy, it only controlled half of Magna Graecia. Recent events had provided plenty of evidence that demonstrated how easy it was for outsiders to interfere in the business of southern Italy, so the Romans were determined to secure their position in the region; they could do so only by dominating both sides of the Straits.

If the actions of the Romans in the following years are taken into account, then it appears that they must have had a larger plan for expansion. By 256, they were successfully waging a full-scale war both on land and at sea, and not only in Sicily but also in Sardinia, Corsica and in Carthaginian territory in Africa. The fact that they could carry through such a policy indicates the strength of their Italian resources and the extent of their ambitions outside Italy. Through their recent conquest of southern Italy they had gained the funds, the abundance of manpower and timber that were important for any state undertaking a naval campaign. Despite war-weariness, the Romans now had larger resources than ever before and the First Punic War was the first occasion when they used them.

The Romans Gain a Foothold in Sicily

The first years of the war form a complex story. The Romans invaded Sicily, clashing with the Carthaginians at the Straits and establishing themselves at Messana. Carthage and Syracuse formed a short-lived alliance against the Romans, who then put pressure on Hiero of Syracuse to switch sides; Hiero became an ally of the Romans and Syracuse a base in Roman operations against Carthage. The Romans took Agrigentum, the most important

Carthaginian base on land in Sicily, and they then built a large fleet. The era of the great sea battles began in 260; ships were, however, used from the beginning of the conflict to transport troops and supplies and for diplomatic missions.

Our information on how the Romans took Messana is far from complete but it is clear that they took an aggressive approach. According to Diodorus and Dio, Roman representatives made several trips to Messana before the Roman army arrived. Negotiations took place between the Romans, the Mamertines and the Carthaginians. The Carthaginians tried to block the Straits and there was a naval battle in which the Romans lost some triremes. The Carthaginians tried to avoid further conflict; Hanno, the Carthaginian commander returned the Roman prisoners taken in the battle as well as the captured ships. He also warned the Romans against becoming involved in naval warfare.

According to Dio and Zonaras, who probably based their accounts on Philinus, a Roman detachment was present in Messana and took an active part in the expulsion of the Carthaginian garrison. Eventually Hanno was compelled to leave the city. According to Polybius, who is probably following Fabius Pictor, the Mamertines dislodged the Carthaginian commander by using a mixture of threats and trickery. They then invited Appius Claudius to enter the city and placed it in his hands. As Thiel puts it, the involvement of Fabius made the agressive character of Roman policy less conspicuous. The Carthaginians crucified Hanno because they thought he had lacked both judgement and courage in abandoning the citadel. They moved their fleet to Cape Pelorias, on the north-eastern tip of Sicily, from where they could continue to check the traffic in the Straits.[16]

The port of Messana was now open. Appius Claudius crossed the Straits at night to avoid the Punic fleet; the Carthaginians attacked his ships and one of the Carthaginian kataphracts ran aground and fell into the hands of the Romans.[17] The Roman army was transported in ships supplied by their allies in southern Italy. Polybius writes: 'When they first undertook to send their forces across to Messana, not only had they not any decked ships, but no long warships at all, not even a single boat, and borrowing pentecontors and triremes from the Tarentines and Locrians, and also from the people of Elea and Naples they took their troops across in these at great hazard.'[18]

Polybius' claim that the Romans did not have any warships cannot be taken literally; the assertion gives an element of awe to his story as it shows how the Romans, against all the odds, managed to win the war at sea against the Carthaginians. It is true that the Romans only started to build quinqueremes a few years later but at this point they certainly had a fleet consisting of triremes and other types of smaller ships, as did their allies in southern Italy. This passage from Polybius gives us a glimpse of how the Romans used the resources of their newly-conquered allies in the south, it being convenient for them to use their allies' ships and crew for an operation in Sicily. This is also one of the many passages in the ancient sources that record how the Romans made use of the ships of their allies in their campaigns. The southern cities concerned probably lent their ships to the Romans later on in the war, too, as the legions needed to be transported to and from Sicily every year but these ongoing arrangements are not referred to in the sources, which shift their focus to the large Roman fleet that was constructed shortly afterwards.

The presence of the Romans at Messana radically changed the situation in Sicily and brought old enemies together. Hiero made an alliance with the Carthaginians that was intended, as Diodorus reports, 'to make war on the Romans unless these should quit Sicily with all speed'. According to Polybius, it was designed 'for expelling from Sicily entirely the foreigners (barbarians) who occupied Messana'.[19] Hiero and the Carthaginians tried to besiege Messana. Appius Claudius responded by attacking Hiero's camp; Hiero lost the battle and retreated to Syracuse. The next day Appius attacked the Carthaginians, inflicting great losses and forcing them to retreat to the neighbouring cities. Appius advanced towards Syracuse and raided its territory.[20] He then returned to Rome.

The conflict escalated in 263. Rome sent two consuls, Manius Valerius Maximus and Manius Otacilius Crassus, who operated together with four legions and four *alae* – in total about 40,000 men. *Alae sociorum* were the cavalry and infantry of the allies attached to Roman legions. They fought on the wings (*alae*) of the battle line.[21] The Romans forced Hiero to give up his alliance with the Carthaginians. Polybius states that, on the arrival of the Roman troops, most of the cities revolted against the Carthaginians and Syracusans and joined the Romans. According to Diodorus, the Romans took action against the cities of Hadranum and Centuripa north of Syracuse, and the subsequent fear of the Romans made sixty-seven cities send envoys asking for peace. The Romans incorporated the forces from these cities into their army and advanced on Syracuse. These cities appear to have taken a pragmatic approach, supporting the party that seemed to be the strongest.

According to Polybius, Hiero saw how confused the Sicilians were and he calculated that the prospects of the Romans were more brilliant than those of the Carthaginians. Also, according to Diodorus, he recognized the level of discontent among the Syracusans. Consequently, he sent messages to the consuls and reached an alliance with them. The Romans hoped that, through this arrangement, Hiero would help them with supplies. Polybius records that Hiero returned prisoners to the Romans without ransom and paid them 100 talents (600,000 drachmas), while Diodorus says that the peace was set to last for fifteen years and the Romans received 150,000 drachmas. Diodorus also describes how Hannibal arrived with a fleet at Xiphonia, north of Syracuse, intending to support the king but when he learned of the deal that had been done, he left.[22]

This was the first indemnity the Romans received in this war to finance their war effort. Hiero's long career as a supporter and supplier to the Romans had begun. In return, he kept his kingdom but by making the treaty he abandoned the traditional Syracusan aim of being the hegemonic power in eastern Sicily. Rome had now taken over that role.[23] Manius Valerius Maximus celebrated a triumph over the Carthaginians and Hiero the king of the Sicilians and received the cognomen 'Messala'.

The treaty with Hiero was ratified by the Romans, who operated with two legions in Sicily for the rest of the year 263. They could rely on the support of Hiero's forces and believed this arrangement would make it easier for their soldiers to be supplied. The Carthaginians, for whom the treaty must have been unwelcome news, enlisted mercenaries – Ligurians, Celts and especially Iberians – and dispatched them to Sicily. They concentrated their troops and supplies in Agrigentum.[24]

Agrigentum had an excellent strategic location in the middle of the south coast of Sicily: it was the end point of roads coming from the north and east coasts to the south and the great road that ran along the south coast went through it. The city was a good base from which the Carthaginians could try to regain control over Sicilian affairs. The Romans, however, were determined to prevent this from happening. The consuls of 262, Lucius Postumius Megellus and Quintus Mamilius Vitulus, laid siege to Agrigentum with four legions, entrapping the new Carthaginian army there. The siege lasted seven months, from June 262 to January 261, and resulted in food shortages, disease and great suffering on both sides.

Hannibal, the Carthaginian commander in Agrigentum, was in contact with Carthage and additional troops and elephants were sent to Sicily to support him. Diodorus, basing his figures on Philinus, states that the Carthaginians transported to Lilybaeum 50,000 infantry, 6,000 cavalry and 60 elephants. Hanno, the other commander defending Agrigentum, received them and concentrated his forces in Heraclea Minoa, a city to the north of Agrigentum. Hanno captured the Roman supply base at Herbesus and the Romans managed to continue the siege only because Hiero sent provisions. The deadlock was finally resolved in two battles between Hanno's troops and those of the Romans. The Romans won, entered Agrigentum, from where Hannibal had managed to flee, and plundered it, taking slaves and booty.

Diodorus' description of the battle has disappeared but the figures he recorded of Roman and Carthaginian gains and losses have survived. He claims that the Romans carried off over 25,000 slaves from Agrigentum and that they lost 30,000 infantry, a number that must be too high. Hanno lost 3,000 infantry, 200 cavalry and 4,000 men taken prisoner; 8 elephants were killed and 33 wounded. Hanno was punished in Carthage by being deprived of his civic rights and being fined; Hamilcar was sent to Sicily to replace him. Diodorus lists a number of cities and fortresses that the Romans also took during the campaign and he notes that they enslaved the people of Mazarin, Mytistratus and Camarina.[25]

As has already been mentioned, Polybius recognized that Roman ambitions gradually increased as the war went on. The capture of Agrigentum was one of the turning points:

When the news of what had occurred at Agrigentum reached the Roman senate, in their joy and elation they no longer confined themselves to their original designs and were no longer satisfied with having saved the Mamertines and with what they had gained in the war itself, but, hoping that it would be possible to drive the Carthaginians entirely out of the island ... now that Agrigentum was in their hands, while many inland cities joined the Romans from dread of their land forces, still more seaboard cities deserted their cause in terror of the Carthaginian fleet ... while Italy was frequently ravaged by naval forces, Libya remained entirely free from damage, they [the Romans] took urgent steps to get to the sea like the Carthaginians.[26]

This is the moment when the nature of the war changed. Roman aims had been growing from the start. The original vote had been to send help to the Mamertines; yet, as soon as the Roman army crossed the Straits, it had fought against the alliance of the Carthaginians and Hiero, then the Romans had won Hiero over to their side and had inflicted significant losses on the Carthaginians. These actions had taken place on land. The consuls did not celebrate a triumph for the conquest of Agrigentum and some scholars consider that Polybius exaggerated the importance of its capture.[27] On the other hand, the Romans had already done everything they could on land. If they were going to continue their campaign in Sicily, which by then had turned into a full-scale war with Carthage, they had to build a large fleet to challenge that of the Carthaginians. In that sense Polybius was right and the victory at Agrigentum was important.

The Romans had sufficient ships to transport troops: tens of thousands of soldiers had been taken to Sicily and back every year, supplies had been shipped and booty carried home. The Carthaginians had tried to intercept these transports and they were also free to send their own troops to Sicily without being stopped by the Romans or by Hiero (interestingly, there is nothing in our sources about the Syracusan fleet in these years). Now, however, the Romans realized that something new was needed. If they were to rival the Carthaginians at sea, they would have to build a fleet with which to wage aggressive, mobile warfare and they would have to attack coastal cities under Carthaginian control. These were the tactics that the Carthaginians themselves had adopted. The Carthaginian fleet operated not only from Sicilian bases attacking targets on the Sicilian coast but ships that were stationed in Sardinia also attacked targets on the coast of Italy.[28] As the Romans upgraded their fleet, sea battles started to occur. The two sides fought for control of the seaboard of Sicily and other islands, thus making their claim to thalassocracy in the western Mediterranean.

Roman Shipbuilding

We do not know who took the initiative to start the new shipbuilding programme in Rome. An anonymous Greek source names Valerius Messala, the consul of 263, as the first person to realize that a new fleet was needed for ultimate victory. This may be true or it may be an attempt by his family to glorify one of its ancestors.[29] According to Polybius, the decision was made in 261 and the ships were completed in the following year. Pliny states that the fleet was sailing sixty days after the first timber was cut.[30]

Polybius' description of the shipbuilding work is a mixture of myths and facts. On the one hand, he highlights the notion that the Romans were beginners and lacked the requisite knowledge:

> When they saw that the war was dragging on, they undertook for the first time to build ships, a hundred quinqueremes and twenty triremes. As their shipwrights were absolutely inexperienced in building quinqueremes, such ships never having been in use in Italy, the matter caused them much difficulty, and this fact shows us better than anything else how spirited and daring the Romans are when they are determined to do a thing ... When they first undertook to send their forces across to Messana ... the Carthaginians put to sea to attack them as they were crossing the straits, and one of their decked ships [kataphract] advanced too far in its eagerness to overtake them and, running aground, fell into the hands of the Romans. This ship they now used as a model, and built their whole fleet on its pattern ... if this had not occurred they would have been entirely prevented from carrying out their design by lack of practical knowledge.[31]

It is possible that quinqueremes had never been built in Italy before. Yet constructing such ships should not have been a problem for the Romans as they could call on Syracusan expertise. Espionage played an important role in any ancient war effort and the capture of the Punic wreck allowed the Romans to analyse the latest development in Carthaginian shipbuilding. Besides, skilful shipbuilders could be hired, just as they had been by Dionysius I in Syracuse at the beginning of the fourth century BC:

He gathered skilled workmen, commandeering them from the cities under his control and attracting them by high wages from Italy and Greece as well as Carthaginian territory. For his purpose was to make weapons in great numbers and every kind of missile, and also quadriremes and quinqueremes, no ship of the latter size having yet been built at that time.[32]

On the other hand, Polybius gives practical information on how the project was executed:

Those to whom the construction of the ships was committed were busy in getting them ready, and those who had collected the crews were teaching them to row on shore in the following fashion. Making the men sit on rowers' benches on dry land, in the same order as on the benches of the ships themselves, and stationing the boatswain in the middle, they accustomed them to fall back all at once bringing their hands up to them, and again to come forward pushing out their hands, and to begin and finish these movements at the word of command of the fugle man. When the crews had been trained, they launched the ships as soon as they were completed, and having practised for a brief time actual rowing at sea, they sailed along the coast of Italy as their commander had ordered.[33]

It was essential that the rowers kept pace. The training and exercising of crews is frequently mentioned in written sources and there is also some evidence in the pottery. Polybius describes a method generally used by fleets around the Mediterranean.[34] Crews had multiple tasks: they could be used for operations on land as fighting soldiers, for instance, and for building siege engines. So it is likely that the new recruits were not only taught to row but were also given some basic military training.

Polybius does not provide any information about where the ships were built, who built them, where the timber came from or where the rowers were recruited from. Nor does he mention the harbours from which they sailed. The gaps in our knowledge need to be filled with the most plausible explanations. There are different opinions about the places where the ships were constructed. Some scholars believe that a centralized building programme was organized, as seems to be suggested by Polybius; others, stressing Rome's lack of shipbuilding experience, believe that the project was spread over several ports, including Rome and the Greek cities of southern Italy.[35] In my opinion, the ships were probably built in dockyards in Rome and then were stored in sheds in the Campus Martius, where the trireme fleet was presumably kept. Timber was available in Latium, Etruria and Umbria and could be taken to Rome using any of the tributaries of the Tiber or Anio. There must have been shipwrights in Rome and they could be hired, as they had been in Syracuse. The ships were probably launched in batches of around twenty-five and in two or three days all of them would have passed Ostia and be sailing south towards the Straits. The triremes required about 4,200 men and the quinqueremes around 35,000. The *socii navales* were obliged to send ships and rowers but Samnites were also recruited, as we know from information that has survived concerning their rebellion.[36]

The naval organization comprised hundreds of thousands of people, including those working at the dockyards and those supplying sails, ropes, food and every other necessity needed on board. An expanding programme of shipbuilding was one of the most expensive policies that any ancient nation could adopt. In the case of Rome, the expansion was dramatic. In 311 the Romans had introduced triremes into their fleet and now, fifty years later, they had the resources to upgrade their fleet once again.

Roman Success at Sea in 260–257 BC

The intensification of the war at sea was demonstrated when the new Roman fleet first approached Sicily and the Carthaginians made an effort to stop it from securing a position on the Sicilian coast.

The consul Gnaeus Cornelius Scipio had given orders to the captains to sail towards the Straits when the fleet was ready, while he put to sea with seventeen ships and proceeded to Messana to prepare for the arrival of the main fleet.[37] However, Scipio was then taken prisoner at the Lipari Islands. Polybius describes how an opportunity came up to capture Lipara by treachery, and so Scipio sailed there with his seventeen ships. The Carthaginians at Panormus learned about Scipio's presence at Lipara. Hannibal dispatched Boödes, a member of the senate, with twenty ships and he blockaded the Romans in the harbour. Scipio surrendered to Boödes, who took him and the captured ships to Hannibal.

Much has been made of this failed enterprise. The Romans gave Scipio the nickname 'Asina', she-ass, but he was released later in an exchange of prisoners and continued his career.[38] Scipio was right to try to take Lipara. It was one of the ports that the Carthaginians could use to protect traffic in the Straits and interfere in Roman transports. If the Romans had captured it, the crossing of their main fleet would have been safer. While they already controlled the ports of Messana and Syracuse and could rely on the support of their ally Hiero along the east coast of the island, the rest of the Sicilian seaboard was dominated by the Punic fleet and was hostile to them. So, for the Romans, Lipara was an important target and the capture of it could have been their first success in the campaign to conquer the Punic ports.

Next, the Roman and Carthaginian fleets clashed off the coast of Bruttium, near a place called the Cape of Italy. This could well have been the Taurianum promontory, known today as Cape Vaticano. Polybius states that Hannibal came upon the main Roman fleet sailing southwards in good order and trim. He does not give details about the battle but claims that Hannibal lost most of his fifty ships before escaping with the remainder. The reasons for Hannibal's voyage are not clear. According to Polybius, he wanted to discover the strength and the general disposition of the enemy and perhaps he intended to combine this reconnaissance with a plundering raid.[39] It is possible that his motive was more ambitious than this. Since the Carthaginians had recently captured seventeen new Roman ships and their commander, he may have felt confident enough to stop the main Roman fleet and take over more of their ships.

When the Roman fleet arrived in Sicily, Gaius Duilius, the consul leading the Roman land forces on the island, was called in to command it. He handed over his legions to the military tribunes before leaving to join the ships.[40] The Romans began to get ready for a sea battle. Polybius states that, since their ships were badly-built and slow-moving, it was suggested that they should equip them with boarding-bridges.[41]

There is no doubt about the historicity of the boarding-bridge or *corvus*. Polybius gives a description of its structure that Wallinga has corrected on some points. It worked as follows: at ramming distance, a gangway located on the bow was lowered onto the enemy deck and the soldiers ran across it in order to fight. The mechanism consisted of a pole with a pulley at the top. A rope ran through the pulley to a gangway that could be raised and lowered. Under the end of the gangway was a pointed pestle that, when the gangway was lowered, pierced the deck of the enemy ship and kept the two vessels locked together.[42]

For anyone who follows Polybius' view that the Romans were novices in maritime warfare and operated with poor-quality ships, the boarding-bridge has come to be seen as the key to their success, especially as, in his description of the battle at Mylae, he states that this device made combat at sea like a fight on land.[43] However, it is doubtful whether the *corvus* had such a decisive impact. The Romans won their first battle on their way to Sicily without it, capturing many Punic ships, and the device is only mentioned twice in the sources: in the sea battles of 260 and 256 – thereafter there is no reference to it.

In my opinion, the *corvus* should not be seen in the context of the Romans' inexperience in maritime warfare; there is a precedent in naval history that points to its real significance. Thucydides describes how the Athenians used grappling irons when they tried to break out from the harbour at Syracuse in 413. They boarded the enemy ships with soldiers and drove their opponents off the deck. According to Thucydides, the sea battle changed into a battle on land. The mass of troops on board made the Athenian ships heavy and hampered their manoeuvres. The Athenian innovation started a new era in naval tactics.[44]

The boarding-bridge was a typical device in the Hellenistic period, when armies and navies were familiar with the strengths and weaknesses of their opponents and experimented with new fighting methods in order to surprise them. Once the Carthaginians had recovered from their surprise, they must have come up with a defence against the *corvus* but the sources do not describe the measures they took. Some of the technical details concerning the operation of the *corvus* remain uncertain, such as the angle at which it could be revolved, and it is not clear why the Romans stopped using it.

As for the alleged slowness of Roman ships, knowledge about the comparative performance of Roman and Carthaginian vessels is based on the outcome of the battle at the Cape of Italy where the Romans captured around fifty Punic ships and the remainder fled. The excessive weight of the Roman ships may have been due to the fact that they were loaded with troops, equipment and supplies, rather than a consequence of poor shipbuilding. However, the Romans had been unable to take a few of the Punic ships. In this context perhaps the boarding-bridge should not be seen as a defensive tool but as a sign of the Roman determination to hunt down every enemy ship at every opportunity. By using the boarding-bridge, they could make sure that no Punic ships could escape.

We do not know how long the preparations for the battle took. Polybius states that the Carthaginians were ravaging the territory of Mylae and that Duilius sailed against them:

They all [the Carthaginians] sailed straight on the enemy, not even thinking it worthwhile to maintain order in the attack, but just as if they were falling on a prey that was obviously theirs ... On approaching and seeing the ravens [*corvi*] nodding aloft on the prow of each ship, the Carthaginians were at first nonplussed, being surprised at the construction of the engines. However, as they entirely gave the enemy up for lost, the front ships attacked daringly. But when the ships that came into collision were in every case held fast by the machines, and the Roman crews boarded by means of the ravens and attacked them hand to hand on deck, some of the Carthaginians were cut down and others surrendered from dismay at what was happening, the battle having become just like a fight on land.[45]

The first thirty ships were taken with their crews. Hannibal, who was commanding the fleet in the seven that had formerly belonged to Pyrrhus, managed to escape in the small boat. Trusting their swiftness, the Carthaginians sailed around the enemy in order to strike from the side or the stern but the Romans swung the boarding-bridges around so that they could grapple with ships that attacked them from any direction. Eventually the Carthaginians, shaken by this novel tactic, took flight. They lost fifty ships.[46]

According to Polybius, Hannibal had 130 ships; according to Diodorus he had 200 ships involved in the battle. Diodorus says the Romans had 120 ships.[47] Information about the type of ships that Scipio Asina lost at the Lipari Islands is not given in the sources but it seems probable that the Romans still had around 100 ships from their original fleet. Possibly they borrowed ships from their allies and made use of captured Carthaginian ships but no information is available. The brief description of the battle that has survived does not indicate whether the Romans arranged their ships in two lines or one. At first it seems the Carthaginians tried a *diekplous* attack. When that failed, they switched to a *periplous* attack but the Romans repulsed that too. If we accept Wallinga's theory that the boarding-bridge could be revolved through 90 degrees, rather than freely in all directions as Polybius claims,[48] then the Romans must have manoeuvred and regrouped their ships during the battle to defend themselves and to target the Punic ships as they approached. So, in practice, they continued to use the traditional tactics that were intended to sink enemy ships with rams and the deployment of the boarding-bridge did not make a significant difference to this aspect of the battle.

Duilius was given extraordinary honours by Rome. He was awarded the first naval triumph in the city's history, '*de Sicul(eis) et classe Poenica*', 'over the Sicilians and the Punic fleet'.[49] Two columns decorated with beaks were built, one in the Forum, probably close to the *Rostra*, and the other perhaps at the Circus Maximus, and a waxen torch was borne before him and a flautist made music whenever he returned from dining out.[50] The *Rostra* and the *Columna Rostrata C. Duilii* were the two most important war monuments of Republican Rome. The *columna rostrata* at the Forum carried an inscription that recorded Duilius' achievements:[51]

As consul, he freed the Segestans – allies of the Roman people –
from the Carthaginian siege, and all the Carthaginian legions
and (their) highest official, by daylight, openly, after nine
days fled from their camp. And the town of Macella
he captured in battle. And in the same magistracy he was
the first consul to successfully wage war in ships at sea; crews
and fleets of warships he was the first to equip and train;
and with these ships the Punic fleets and likewise all
the mighty hosts of the Carthaginians, with Hannibal – their
dictator – present, he defeated in battle on the high seas.
And by force he captured, with their crews, one septireme
and 30 quinquiremes and triremes, and he sank 13 ships.
Gold coins captured: 3,700 (?)
Silver coins captured and from the sale of booty: 100,000 (++?)
All captured in bronze: 1.4 million (or more, plus)
1.5 million (or more)
And at his triumph he presented the people with naval booty,
and many freeborn Carthaginians he led before
his chariot. ----------------- captured --------------- [52]

Polybius sees the victory at Mylae as one of the important moments of the war; he states that the determination of the Romans to prosecute the war became twice as strong. This is plausible. The victory and the retreat of the Carthaginian navy opened the north coast of Sicily to the Romans, who used their fleet to take troops westwards when they raised the siege of Segesta and took Macella.[53]

No figures are available for the size of the fleets of 259–257, when the Romans extended their operations to other islands and attacked important Punic harbours. The consul of 259, Gaius Aquillius Florus, operated in Sicily against Hamilcar and celebrated a triumph '*de Poeneis*', 'over the Carthaginians'. We do not know exactly what he accomplished. According to Polybius, Roman troops did nothing worthy of note in Sicily that year. Perhaps events on land were slow; as Lazenby puts it, it is most likely that Aquillius had two legions with him consisting of about 20,000 men. This was not a large enough force to take on Hamilcar's army in which there might have been up to 50,000 men after the fall of Agrigentum. Diodorus, however, states that Hamilcar took Camarina and Enna and fortified Drepana on the north-west coast and that people were moved there from Eryx.[54] Drepana was one of the most important Carthaginian harbours in Sicily. The Carthaginians reacted to the presence of the Roman navy and the threat it posed to them.

According to Polybius, the Romans – from the moment they concerned themselves with the sea – began to entertain designs on Sardinia.[55] Sardinia and Corsica were strategically important and taking Sardinia would put a stop to Carthaginian attacks on the Italian coast from that direction. Moreover, the Romans had a long-standing interest in both islands, demonstrated by their attempts to found colonies on them.

The second consul of 259, Lucius Cornelius Scipio, brother to Gnaeus Cornelius Scipio Asina, was awarded a triumph for his campaign against the Carthaginians on both Corsica and Sardinia.[56] His opponent was Hanno. Scipio started on the east coast of Corsica, capturing Aleria and other ports that are not named in the sources. While sailing towards Sardinia, he spotted a Carthaginian fleet, which turned and fled. He went on to Olbia on the north-east coast of Sardinia. There a Carthaginian fleet put in an appearance but Scipio decided to sail home, judging that his infantry was insufficient to give battle.[57] Scipio's funerary inscription records his success in Corsica:

He took Corsica and the city of Aleria
He dedicated a temple to the Storms as a just return.[58]

The reference to 'Storms' in the dedication presumably alludes to a particular storm that Scipio was fortunate to escape and probably it was Hannibal's Carthaginian fleet that caused him to turn back. Polybius does not record previous events in Corsica and Sardinia but he continues the story of Hannibal, who had sailed to Carthage after the Battle of Mylae. He collected additional ships and recruited some of the most celebrated Carthaginian naval officers, then returned to Sardinia. There he was blockaded in one of the harbours by the Romans and, after having lost many ships in a battle, he was arrested by his men and crucified in Sulci, in the south-west corner of the island.[59] The Roman consul who defeated

Hannibal was probably Scipio's successor, Gaius Sulpicius Paterculus. He was awarded a triumph 'over the Carthaginians and Sardinia'.[60] We have no further information about subsequent events in Sardinia until the great mutiny of the Carthaginian mercenaries in the aftermath of the war and the consequent Roman annexation of the island.

The other consul of 258, Aulus Atilius Caiatinus, operated in Sicily. He attacked the Carthaginian winter quarters in Panormus but withdrew his forces when the Carthaginians refused to give battle. The Romans took Hippana, Mytistratus, Camarina and Enna and besieged Lipara. Surviving inhabitants were sold into slavery.[61] Lipara and Panormus were important Punic naval bases and the Roman attacks demonstrate the powerful position the Roman fleet had gained on the north coast of Sicily. Atilius celebrated a triumph 'over Sicily and the Carthaginians'.[62]

In 257 both consuls operated in Sicily. Information about Gnaeus Cornelius Blasio's campaign has not come down to us; Gaius Atilius Regulus, however, was awarded a naval triumph 'over the Carthaginians'. It is hard to say what he achieved; Polybius states that, in a sea battle off Tyndaris on the north coast of Sicily, the Romans took ten Carthaginian ships with their crews, sinking eight. Details of the battle have been lost but he describes the consul's ship as well-manned and swift. The rest of the Punic fleet withdrew to the Lipari Islands. A surviving fragment in the works of Naevius mentions the ravaging of Malta. Orosius, Zonaras and Polyainos state that Atilius operated against the Lipari Islands and Malta.[63] Certainly, operations against these two islands helped to make the route safe for the invasion of Africa that began in the following year.[64] Atilius' triumph was the seventh that had been celebrated during the war and the second for naval operations. Once again, naval paraphernalia must have been displayed in the triumphal procession; there is no record of a monument being built to commemorate the victory.

What made a naval triumph? All the Roman operations of this period depended on cooperation between the army and the fleet, in particular on the rapid transport of troops, which could only take place in areas where the navy had cleared the coast of the enemy fleet and made safe landing possible. Scipio's operations in Corsica, which included the capture of important Punic harbours, had not earned him a naval triumph. As for Atilius, we do not know exactly what he achieved but we must assume that he inflicted a serious loss on the Punic navy that could be counted in terms of booty and a significant number of captured or sunken ships. Perhaps his success at the Battle of Tyndaris fulfilled the criteria for a triumph and in addition he may have fought the Carthaginians at the Lipari Islands or Malta, in sea battles of which we know nothing.

The Roman Invasion of Africa, 256–255 BC

The Roman expedition to Africa should be considered in the light of Agathocles' campaign against the Carthaginians half a century earlier. The similarities were many. According to Diodorus, Agathocles was hoping to 'divert the barbarians from his native city and from all Sicily and transfer the whole war to Libya.'[65] The Syracusan attack had come as a surprise. Agathocles had escaped from the siege of Syracuse and his fleet reappeared close to the African coast. The Carthaginians had chased it but had failed to stop it. The Syracusans landed near the Latomiae on Cape Bon. After seeing the beached Sicilian ships burning – Agathocles had ordered them to be set on fire so that his soldiers would have no option but to fight for victory – the Carthaginians spread hides over the prows of their ships to mark the misfortune that had befallen their city and they took the bronze beaks of Agathocles' ships on board their triremes.[66] Agathocles conquered cities in Carthaginian territory, yet his campaign had been made easier by revolts launched by inhabitants who resented the exactions that came with Carthaginian rule. Polybius makes it clear that the Carthaginians were well aware that the local people could easily be subdued by an invader and they were prepared to run the risk of a sea battle to prevent the Romans from crossing to Africa.[67] The Romans planned 'to sail to Libya and deflect the war to that country, so that the Carthaginians might find no longer Sicily, but themselves and their own territory in danger.'[68]

We do not know when the plans for the invasion were made. Polybius states briefly that the Romans, after making preparations for the coming summer, went to sea with a fleet of 330 decked ships and two sixes and put in to Messana, then started again and sailed southwards, doubled Cape Pachynus at the south-east corner of Sicily and came round to Ecnomus, where their land forces were. The Carthaginians set sail with 350 decked vessels, touched at Lilybaeum and anchored off Heraclea Minoa.[69] Heraclea Minoa was the furthest point under their control on the south coast. Both Heraclea Minoa and Ecnomus were well-suited as staging areas for the two fleets before the battle as they were located on rivers Halycus and Himera, respectively, which would provide the fleets with drinking water.

The route the Romans used was safe until they turned onto the south coast. They wanted to follow the coastline as far as possible in order to reduce the distance of the sea voyage. However, they were likely to encounter the Punic fleet, which was determined to stop them from making the crossing. Polybius does not say where the battle took place. It is a modern assumption that it occurred off Ecnomus but Zonaras places it off Heraclea and this makes sense since the Carthaginians found the Romans towing their horse transports. If the Romans had been near Ecnomus, it would not have been necessary for them to do this, so clearly they must have left their staging area and been on their way to the west.[70]

Polybius states that the Romans had prepared for action at sea and for a landing on enemy territory. Around 140,000 men were embarked on the Roman ships, each ship carrying about 300 rowers and 120 marines. The Carthaginians adapted their preparations to fight at sea and, based on the number of ships, over 150,000 of their men were involved.[71] These figures are essentially credible, except that the number of staff on board the Punic ships may well be too high. Polybius probably made a mistake by multiplying the number of warships by a Roman complement of 420 per ship; the Carthaginians almost certainly had fewer soldiers on board as they were expecting to fight at sea, not on land.[72] As discussed above, some researchers have seen numbers of ships over 300 as too high and have tried to reduce them. There are nevertheless reasons for keeping them as they are. This battle probably involved the largest number of men in any naval battle in history.

The figures for the number of ships refer to both new and old ships that were used in the operation; it was customary to see how many old ships were seaworthy and then build new ships to fulfil the number required. Rome had built 120 ships in 260; most of these were probably still in operation. At this time the Romans had over 100 Punic ships and possibly some of these were repaired and used in the Roman fleet. Thus the invasion would require the building of 100–200 additional ships. The Punic fleet was probably put together in the same way but for Carthage we have no information of the pace of their shipbuilding. However, the number of captured Roman ships was very low and they did not play a role in the Punic fleet.

Polybius wrote a detailed description of the battle, the most complete account we have of all the sea battles of the Punic Wars. The Romans took up a protective wedge formation, with their three sections of ships in a triangle. The commanders, consul suffectus[73] Marcus Atilius Regulus and consul Lucius Manlius Vulso Longus, were placed at the front of the triangle, each commanding a six. The third section, at the base of the triangle, towed the horse transports and behind it was the fourth squadron, the *triarii*, in a single long line.[74]

The Carthaginians adapted their formation to that of the Romans. Polybius states that they tried to surround the Romans and deployed their ships so that the left wing, commanded by Hamilcar, was close to the coast. The swiftest quinqueremes were on the seaward wing, commanded by Hanno. Three separate engagements followed at a long distance from each other. The first began when the Romans, in their wedge formation, noticed that the Carthaginian line was thin and attacked in the centre:

> The Carthaginian center had received Hamilcar's orders to fall back at once with the view of breaking the order of the Romans, and, as they hastily retreated, the Romans pursued them vigorously. While the first and second squadrons thus pressed on the flying enemy, the third and fourth were separated from them ... When the Carthaginians thought they had drawn off the first and second squadrons far enough from the others, they all, on receiving a signal from Hamilcar's ship, turned simultaneously and attacked their pursuers.[75]

Polybius says the Carthaginian ships were superior in speed so they could move around the enemy's flank and approach and retire rapidly. In contrast, the Romans relied on their strength, grappling each Carthaginian ship with a boarding-bridge as soon as it approached.

The second phase of the battle started when the Carthaginian right wing attacked the ships of the *triarii*, causing them great distress, and the third phase began when the third Roman squadron towing the horse transports was attacked by the Carthaginian left wing. The Romans released the tow lines and engaged the enemy. Hamilcar's division was forced back and took to flight. Lucius took the prizes in tow. Marcus went to help the *triarii* and the horse transports with those ships from the second squadron that were undamaged. Hanno's division soon found themselves surrounded by the Romans and began to retreat out to sea. Both consuls hastened to relieve the third squadron, which was shut in so close to the shore, according to Polybius, that it would have been lost if the Carthaginians had not been afraid of the boarding-bridges. When the consuls came up and surrounded the Carthaginians, they captured fifty ships with their crews, although a few managed to slip away along the shore and escape. The Romans lost twenty-four ships sunk, the Carthaginians more than thirty. No Roman ship was captured but in all the Romans captured sixty-four from the Carthaginians.[76]

The detailed information that has come down to us allows a full analysis of the battle but does not necessarily make it easy to understand. Some scholars have rejected the triangle formation on the grounds that it would have been impossible to organize.[77] However, as Tipps has demonstrated, the alleged difficulties have been overstated as the wedge was hardly anything more than a variation of the line-astern formation that offered safety: the outer flank of each ship in the wedge was covered by the ship on its quarter, thus any ship that was attacked was defended by its neighbour with a ram or boarding-bridge.[78]

Other areas of debate are the Punic plan and the reasons for the Roman victory. According to Tipps, forming a trap to lure the enemy was a common Punic manoeuvre in the period of the First Punic War and the Carthaginians expected the Romans to keep their formation. The partial retreat of the Carthaginian centre was a part of the plan. They wanted to draw the Roman fleet forward so that the Carthaginian wings could close around the Roman formation. The Romans were saved because they allowed their formation to split when the consuls made a vigorous charge towards the centre of the Carthaginian line.

Goldsworthy argues that it was Hamilcar's plan to break the Roman formation in order to produce small-scale encounters between different parts of each fleet and in these clashes the Carthaginians could use ramming tactics. According to Lazenby and Goldsworthy, the Roman victory depended on the boarding-bridge, which turned out to be especially effective in a battle taking place near the shore. At this point in the conflict the Carthaginians had not yet found a way of counteracting it. Moreover, Goldsworthy points out the speed and the skill with which the consuls finished the first battle and came to help in the second and third battles. Most of the damage the Carthaginians suffered was inflicted in the last two battles.[79]

The Carthaginians had lost a crucial battle. Using the boarding-bridges, the Romans had captured a significant number of Punic ships but the boarding-bridges are not the sole explanation for their victory; the speed and mobility of the Roman ships were also important factors. It is intriguing that there must have been a considerable difference between the weights of the ships in the opposing fleets, just as there had been in 260 when the Carthaginians lost to the Romans off the coast of Bruttium. The Roman ships were carrying soldiers and equipment needed in Africa, whereas the Carthaginians had prepared for the sea battle only and had made their ships as light as possible – they had probably left the main masts and rigging on shore. Despite this, the Roman ships managed to move from one side of the battle to another, always giving each other support.

The Romans spent some time, probably at Ecnomus, taking on extra supplies, repairing the captured ships and giving prizes to their men for their success. Then they crossed the sea, meeting no resistance on the way. First a group of thirty of their ships reached Cape Bon, east of the Bay of Carthage. Then, when their remaining ships arrived, the fleet was united and sailed along the coast and landed at Aspis on Cape Bon. The ships were beached and surrounded with a trench and palisade; then the siege of the town began. The Carthaginians watched the situation as it developed. The Punic ships that had escaped from the naval battle had sailed for home and the Carthaginian land and sea forces kept a lookout at different points over the approaches to their capital. When they learned that the Romans had landed, they brought their forces together to protect the city and its environs.

The Romans took Aspis and garrisoned the town and the district, then sent a mission to Rome to report and ask for instructions. In the meantime, they pillaged the fertile countryside, destroying rich country houses and taking many cattle. They also captured over 20,000 slaves and took them back to their ships. Then messengers arrived with the senate's instructions: one of the consuls, Marcus Regulus, was to remain with forty ships, 15,000 infantry and 500 cavalry, while Lucius was to return to Rome with the ships' crews and the slaves. He celebrated a naval triumph 'over the Carthaginians'.[80]

At first the Roman plan worked. The Carthaginians elected two generals, Hasdrubal and Bostar, and summoned Hamilcar back from Sicily; he sailed from Heraclea Minoa to Carthage with 500 cavalry and 5,000 soldiers. The first Carthaginian attempt to stop the Romans at Adys failed. The Romans continued their advance and captured Tunis, which they used as a base for raids against the area surrounding Carthage. The Roman invasion also gave a boost to the rebellion of the Numidians and Polybius states that the Numidians inflicted even more damage on the country than the Romans did. Terror-stricken inhabitants sought refuge in Carthage, where despondency and famine prevailed. Consequently, Hamilcar was sent with an army into Numidia and Mauretania to suppress the rebellion, which he did with great cruelty.[81]

Peace negotiations were started. Polybius states that Regulus initiated them because he was worried that his successor would arrive before Carthage fell and thus receive the credit for the success. According to Dio the Carthaginians, fearing defeat, contacted the Romans, seeking an arrangement that would persuade them to leave. However, both Polybius and Dio agree that the negotiations failed as the Carthaginians were disgusted by the harsh conditions set by Regulus. Dio is the only source for the conditions and there is some doubt about the authenticity of his information.[82]

The two sides had different ideas about peace treaties. The Carthaginians followed the Hellenistic practice in which a war was brought to an end through a peace treaty that reflected the current balance of power without binding the defeated enemy in a subordinate position. To give one example, in 306, Agathocles evacuated the towns he had taken in Carthaginian *epikrateia* in Sicily and in return the Carthaginians gave him grain and gold.[83] The Romans, on the other hand, aimed to ensure that an enemy ceased to be a threat by forcing them to admit total defeat and making them subordinate to Rome.[84] This unyielding approach partly explains the triumphs and the landscape of monuments commemorating military achievements in the Forum.

However, the Romans, despite having landed on Carthaginian soil, were not in a position to put significant pressure on Carthage. Their army was not large enough to conquer Carthaginian cities one by one, as the cities would have to be garrisoned and they had no allies in the area. Also, they did not intend to secure a permanent foothold in Africa, so Carthage was by no means defeated. After the failed negotiations, the Carthaginians sent messengers to Greece and hired the Spartan mercenary commander Xanthippus and his men. The Romans were unable to interfere with this arrangement and so Carthage, although it was forced to fight the Romans and the Numidians at the same time, retained the initiative.

Xanthippus reorganized and trained the Carthaginian army over the winter of 255. With renewed confidence, the Carthaginians defeated Regulus' army in 255 in the vicinity of Tunis and Carthage. They pitted 12,000 soldiers, 4,000 cavalry and nearly 100 elephants against Regulus' 15,000 infantry and 500 cavalry. The Carthaginians lost 800 mercenaries; the Romans all of their army except for 2,000 who managed to make their way back to Aspis. Regulus was captured with 500 men and taken to Carthage.[85]

The Carthaginians besieged Aspis, where the remaining Romans were waiting to be rescued. When the Carthaginians learned that the Romans were preparing a fleet, they repaired the ships they had and built new ones, thus creating a fleet of 200 vessels, and put to sea. This time the Punic fleet did not sail to Sicily to stop the Roman expedition but stayed on the African coast and waited for the enemy. In the early summer of 255 the Romans launched 350 ships and sent them off under the command of the consuls Servius Fulvius Paetinus Nobilior and Marcus Aemilius Paullus. They proceeded along the coast of Sicily, then made for Africa. On their way they took Cossyra, a small island near Malta.[86] A detailed account of the battle they then fought with the Carthaginians has not come down to us but Polybius briefly states that the Romans encountered the Carthaginian fleet off Cape Bon, north of Aspis, fell on them and easily routed them, capturing 114 ships with their crews. They proceeded to Aspis, took on board their soldiers and set sail for Sicily.[87] If the figures are correct, this was a notable evacuation – 350 warships were used to rescue 2,000 soldiers – but there is not enough information to describe the operation in detail.

Thus the Roman attempt to wage war in Africa, like that of Agathocles, had failed after an initial success. However, the idea of attacking Carthaginian territory to put pressure on the Carthaginian government became the main Roman goal in the Punic Wars.

The Romans returning from Aspis lost their fleet in a storm near Camarina on the south coast of Sicily. Polybius describes the disaster: 'Of their 364 ships only 80 were saved; the rest either foundered or were dashed by the waves against the rocks and headlands and broken to pieces, covering the shore with corpses and wreckage.'[88] Diodorus records the same story in more detail:

[The Romans] while sailing across to Sicily ran into danger near Camarina and lost 340 warships, as well as cavalry transports and other vessels to the number of 300; bodies of men and beasts and pieces of wreckage lay strewn from Camarina as far as Pachynus. Hiero received the survivors hospitably, and having refreshed them with clothing, food and other essentials, brought them safely to Messana.[89]

According to Eutropius, the Romans had a fleet of 464 ships; according to Orosius, they had 300. Both claim they lost all but eighty ships.[90] We do not know whether the captured Punic ships were attached to the Roman fleet. Eutropius' figure seems to indicate that they were but other estimates do not support him. The number of soldiers on board is also uncertain but if we take Polybius' figure of 284 lost ships as a starting point and assume that there were 300 rowers and 120 marines on every ship, as there had been at Heraclea, the disaster would have involved about 85,000 rowers and 34,000 marines. We cannot say how many survived and how many perished anyway; these numbers are pure guesswork.

The disaster occurred between the rising of Orion and the rising of Sirius – that is, between 4 and 28 July, within the normal sailing period when storms were less likely. Polybius says the commanders tried to strike terror into the inhabitants of some of the cities they passed; they drew attention to their recent success and hoped to win them over to their side. He is highly critical of the route the commanders chose, sailing eastwards along the south coast and round Cape Pachynus. However, Walbank believes this criticism entered the tradition later and that there was no alternative route because the Carthaginians still controlled Lilybaeum, Drepana and Panormus.[91] The episode has been interpreted, perhaps unnecessarily, as yet another proof of Roman incompetence at sea. The question has also been raised as to whether the boarding-bridges would have made the ships dangerously unseaworthy in bad weather but Wallinga points out that the total weight of a boarding-bridge, about 1 ton, would not have upset the stability of a quinquereme.[92]

Fleets had been lost in similar circumstances before. For instance, the Carthaginians had lost one in a storm in 311 during the war against Agathocles. They had sent 130 triremes from Carthage to Sicily with Carthaginian nobles, citizen soldiers and mercenaries, money and supplies onboard; sixty triremes and 200 transport ships were wrecked. Carthage instituted public mourning and the walls of the city were covered with black sackcloth.[93]

Polybius records that the Romans were deeply grieved when they received the news.[94] Despite the staggering losses, the senate must have looked at the overall result of the campaign. We cannot be sure of the number of ships captured by the Romans but any reduction in the size of the Carthaginian fleet would make it easier for them to operate against Punic dominions in future. Servius Fulvius Paetinus Nobilior and Marcus Aemilius Paullus celebrated a triumph over Cossyra and a naval triumph over the Carthaginians. The triumphal processions probably did not display much booty as most of it lay at the bottom of the sea but the *Columna Rostrata M. Aemilii Paulli* was built on the Capitol.[95]

The War Continues in Sicily, 254–250 BC

The Romans had taken over Syracuse's traditional role as the hegemonic power in eastern Sicily and they wanted to control the entire island. The Carthaginians were faced with a difficult question: what could they do to make peace with the Romans without giving up Sicily? Over the course of ten years they had equipped a larger fleet than ever before, had revitalized their army and they had forced the Romans out of Africa. Yet they showed no sign of being able to defeat the Roman navy. Never before had they had to run a fleet of hundreds of quadriremes and quinqueremes in the way that was now required against the Romans. In 368, despite a fire that destroyed the dockyards in Carthage,[96] they had deployed 200 triremes and defeated Dionysius' fleet at Drepana. In the war with Agathocles, they had blockaded the harbour of Syracuse with thirty triremes and during the Pyrrhic War they had again blockaded the harbour with about 100 ships of unknown type. They had been threatened when Pyrrhus started to operate in Sicily because he commanded a fleet made up of his own ships and ships from Syracuse but in the end the Carthaginians did not have to increase their naval effort as Pyrrhus lost the support of the Siceliots and left the island. The First Punic War forced the Carthaginians and the Romans to make an extraordinary naval effort and certainly the war at sea with Rome was on a scale that the Carthaginians were not accustomed to.

In Sicily the war continued and Polybius describes how the Carthaginians, when they had heard of the destruction of the Roman fleet, made extensive military and naval preparations. They sent Hasdrubal to Sicily, giving him 'the troops they previously had and a force that had joined them from Heraclea, together with 140 elephants'. This sentence of Polybius probably means the troops that were already in Sicily and those that Hamilcar had brought from Sicily to Africa in 256. So now they thought it was time to send the troops back. They also equipped 200 ships and made preparations for a naval expedition. Hasdrubal crossed safely to Lilybaeum and started to drill the elephants and the rest of his force. Carthalo besieged Agrigentum, captured it and razed it to the ground. The date of Hasdrubal's arrival has been debated because the sources only mention him in the context of an action that took place in 250.[97] Before then, the Carthaginians lost control of several ports. So far the Romans had made only a few attempts against the ports but now they became the target of the joint operations of the Roman navy and army.

In 254 the Romans built 220 ships in three months. The consuls Aulus Atilius Caiatinus and Gnaeus Cornelius Scipio Asina put to sea and, after passing through the Straits, picked up at Messana the ships that had escaped shipwreck. Panormus is the only target for the expedition mentioned by

Polybius and he says the Romans besieged and took it using 300 ships. Diodorus, however, says the Romans first proceeded to Cephaloedium with 250 ships and captured it through an act of treason. They then moved on to Drepana and besieged it but when Carthalo came to its aid they were driven off and attacked Panormus instead. The Romans moored their ships in the harbour close to the walls and disembarked their men. They invested the city with a palisade and a trench and broke the city wall by using siege engines. When the Romans had taken the city, 14,000 of the inhabitants were allowed to buy their freedom by paying 2 minae each, while 13,000, along with their household goods, were sold by the Romans as booty. Other cities – Iaetia, Solus, Petra and Tyndaris – expelled their Punic garrisons and submitted to the Romans. The consuls then withdrew to Messana. Dio and Zonaras record that the Carthaginians kept a close watch on the Roman operations and captured a group of Roman ships that were on their way home from Panormus carrying a large sum of money. We do not know where this interception took place or who commanded the ships. At about the same time the Punic navy retook Cossyra. Gnaeus Cornelius Scipio Asina celebrated a triumph 'over the Carthaginians'.[98]

These events show the power of the Roman navy on the north coast, where cities had surrendered to it. This is what the commanders in the south had tried to achieve in 255 before they were shipwrecked. Clearly, the Punic fleet that rescued Drepana came from Lilybaeum, which is only 24 kilometres away. Lazenby plausibly suggests that the Romans divided their forces: Scipio taking Panormus and Atilius making the unsuccessful attempt on Drepana. As to Scipio Asina, perhaps he was given a second chance as consul after the failure in 260 because the Cornelii Scipiones were one of the most powerful families in Rome.[99] Yet in his two terms as consul he achieved – or had come near to achieving – significant successes. For instance, had he managed to take the Lipari Islands in 260, the Roman fleet would have been much safer on its arrival in Sicily and he now took a number of important coastal cities, including the wealthy Panormus, which had served as Carthaginian winter quarters and where he had been held as a prisoner. The possession of these cities also opened up the possibility of sailing around Sicily using the northern route.

Zonaras records that, in 253, the Romans made their attempt to take Lilybaeum. This is the first time Lilybaeum is mentioned in the sources as a Roman target. The Romans were repulsed but their campaign continued with a raid on the rich area of Syrtis Minor in Africa. The sources relate that both consuls participated but only Gaius Sempronius Blaesus celebrated a triumph; the other consul, Gnaeus Servilius Caepio, probably stayed in Sicily. According to Polybius, the Romans sailed along the coast and made a number of landings but achieved nothing important. Then, at Meninx, the modern Djerba, they ran aground on some shoals. They only managed to refloat their ships at high tide by throwing overboard all heavy objects and their departure was so hasty that it resembled flight. On their way back, they rounded Cape Lilybaeum and anchored at Panormus. Diodorus describes briefly how the Carthaginians prevented the Romans from mooring their ships in Africa so they went on to Panormus. According to Orosius, the Romans laid waste the coast near the Syrtes. Advancing inland, they captured many cities and brought a huge amount of booty back to their fleet. The Romans probably encountered the spring tide, which can be exceptionally high for the Mediterranean: 1.8 metres to the north-west of Djerba, and 0.9–1.5 metres elsewhere in the Syrtis Minor. These operations were not intended solely as raids to gain booty and glory for the consuls; their more important goal was to stir up renewed trouble for Carthage in Africa. This would prevent the Carthaginians from sending reinforcements to Sicily and might lead to a resumption of peace negotiations.[100]

On their way home, the Romans suffered a great shipwreck off the coast of Lucania, near the promontory of Palinurus. Polybius states that the Romans rashly crossed the open sea. The sources describe the Roman losses in different ways but it can be concluded that they amounted to around 150 warships as well as transport ships and booty. The senate seems to have treated the victories and losses as separate issues, since Gaius Sempronius Blaesus was awarded a triumph 'over the Carthaginians'. Nevertheless, the disaster shows that there were limits to the Romans' ability and willingness to furnish another fleet. Polybius says that, 'owing to the magnitude and the frequency of the disasters they met with, they were obliged by the force of circumstances to renounce the project of getting another fleet together.' Zonaras adds that 'the people believed that their misfortunes were due to their inexperience in naval affairs, and voted to keep them away from the sea with the exception of guarding Italy with a few ships.' The ships were needed to guard the Italian coast from raids.[101]

This change cannot be explained by any change in the generals' strategy or because the senate would have switched from naval to land war but it shows that resistance of the people to recruitment for naval service increased.[102] The consuls of 252, Gaius Aurelius Cotta and Publius Servilius Geminus, took Therma and Lipara. Some ships from Hiero were involved in this action. Taking Lipara had been on the agenda since 260. Aurelius celebrated a triumph 'over the Carthaginians and Sicilians'.[103] Once again the Romans had managed to erode a small part of the Carthaginian empire in Sicily.

The consuls of 251, Lucius Caecilius Metellus and Gaius Furius Pacilus, operated in Sicily and the Romans sent sixty ships to revictual the legions on the island but there was little fighting. Polybius relates that Carthaginian and Roman troops were often present at the same time in the district of Lilybaeum and Selinus, often only 5 or 6 stades [a stade = approx. 185 metres] from each other but the Romans avoided battle. They did not want to come down to meet the enemy on flat ground because of the bad experience they had with Carthaginian war elephants during the African expedition. This quiet period apparently continued throughout 251 and only came to an end in June 250, when the Carthaginians attacked the Romans in Panormus.[104]

According to Diodorus, the Carthaginian commander Hasdrubal had been berated by his own people for not fighting. Now, though, he seized the moment, taking advantage of the absence of Furius, who had returned to Italy. Metellus was left with two legions at Panormus protecting the local people who were collecting the harvest. Hasdrubal moved his forces from Lilybaeum and encamped on the frontier of Panormus.

By now the Romans had finally found a way of dealing with the Carthaginian elephants and they were confident about facing the Carthaginians in the open country. Caecilius apparently exploited the notion that the Romans lacked the courage to meet the Punic army and in this way he provoked a Carthaginian attack. They advanced right to the city walls. The elephants were rendered harmless by light troops who were given the task of targeting the animals with their missiles. Once wounded, the beasts turned on their own troops, trampling down and killing them and breaking their ranks. Caecilius made a sally from the city into the disordered Carthaginian army, killing many men and forcing the rest into a headlong rout.

The Punic navy also played a role in the action but we cannot say whether they intended to besiege the city from land and sea. According to Zonaras, the Carthaginian fleet, which was approaching the coast, became the agent of their army's destruction, for the fugitives, seeing the ships, rushed towards them and tried to force their way on board, some falling into the sea and perishing. Lucius Caecilius Metellus celebrated a triumph over the Carthaginians and the captured elephants were shown in the triumphal procession, then slaughtered in the circus.[105]

The Roman Siege of Lilybaeum and Drepana: Contest for the Last Punic Corner in Sicily

Surviving information about the last nine years of the war down to 241 focuses on Roman attempts to take the last Carthaginian naval bases in Sicily – Lilybaeum and Drepana – and the resistance put up by the Carthaginians. The victory at Panormus boosted the confidence of the Romans. Polybius reports that the news encouraged them 'to revert to their original plan of sending out the consuls to the campaign with a fleet and naval force; for they were eager by all means in their power to put an end to the war.'[106]

Polybius says the Romans built fifty new ships and enrolled sailors. The consuls Gaius Atilius Regulus and Lucius Manlius Vulso set sail for Sicily with a fleet of 200. According to Diodorus, they had 240 warships, 60 *kerkouroi* and a large number of transport ships.[107] These figures indicate that, during the two-year period when the Romans tried to wage war without any great input from the fleet, they were probably short of sailors rather than ships. The year 250 marks the peak of Roman naval power in Sicily. Since 260, they had significantly enlarged their territory, defeating Punic fleets and taking control of the south and north coasts. This expansion culminated in their attempt to take Lilybaeum.

Just before the siege of Lilybaeum began, the Carthaginians razed Selinus to the ground and moved its population to Lilybaeum, obviously because they could not protect Selinus and did not want the Romans to have it; this measure also increased the number of people available to defend Lilybaeum. Polybius makes it clear that both the Romans and the Carthaginians knew what was at stake. The Romans sailed along the north coast of Sicily; first landing at Panormus, then anchoring off Lilybaeum. There they were joined by their land forces and the siege began. They blockaded the city from sea to sea by means of a trench that connected the Roman camps on either side of the city. They constructed catapults and battering rams, which they used to attack the city's towers. They blocked the entrance of the harbour by sinking fifteen *kerkouroi* loaded with stones. The fleet stayed at sea outside the city and waited. Lilybaeum was defended by 7,000 infantry and 700 cavalry. Polybius says that, in addition to the civilian population, there were 10,000 mercenaries in the city. According to Diodorus, the Roman force amounted to 110,000 soldiers. This figure was probably made up of four legions and the crews and marines of 200 ships.[108]

The western tip of Sicily had served for centuries as a relay point for Carthage's maritime trade. Dionysius I had attacked the old Phoenician colony of Motya. The Carthaginians defended it by destroying ships in Syracuse and attacking those ships that had been taken on shore at Motya. After the city was besieged and destroyed, the Carthaginians founded Lilybaeum in 396 BC. In 368, Dionysius I occupied Selinus, Eryx and Drepana, and laid siege to Lilybaeum but failed to capture the city.[109] During his campaign, Pyrrhus took Eryx, Panormus and all the Carthaginian dominions except Lilybaeum, which he besieged in vain for two months. The Carthaginians brought over a considerable army from Africa, including grain as well as engines of war and missiles to defend the city. They walled off the land approaches, built towers at short intervals and dug a great ditch. Pyrrhus constructed siege engines, which Diodorus explains were more powerful than those he had transported from Syracuse, and tried to undermine the walls. The project failed and he left Sicily.[110]

Therefore, Lilybaeum was the only Carthaginian base that had withstood previous attacks on their territory. It was strongly fortified. Walls and a deep ditch defended the landward side and, on the side facing the sea, shoaly water made the way into the city very difficult for anyone who did not know the exact route. The Carthaginians had also fortified Drepana in 259, as soon as they had seen the power of the new Roman navy.

The Romans built more sophisticated siege works than ever before and the Carthaginians did everything they could to counteract them. As Goldsworthy puts it, this was the first siege to rival the complex sieges of the Hellenistic world, where the attackers devised elaborate siege engines and the defenders took equally elaborate countermeasures.[111] However, his comment is only relevant to the conduct of operations on land, for the siege of Lilybaeum by sea did not reach the magnitude of, for example, the siege of Rhodes by Demetrius in 305/4. There Demetrius used onboard siege engines to crack the city's defences, while the Rhodians responded by using catapults and ballistae against the ships.[112] The Romans did not have a naval siege unit. The Carthaginians used swift ships to carry envoys, just as the Rhodians had done, and they targeted some of the Roman vessels.

Help arrived from Carthage; according to Polybius, the Carthaginians filled fifty ships with 10,000 troops and sent them off under the command of Hannibal with orders to make a bold attempt to relieve the besieged city. Diodorus gives the lower figure of 4,000 men. First, they landed at the Egadi Islands to wait for favourable weather:

> As soon as he [Hannibal] had a fine stern breeze he hoisted all sail and running before the wind sailed straight for the mouth of the harbour ... The Romans, partly owing to the suddenness of the fleet's appearance and partly because they feared being carried into the hostile harbour by the force of the wind together with their enemies, made no effort to prevent the entrance of the relieving force, but stood out at sea amazed at the audacity of the Carthaginians.[113]

Hannibal also sailed to meet Adherbal, the commander of Drepana, and the Carthaginians managed to transport their cavalry from Lilybaeum to Drepana.[114] A Carthaginian called Hannibal the Rhodian worked as messenger between Lilybaeum and Carthage, making several trips. Roman ships were guarding the entrance to the harbour but they could not stop him because his ship was too fast. Several other ships whose captains had local knowledge followed his example. Polybius does not give any details but explains that they all succeeded as they knew how to navigate through the shoals when they entered the harbour. The Romans, in response, tried to fill the mouth of the harbour but the material they used either sank to the seabed or was carried away by the current. However, after several unsuccessful attempts, they finally managed to capture two Carthaginian ships in one night. First they caught a Carthaginian quadrireme that came out at night and ran aground. Then, after manning this ship, they captured the Rhodian as he was leaving the harbour. Both the Carthaginian ships were added to the Roman navy. Polybius claims that, after this success, the Romans stopped the blockade-running.[115] He is probably exaggerating here, since the acquisition of two fast ships would not have given the Romans the means to prevent all traffic to and from the city.[116]

Much has been made of the Roman failure to block the entrance to the harbour. Thiel and Wallinga, who generally see the Romans as beginners at sea, look for the explanation in terms of the comparative quality of the ships, reiterating the idea that the Carthaginian vessels were light and well-built, while those of the Romans were heavy and difficult to handle.[117] I am not convinced by this argument, because there is a practical explanation as to why the Roman blockade failed: the geography of the area favoured the Carthaginians. The Roman ships had to avoid being carried into the enemy harbour by the wind and there was also the risk of being caught on the nearby sandbanks, as had happened off the Syrtes. As to the heaviness of the Roman ships, being stationed in the open sea was a difficult position to keep and if the ships were kept there for weeks, they were bound to become waterlogged and heavy to manoeuvre.

There had been other blockades during the war: in 264 the Carthaginians had tried to prevent the Romans from crossing the Straits and failed; in 260 they had blockaded Scipio's ships successfully in the harbour of Lipara and Scipio was taken prisoner; and in 259 the Romans had blockaded Hannibal effectively in one of the harbours in Sardinia. There are other examples from the conflicts of the period. During the war with Agathocles, Etruscan ships, which had helped to relieve the blockade of Syracuse in 307, slipped into the harbour at night undetected by the Carthaginians. Similarly, during the war with Antiochus in 191–188, the Romans considered blockading the harbour of Ephesus, which was the headquarters of the Seleucid navy. The plan was to sail their fleet to Ephesus and, by sinking cargo boats, block the entrance. The idea was abandoned as a waste of resources. The fleet would have had to stay on the open sea outside the port in order to monitor the blockade. This would have exposed it to storms and stopped it from being used for any other purpose.[118] These examples demonstrate that the Roman fleet was as capable of enforcing a blockade as any other fleet but that the layout of the harbour at Lilybaeum made the operation more difficult. They did what they could with their fleet of quinqueremes and quadriremes. Restrained finances probably explains why Rome never built naval siege units like the ones used in the east: the largest ship Rome used was a six. A siege unit might have helped to crack the defence of Lilybaeum and Drepana.[119]

The siege of Lilybaeum continued until the end of the war. The campaign season of 250 ended with many problems on the Roman side. Pestilence and famine forced one of the consuls to return home with his forces. The Carthaginians managed to destroy the wooden siege engines by setting them on fire and so the Romans dug a trench and built a stockade all around the city and waited for it to surrender. The garrison in Lilybaeum rebuilt the fallen sections of the wall and continued to resist. According to Diodorus, the Romans would have been ready to give up the siege at this point, had not Hiero sent them an abundant supply of grain. Zonaras also makes it clear that the cavalry, setting out from Drepana, prevented the Romans from getting provisions and overran the territory of their allies. Adherbal, who apparently operated from Drepana, ravaged the shores of Sicily and Italy.[120]

The Romans did not succeed in challenging the Carthaginians to a sea battle. The Carthaginians could have taken their fleet out from Lilybaeum or Drepana and expelled the Romans but they did not try to do this. They could also have sent a substantial fleet from Carthage to fight the Romans but they only sent reinforcements to the city. This restrained response indicates the weakness of the Carthaginian navy but it also shows that the Carthaginians were prepared to refuse battle and wait because, thanks to their reinforcements, they suffered less than the Romans besieging the city.

Roman naval power in Sicily was at its peak in 250. In the following year, during the mandate of the consuls Publius Claudius Pulcher and Lucius Iunius Pullus, they lost practically everything they had built up in the previous decade. Publius Claudius Pulcher continued operations on the west coast and became famous for the failed attempt to take Drepana which cost him most of his fleet. The sources concentrate on his personality and the grave mistakes that were made in the execution of the project; nevertheless, there was an urgent strategic reason for the operation. The Carthaginians had blocked the route along the north coast of Sicily that the Romans used to send shipments. Consequently, the 10,000 sailors that were dispatched to Sicily to replace the men who had perished during the siege had to be ferried over the Straits and then they had to proceed to the camp on foot.[121] The Carthaginians, on the other hand, were able to support their army in Lilybaeum from Carthage and Drepana; and to send ships from Drepana to ravage the shores of Sicily and Italy. So from the Roman point of view, it was extremely important that Carthaginian naval operations from Drepana should be stopped.

Diodorus describes how Claudius first tried to block the harbour of Lilybaeum but again the sea smashed the barrier to bits. After this setback, he equipped his best ships and sailed to Drepana.[122] Polybius states that the consul planned to attack Drepana with the whole fleet as he thought the Carthaginian general Adherbal would be unprepared for such a contingency, as he did not know the new crew had arrived in Lilybaeum and was convinced that the Romans would be unable to take to sea owing to the heavy loss of men in the siege: 'On the tribunes readily consenting, he at once embarked the former crews and the new arrivals, and chose for mariners the best men in the whole army, who readily volunteered as the voyage was but a short one and the prospect of booty seemed certain.'[123]

The Romans put to sea at midnight; the first ships arrived at Drepana at daybreak. Adherbal saw the risk of being blockaded and collected the crews on the beach and summoned by crier the mercenaries from the city. He made his escape close under the rocks on the opposite side of the harbour from the Romans.[124] So, when the first Roman vessels entered the harbour, they found it empty. Claudius realized that the Carthaginians were prepared to fight him and ordered the ships to sail out again. At that point part of the fleet was inside the harbour, part was at the entrance and part was still approaching: 'On the ships already in the harbour fouling those which were entering owing to their sudden turn there was not only great confusion among the men but the ships had the blades of their oars broken as they came into collision.'[125]

The Romans soon recovered, however. They arranged their ships in a battle line outside the harbour, drawing them up close to the shore with their prows to the enemy. The Carthaginians attacked them from the sea while the Romans were still waiting for the last ships to sail out from the harbour. Polybius writes that at first the battle was equally balanced, as the marines in both fleets were the very best men from the Roman and Carthaginian land forces. The Carthaginians, though, began to get the best of the fight as they had many advantages. They surpassed the Romans in speed, because their ships were better built and their rowers better trained. Their position was also favourable as they had been free to arrange their line in the open sea. If any of their ships were hard-pressed by the enemy, they had room to retreat and they could ram and sink the Roman ships that pursued them. In contrast, the Romans could not defend themselves and turn their ships quickly because of the weight of the hulls and the poor oarsmanship of the crews; there was also nowhere for them to escape to because they had their backs to the shore. As a result, some of their ships ran onto the shallows stern-first or made for the shore and grounded. The Romans could not execute the *diekplous* attack and there was no space for them to rescue ships in distress. When the Roman commander saw what was happening, he fled with about thirty ships that were nearest to him. The rest – ninety-three ships, according to Polybius – were captured by the Carthaginians, including the crews, except for those who ran their ships ashore and escaped. Diodorus gives no further details but states that of the 210 ships, Claudius lost 117 ships and 20,000 men. Polybius' figure is probably more reliable. The sources do not give any figures for the Carthaginian fleet.[126]

There are several possible explanations for the Roman defeat. Thiel calculates that the ships were undermanned and some of the rowers were untrained and I agree with this analysis. He also makes the point that the Carthaginians did not hesitate to attack when the Roman ships were pressed against the coast, as they had done in Heraclea. According to him, this indicates that the Romans were not using boarding-bridges.[127] Rather, I believe that the Romans would have lost this battle even with the boarding-bridges. Instead of deploying their ships in a conventional battle line extending from the coast towards the open sea, they found themselves fighting with their backs against the coast and this gave them very little room for manoeuvre. Moreover, they entered the battle with broken oars. In this position, it is unlikely that any fleet could have survived, so Claudius did the only sensible thing: he fled.

The Carthaginian victory changed the balance of power at sea. Adherbal sent the Roman prisoners and captured ships to Carthage and he gained a high reputation in the city. Hannibal the trierarch sailed to Panormus with thirty ships on a raid and carried off to Drepana the store of Roman grain. Then he sailed on to Lilybaeum, carrying other useful provisions, and provided the besieged population with an abundance of supplies. Carthalo arrived from Carthage with seventy warships and a similar number of transports loaded with provisions. Adherbal gave him an additional thirty ships and sent him off to make a surprise attack on the Roman fleet that was moored near Lilybaeum. His mission was to capture as many of the ships as he could and to set fire to the rest. As the ships began to burn and others were carried off, Himilco, the commander at Lilybaeum, sent mercenaries from the town to attack the Romans. Then Carthalo left Lilybaeum and sailed towards Heraclea on the south coast in order to intercept Roman ships that were on their way to join the army at Lilybaeum.[128]

Carthalo made sure that the Roman transports and warships bringing supplies to the besiegers of Lilybaeum never got there. The consul Lucius Iunius Pullus manned sixty ships to act as a convoy. He sailed from Italy to Messana, where he was joined by ships from Lilybaeum and the rest of Sicily, and he then followed the coast to Syracuse. In all, his fleet consisted of 120 warships and about 800 transports carrying supplies. At Syracuse, the fleet was divided into two convoys. The Carthaginians intercepted the first convoy led by the quaestors somewhere on the south coast. The sources give conflicting information about the damage the Roman convoy suffered but there is no doubt that it could go no further.[129] The second convoy, led by Iunius Pullus, rounded Cape Pachynus and sailed in the direction of Lilybaeum; to avoid battle with Carthalo, he anchored off a rugged part of coast. There he was caught in a storm; all the transports and warships were lost. The first Roman convoy was also caught by the storm and destroyed. The Carthaginians avoided the storm by rounding Cape Pachynus. Iunius made his way to the army camp at Lilybaeum with the two surviving ships and their crews. He occupied Mount Eryx, located between Drepana and Panormus, taking both the temple of Venus and the town. According to Diodorus, he also fortified a place called Aigithallos and Zonaras says Carthalo captured him there.[130]

According to Roth, the fact that a consul had to organize a fleet to carry provisions suggests that the Romans had not yet set up a regular system for supplying their overseas armies.[131] However, it seems to me that both of the major tasks of that year – putting an end to Carthaginian naval activity at Drepana and using the southern supply route instead of the north – indicate that the Carthaginians had succeeded in interfering with the Romans' existing supply system. Therefore, both consuls were involved in mending a situation that had already become difficult and they failed.

The command of Sicily was given to the dictator Aulus Atilius Caiatinus and master of horse Lucius Caecilius Metellus. In Rome Publius Claudius Pulcher was brought to trial. He was accused of having acted so rashly that he had done all a single man could to bring about a great disaster. He was found guilty and heavily fined.[132] Diodorus gives a very negative description of his character.[133] There is a later tradition that both consuls were accused of having disregarded the auspices and that Iunius Pullus committed suicide rather than stand trial in Rome. Some scholars have suggested that the trial may have been prompted by Claudius' political enemies and that it was part of the agitation directed against the continuation of the naval war.[134]

The events of 249 had wide and long-lasting consequences for the campaign. Had Claudius simply lost the battle at Drepana without major casualties, the Romans could have maintained their position at Lilybaeum and protected their supply route along the south coast but the defeat was so severe it had a domino effect. Not only had they lost an immense number of men and ships, they had lost control of the Sicilian coast that they had gained over the course of the previous decade. Now the only safe area for their navy to use was the stretch of the east coast controlled by Syracuse. As the supply line by sea was closed, their troops at Lilybaeum had to be supported by land. The Romans also had to cope with renewed Carthaginian raids on the coast of southern Italy, as they had done at the beginning of the war. Therefore, the work of the last eleven years had come to nothing and their concern must have been so great that it went beyond any political battle lines.

Sicily Saved and Lost

After this victory over the Romans, the Carthaginians divided their forces so that Hamilcar Barca operated in Sicily and Hanno the Great in Africa. In 254 the Carthaginians, led by another Hamilcar, had suppressed a rebellion among the Numidians and now Hanno led a campaign that ended in the capture of Theveste 250 kilometres south-west of Carthage.[135] Hoyos dates the end of this campaign to 247, Lancel between 247 and 243 and Lazenby between 247 and 241.[136] Polybius describes how the Libyans endured the burden of funding the Carthaginian war effort:

> [The Carthaginians] had thought themselves reasonably justified in making their government of the Libyans very harsh. They had exacted from the peasantry, without exception, half of their crops, and had doubled the taxation of the townsmen ... They had applauded and honoured not those governors who treated the people with gentleness and humanity, but those who procured for Carthage the largest amount of supplies and stores and used the country people most harshly – Hanno for example.[137]

Historians have been critical of the Carthaginian decision to divide their forces, seeing it as a lost opportunity to deal with the Romans. Lazenby, for example, writes that the Carthaginians failed to press home the advantage they had gained by the destruction of the Roman fleet: they did not send troops to Sicily to relieve the siege of Lilybaeum, nor did they attempt to recapture Panormus. They could have put pressure on Hiero, whose original agreement with Rome probably ran out in 248 and they could have made proper use of their newly-recovered sea power by attacking southern Italy but they pursued these policies in a half-hearted way. Scullard also believes that the Carthaginians missed a splendid opportunity and Thiel argues that the interests of the landowners were advanced while the Punic navy was allowed to decline. However, as Hoyos points out, the expansion of

Carthage's territory meant fresh taxpaying sources that were badly needed as the Carthaginian *epikrateia* in Sicily kept shrinking.[138]

There are many factors that are uncertain, which makes it difficult to assess the situation accurately. The numbers of troops the Carthaginians deployed in Africa and in Sicily, for instance, is not known, so we cannot estimate the proportion of their military capacity that was directed towards Africa. The Carthaginians had significantly improved their position in Sicily. They had plenty of ships – their own and a substantial number captured from the Romans – so they probably sent regular supplies to their troops at Drepana and Lilybaeum and the Romans were powerless to stop them. All things considered, the Roman threat to Sicily was now less acute than it had been in previous years and the island did not demand the total attention of the Punic army. Carthage was also capable of waging war on two fronts at the same time, whereas Rome, after its defeat, could only send troops and supplies to the island where it no longer managed to use the fleet for war at sea and it therefore achieved nothing. The war had started to resemble those campaigns Carthage had fought against Syracuse or Pyrrhus, where the enemy had failed to take the last Punic strongholds, especially Lilybaeum, and the conflict was soon brought to a close with a peace treaty. Perhaps the Carthaginians thought that the Romans would give way in the same fashion as their previous opponents.

Certainly the ability of Rome to prolong operations on the island looked doubtful. It is likely that Rome's original agreement with Hiero was due to expire in 248. Polybius does not say this but according to Diodorus the peace treaty was supposed to last for fifteen years and Zonaras states that in 248 the Romans concluded a treaty of perpetual friendship with Hiero, remitting all the tribute which they were accustomed to receive from him annually.[139] Any continuation of the Roman campaign in Sicily depended on Hiero's uninterrupted support, especially now, when sailing along the Sicilian coasts had become so difficult. It is plausible that Hiero understood the value of his support and found himself in a position to renegotiate the terms but the Romans would have been reluctant to forgo his annual payments.

Polybius states that the Romans gave up their attempts to dominate at sea but they maintained their hold on the country. They continued the siege of Lilybaeum, supplying the besieging army by land.[140] Carthalo campaigned against the consuls of 248 – Gaius Aurelius Cotta and Publius Servilius Geminus – but accomplished nothing and he mounted a naval raid against Italy. Zonaras does not indentify the area he targeted but states that he made no headway and, on learning that the *praetor urbanus* was approaching, sailed back to Sicily. Mercenaries in his army now mutinied because they had not been paid. He responded by marooning many of them on deserted islands or sending them back to Carthage. When other mercenaries learned of his actions, they were indignant and were ready to mutiny as well. Hamilcar Barca, Carthalo's successor, managed to put an end to the unrest[141] and he continued the policy of naval raids initiated by Adherbal and Carthalo: 'The Carthaginians shortly afterward appointed Hamilcar surnamed Barca to the command and entrusted naval operations to him. He started with the fleet to ravage the Italian coast and after laying waste Locri and the Bruttii quitted those parts and descended with his whole fleet on the territory of Panormus.'[142]

Hamilcar seized Hercte, which was on the coast between Eryx and Panormus. According to Polybius, it possessed particular advantages for a safe and prolonged stay by an army. It also commanded a harbour, which was convenient for ships making the voyage from Drepana and Lilybaeum to Italy, and there was an abundant supply of water. From here, Hamilcar would sally out with his fleet and devastate the coast of Italy as far as Cumae.

The Romans took up a position in front of Panormus about 5 stades from Hamilcar's camp and the two sides struggled against each other for three years. Polybius gives no details of the battles but he compares the situation to a boxing match in which two champions trade blows. In 244 Hamilcar sailed at night from Hercte to Eryx and besieged the Romans who held the summit of the mountain. He defeated them and forced the inhabitants of Eryx to move to Drepana. The situation then remained stable for two years, although both sides suffered considerable hardships and repeatedly attacked each other.

Diodorus records that Hamilcar raided a fort called Italium near Longon in Catanian territory. The locations of Italium and Longon are not known to us but Catana is situated about 50 kilometres north of Syracuse. This episode shows that the Carthaginians could now sail where they liked in

Sicilian waters, a freedom they had not had for years. Zonaras describes an incident on the west coast in 247 involving a battle between the consul Numerius Fabius and Hamilcar for possession of the island of Pelias, which confirms that the Carthaginians took advantage of this situation.[143]

The Romans founded new colonies at Alsium in 247, Fregenae in 245 and Brundisium in 244. These measures strengthened the defence of the coast where the colonies of Cosa, Castrum Novum and Pyrgi had been founded before the war.[144] The Romans also raided the African coast. Zonaras describes how private citizens took over ships on the understanding that, if they restored them and took part in the raids, they could keep any booty they gained. Hippo, probably Hippo Acra, the modern Bizerte, to the west of Carthage, was one of the cities that was attacked; the ships there were burned as well as many of the buildings. The raiders also defeated a Carthaginian squadron off Panormus.[145] We have no information on the size of the Roman fleet and the type of ships that were used but evidently there was considerable interest in the venture and financial support for it. The Romans targeted a rich area. In addition to the booty that was taken during these raids, and their terrorizing effect on the local population, they were valuable to the Romans because of the information about Carthage that was gained during the course of them.

The Carthaginians never tried to recapture Messana or to interfere with the Roman supply route across the Straits. The crossing to Messana was probably protected by warships from Syracuse. In the absence of the Roman fleet, the cities on the seaboard may well have deserted the Roman cause; however, the sources do not confirm this and give very little information about these years.

The huge cost of the war was an issue for Carthage and for Rome. Carthaginian coinage was debased: silver coins fell to about 33 per cent purity during the war.[146] Polybius and Appian make it clear that both sides were severely weakened. Their resources were exhausted by protracted taxation and expenditure and lack of money prevented the Romans from building ships. Appian also states that the Carthaginians at some point sent an embassy to Ptolemy seeking to borrow 2,000 talents but the request was declined, probably as Ptolemy had made an *amicitia* with Rome in 273 and wanted to remain neutral. We cannot date the Carthaginian request to a year or tie it in with a particular event. The Roman losses are visible in the census of 247 which shows a decline of 50,000 adult male citizens in the last twenty years. Scullard concludes that Rome's allies must have suffered similar losses.[147] However, Hamilcar's resources and the operations he conducted were strong enough to force Rome to consider a new shipbuilding programme to make some progress.[148] The war in Sicily had come to a stalemate, which nevertheless required the constant presence of both consular armies. It had produced no profit for years; the last triumph with booty had been celebrated by Lucius Caecilius Metellus in 250. The Romans had not received any annual payments from Hiero after 248. So, for all these reasons, there was no money in the public treasury for the shipbuilding project. The alternative was to fund the building of a fleet through private enterprise, as had been tried successfully on a small scale a few years earlier. Polybius explains that:

> There were no funds in the public treasury for this purpose; but yet, owing to the patriotic and generous spirit of the leading citizens, enough was found to carry out the project; as either one, two, or three of them, according to their means, undertook to provide a quinquereme fully equipped on the understanding that they would be repaid if all went well. In this way a fleet of two hundred quinqueremes was rapidly got ready, all built on the model of the 'Rhodian's' ship.[149]

According to Diodorus, the Romans sailed to Sicily with 300 warships and 700 transports.[150] The names of the leading citizens who took part have not come down to us. The project resembles the Greek *leitourgia*, liturgy, known especially from Athens, according to which rich men were required to undertake work for the state at their own expense.[151] In Rome, *tributum* was collected to meet a particular public expense but Polybius is probably referring to an arrangement that went beyond that. Patriotic spirit may not have been the patrons' sole motivation since they must have been aware of the profits that could be made in Sicily from grain production and trade.

The reference to the Rhodian's ship serves in my opinion the same purpose as the story that the Romans copied a Carthaginian ship at the beginning of the war. Of course, the Romans would have wanted to examine the latest development in their enemy's shipbuilding technology. It has been argued that this exercise prompted a revolution in Roman shipbuilding and that, by using this new design, the Romans could succeed even without the boarding-bridge.[152] However, this interpretation is based on the questionable assumption that the Romans, at the outbreak of the war, were beginners at sea and needed the *corvi* to survive.

Polybius states that the whole Carthaginian navy had retired to their own country when the consul Gaius Lutatius Catulus appeared off the coast of Sicily in the summer of 242 and seized the harbour of Drepana and the roadsteads near Lilybaeum. Lutatius trained his fleet carefully:

> He was not forgetful of the original motive of the expedition, the belief that it was only by a sea battle that the war could be decisively finished. He did not, then, allow the time to pass uselessly and idly, but every day was spent in exercising and practising the crews properly for this purpose. He also paid unremitting attention to the matter of good food and drink, so that in a very short time he got his sailors into perfect condition for the anticipated battle.[153]

These thorough preparations are easy to understand: the Romans had to regain their position on the Sicilian coast and they could not afford to lose this fleet. Its arrival meant a new intensification of the war.

> When the unexpected news reached Carthage that the Romans were at sea with a fleet and were again disputing the naval supremacy, they at once got their ships ready, and filling them with corn and other provisions, dispatched their fleet on its errand, desiring that the troops at Eryx should be in no need of necessary supplies. Hanno, whom they had appointed to command the naval force, set sail and reached Hiera [the modern Marettimo, the westernmost of the Egadi Islands], from where he designed to cross as soon as possible to Eryx, unobserved by the enemy, and, after lightening the ships by disembarking the supplies, to take on board as mariners the best-qualified mercenaries together with Barca himself and then engage the enemy.[154]

According to Diodorus, Hanno had 250 warships and transports.[155] The battle has been dated to 10 March in 241,[156] so the Carthaginians' fleet arrived right at the beginning of the sailing season and they needed to lighten their ships and take Hamilcar on board before encountering the Romans. However, Lutatius' swift action made the Carthaginian plan come to nothing. The battle was fought between the well-prepared Roman fleet and a Carthaginian fleet that cannot be called anything more than a supply convoy at that point. Polybius explains that the Romans dreaded Hamilcar's bravery. Lutatius embarked a picked force from the army and sailed to the island of Aegusa off Lilybaeum. Rough weather made him hesitate for a moment but then he decided to attack:

> The Carthaginians, seeing that the Romans were intercepting their crossing, lowered their masts and, cheering each other on, each ship closed with the enemy ... The Romans had reformed their system of shipbuilding and had also put ashore all heavy material except what was required for the battle; their crews rendered excellent service, as their training had got them well together, and the marines they had were men selected from the army for their steadfastness. With the Carthaginians it was just the opposite. Their ships, being loaded, were not in serviceable condition for battle, while the crews were quite untrained, and had been put on board for the emergency, and their marines were recent levies whose first experience of the least hardship and danger this was.[157]

We have no proper description of the battle. According to Polybius, fifty Carthaginian ships were sunk and seventy captured with their crews. The ships in the rest of the fleet raised masts and fled, using a fair wind to get back to Hiera. Lutatius, sailing to Lilybaeum, joined the legions there and occupied himself with the disposal of the captured ships and 10,000 prisoners. Diodorus briefly relates that the battle was fierce. According to him, the Carthaginians lost in all 117 ships, of which twenty were captured with their crews. The number of Carthaginian prisoners was 6,000, according to Philinus. The Romans lost eighty ships; fifty were damaged and thirty destroyed. The surviving Carthaginian ships fled, aided by a favourable wind, to Carthage. Gaius Lutatius celebrated a naval triumph 'over the Carthaginians in Sicily'; the praetor Quintus Valerius Falto was awarded a naval triumph 'from Sicily'.[158]

Had the Carthaginians sent a fully-equipped battle fleet to fight the Romans, the battle would have been more evenly fought. Certainly the Carthaginians would have resisted more strongly if they had been able to unload the supplies to lighten their ships, if they had had the chance to replace the untrained crews Polybius mentions with Hamilcar's more experienced men and if Hamilcar had been given command of the fleet. The Carthaginians came to the conclusion: 'they were no longer able to send supplies to their forces in Sicily as the enemy commanded the sea, and if they abandoned and in a manner betrayed them, they had neither other men nor other leaders with whom to pursue the war.'[159]

Carthage sent a message to Hamilcar, giving him full powers to deal with the situation. Polybius praises the practical good sense he showed when he yielded to circumstance and dispatched an embassy to the Romans to discuss peace: 'a general ought to be qualified to discern both when he is victorious and when he is beaten.'[160]

The final terms of the peace treaty were only settled in Rome after the people, the *comitia centuriata*, had rejected the initial terms as being too lenient. Ten commissioners were sent to Sicily to investigate the situation (using commissioners later became common practice but this was the first time it had been done). The treaty stated that the Carthaginians had to evacuate the whole of Sicily and all the islands lying between Sicily and Italy and that they should not make war on Hiero or bear arms against the Syracusans or the allies of the Syracusans. The allies of both parties were to be secure from attack by any of the others. Neither party was entitled to impose any contribution to construct public buildings, or to enrol soldiers, in the dominions of the other, nor to form alliances with the allies of the other. In addition, the Carthaginians had to give up to the Romans all the prisoners they held without ransom and to pay 3,200 Euboean talents over ten years.[161]

The Romans had succeeded in taking Sicily; an accomplishment that neither the Syracusan leaders nor Pyrrhus had achieved. The Syracusan campaigns had lacked the united support of the Greek states needed to provide the resources to drive out the Carthaginians. Pyrrhus had had a large coalition from the Hellenistic east supporting his campaign and in Sicily he received support from Syracuse and the other cities that had invited him to intervene; nevertheless his campaign failed as soon as he lost the support of the Siceliots. The Romans, on the other hand, brought their troops and allied forces from Italy and could always rely on that source of manpower. They needed the alliance with Syracuse but were not dependent on the people in Sicily.

The heavy losses of men and ships during the war did not go unnoticed in Rome. The ability to build and man ships is an important indicator of the condition of a state's economy; therefore the postponement of shipbuilding programmes shows a shortage of money and, perhaps most important, a shortage of rowers. These factors influenced the course of the conflict. The sources tell us how bad news was received in Rome itself, where the people grieved and shipbuilding projects were postponed. The losses sustained by the allies must have been at least as large as those of the Romans. The rebellion of the Falerii in 241, which ended in their destruction, shows a reaction to the casualties and costs; it also shows how determined the Romans were to keep the Italian federation in order. While during the Second Punic War the Roman war effort grew to such an extent that it damaged the economy and demography of Rome and its allies, this effect was already visible during the First Punic War.

For Carthage, this was a most unsatisfactory conclusion. The arrival of the new Roman fleet must have come as a nasty surprise as they had done everything to stop the Romans, expelling them from Africa and defeating their fleet so that they had lost their hold on the coast of Sicily. With any other enemy a peace treaty would have been written long ago. Had the Carthaginians been able to send a battle-ready fleet into the last battle and had their preparations gone according to plan, Hamilcar Barca might have defeated the Romans at sea, forcing them to abandon their campaign for Sicily. However, now Lilybaeum, Drepana and Eryx were still firmly held by Carthage and the Carthaginians had to evacuate their undefeated army and the remains of their fleet, which was no longer strong enough to challenge the Romans at sea. The indemnities further weakened the Carthaginian economy, which had already been damaged by the war. Moreover, the loss of

Sicily directly threatened their security, for the Romans at Lilybaeum were only 140 kilometres from Carthage. This was a far more alarming situation than the Roman presence at Messana that had prompted their original objection.

Chapter 4

A Short Period of Peace: The Contest for Sea Power Continues

T he end of the longest continuous war in ancient history did not bring peace to the western Mediterranean. Carthaginian power in Africa was undermined by the rebellion of unpaid mercenaries and the mutiny spread to Sardinia. At first the Romans supported the Carthaginians but then they threatened to start a new war and forced the Carthaginians to give up Sardinia and Corsica as well. Having lost a large part of their empire in a few years, the Carthaginians, led by Hamilcar Barca, turned to the conquest of the Iberian Peninsula. The Romans fought two wars against Illyria and took Gallia Cisalpina.

The First Punic War did not automatically lead to the Second. Events in the interwar period cannot be seen simply in terms of preparation for a fresh conflict. There was no single compelling reason for war and, when it started, the parties could not have anticipated the profound effect it would have on the balance of power in the Mediterranean. However, developments during this period suggest some reasons for the renewal of hostilities, although it should be emphasized that our view of events is incomplete. The Romans did not only defeat the Carthaginians but the Second Punic War was a milestone in terms of the image the Romans created of themselves and of the Carthaginians and the justification the Romans sought for their wars.

For Polybius, the war was the starting-point of the fifty-three-year period during which Rome brought nearly the whole of the known world under its rule; he saw it as the defining moment in Rome's foreign expansion. By the end of the republic, the transformation of the Mediterranean into a Roman sea was seen as an inevitable development. The defeats Hannibal inflicted on the Romans at the beginning of the war were explained away by Augustan propaganda which represented them as tests of Roman endurance. After the war with Hannibal, the term *Punica fides*, Punic fidelity, entered common usage in Rome as a reference to notorious unfaithfulness. Thus anything Punic was stigmatized, while the Roman virtues of loyalty and justice were lauded.

The reasons for the war on the Roman side are relatively well-known through the writings of Quintus Fabius Pictor, Lucius Cincius Alimentus, Marcus Porcius Cato and Quintus Ennius. Only fragments of their works have been preserved but their interpretations resonate through the works produced by Polybius and Livy. The Carthaginian historical tradition, however, has been erased. Two professional historians, Sosylus of Sparta and Silenus of Caleacte, were selected by Hannibal to record his campaigns. Philinus also recorded important information about Roman–Carthaginian relations before the Hannibalic War but these writings have been lost except for a few fragments. It has been shown that Polybius interwove the accounts of his forerunners into his own narrative, so it is practically impossible to distinguish the contribution of Philinus from the other sources.

We have no way of knowing directly what the pro-Carthaginian authors wrote, as the little of their work that is left has been passed on through sources that were highly critical and openly hostile to their interpretation. This needs to be kept in mind when the reasons for the outbreak of the new war are assessed. As Beck points out, the narrative has been transmitted to us through the filter of the Roman tradition, which bears the marks of innate sociocentrism. The Romans did not question its validity and, as Rome's empire expanded, so did their confidence in their cause.[1]

The question of the development of the Punic navy during the interwar period is an interesting one. It has been argued that the Carthaginians neglected the fleet. Hoyos, for instance, maintains that after 244 the Barcids did not show any enthusiasm for naval warfare. While they built their new empire in Spain using its human and financial resources, the navy contracted. Rich points out that the construction of a strong fleet by the Carthaginians would have run the risk of provoking Roman retaliation before the Barcids were ready, since the purpose of such a navy could only be to rival Roman sea power.[2] Yet, the First Punic War could have ended differently, had Hamilcar Barca and his crew confronted the Romans at the Egadi Islands. Naval warfare was very much on the agenda of the Carthaginian government and they were fully prepared at the beginning of the Second Punic War, challenging the Romans both on land and at sea.

The Mercenaries' War

The Carthaginians suffered further setbacks during the first four years of peace. Under the terms of the peace treaty they lost Sicily and the indemnities they were required to pay were so high that they did not have sufficient funds left to pay their mercenaries who had to be evacuated from the island. It has been estimated that, at the outbreak of the First Punic War, the state revenues had been about 2,000 talents a year;[3] this income reduced during the war. The Carthaginians had tried to improve their financial situation by making a failed request to borrow 2,000 talents from Ptolemy and by extracting money from the Libyans. By the time the mercenaries' rebellion and war broke out, the first instalment of 1,000 talents had probably been paid out to the Romans.

The Mercenaries' War lasted from the autumn of 241 to the end of 238 and probably into 237.[4] Hamilcar Barca transferred his forces from Eryx to Lilybaeum and resigned his command. Then Gisco, the commandant of Lilybaeum, took the necessary steps to send the 20,000 troops over to Africa. His plan was to embark them in detachments at intervals in order to give the Carthaginians time to pay them their arrears and pack them off to their own countries before the next batch arrived. The sources do not give any details about these transports. At Carthage, however, there was a shortage of funds and the mercenaries were first confined in the city and then transferred to Sicca, the modern El Kef, 200 kilometres away, to wait for the money. Hanno's negotiations with them failed as they did not recognize his authority and they refused to accept the reduced payments he proposed. The situation was aggravated by language problems as it was difficult to communicate with the Iberians, Celts, Ligurians and people from the Balearic Islands who made up the mercenary army. There were a good many men of part-Greek origin among them, mostly deserters and slaves, but the largest contingent were Libyans. Polybius says:

> It was therefore impossible to assemble them and address them as a body or to do so by any other means; for how could the general be expected

to know all their languages? And again to address them through several interpreters, repeating the same thing four or five times, was, if anything, more impracticable. The only means was to make demands or entreaties through their officers, as Hanno continued to attempt on the present occasion, and even these did not understand all that was told them, or at times, after seeming to agree with the general, addressed their troops in just the opposite sense either from ignorance or from malice.[5]

The mercenaries marched on the capital and encamped at Tunis. Gisco reached Tunis by sea, bringing the money, and paid off each nationality separately. The situation could have been resolved there but now two mercenaries – Spendius, a runaway Roman slave from Campania, and Mathos, a Libyan freeman who had taken a leading part in the late disturbances – were afraid of the penalty for their actions and acted to break off the negotiations with Carthage. They managed to convince the Libyans that, once the foreign troops had been paid and sent home, the Carthaginians would take their vengeance on the Libyans. With the support of the Libyans, Spendius and Mathos were elected as generals. The mercenaries started to besiege Utica and Hippo Acra. By besieging Utica and keeping Tunis, they shut off Carthage from outer Libya. They also started to besiege Carthage. The war is known for the extreme cruelty and ruthlessness shown by both sides. Hanno and Hamilcar quarrelled and the Carthaginians ordered one of the two to leave his post and the other to remain in sole command, leaving the choice to the troops. They voted for Hamilcar to stay. In the final stages of the conflict Hanno and Hamilcar worked together to save their state.[6] According to Polybius' account, Hamilcar was the general who restored order and saved Carthaginian civilization[7] but the level of Hanno's incompetence is probably overstated.[8]

During the great rebellion in 396, the Carthaginians had transported supplies from Sardinia. The rebels, who had no capable commanders, had run out of supplies and eventually they had broken up and scattered to their native lands.[9] Now, though, the situation was much more complicated. Polybius records that the rebels received plenty of funds, troops and supplies from the Libyan towns and were able to pay the soldiers their arrears.[10] The Carthaginians were 'deprived of all these resources at one blow, but actually saw them turned against themselves ... neither had they a sufficient supply of arms, nor sailors, nor any supply of ships, so many had been the battles in which they had been engaged at sea.'[11]

Coins from this period show a further debasement; their silver content fell to 15–23 per cent.[12] The Carthaginians enrolled mercenaries and armed citizens of military age, mustered and drilled their civic cavalry and prepared triremes, pentecontors and the largest of the *akatia* (oar-propelled boats). Rome gave permission for mercenaries to be hired from Italy, though it had been forbidden in the peace treaty.[13] The use of citizens and civic cavalry indicates how urgent the situation was. Some of the larger ships may have been excluded from this effort, probably because of the shortage of crews.

The Carthaginians transported supplies from Emporia in Syrtis Minor but we do not know how frequently this was done; Polybius records one occasion on which a convoy on its way to Carthage was lost in a storm.[14] Hiero sent supplies; Polybius says Hiero was convinced that it was in his own interest to secure his Sicilian dominions and his friendship with the Romans and that Carthage should be preserved.[15] Thus Carthage would exist as a balance to Roman power.[16] Land links between Carthage and Utica were cut by the rebels but the Carthaginians communicated by sea and ships were used to take Hanno's army to Utica.[17] The Punic fleet was also used to patrol the African coast to intercept supplies coming from Italy to the mercenaries. Up to 500 traders who were captured during these operations were imprisoned in Carthage:

> The Romans were annoyed at this, but when on sending an embassy, they recovered all the prisoners by diplomatic means ... in return they gave back to the Carthaginians all the remaining prisoners from the Sicilian war and henceforth gave prompt and friendly attention to all their requests. They gave permission to their merchants to export all requirements for Carthage, but not for the enemy.[18]

Rome Takes Sardinia and Corsica

The events leading to the Roman annexation of Sardinia are difficult to explain. The unrest on the island had begun in 239 when mercenaries there, following the example of the rebellious mercenaries in Africa, attacked the Carthaginians. The Carthaginians sent over a commander called Hanno with a fresh force but we do not know what kind of ships were used to transport them or how many troops were sent. These men deserted Hanno and joined the rebels. Hanno was crucified and the mutineers murdered all the Carthaginians on the island. They took control of all the towns on the island but then quarrelled with the local population and were driven out to Italy. There are no details of how many mercenaries went to Italy or where they landed. The rebels suggested to the Romans that they should occupy Sardinia but the Romans refused. Likewise, the citizens of Utica offered to surrender to Rome but the Romans turned down the offer.[19]

Apparently, the change in Roman policy took place at the moment when the Carthaginians had dealt with the mercenaries in Libya and were preparing to recover Sardinia and invade Spain.[20] Polybius states:

> The Romans about the same time, on the invitation of the mercenaries who had deserted to them from Sardinia, undertook an expedition to that island. When the Carthaginians were angered on the ground that the sovereignty of Sardinia was rather their own than Rome's, and began preparations for punishing those who were the cause of its revolt, the Romans made this the pretext of declaring war on them, alleging that the preparations were not against Sardinia, but against themselves.[21]

The Carthaginians were in no position to resume hostilities with Rome. They sent several envoys to Rome and then, after failed negotiations, gave up Sardinia and agreed to pay 1,200 talents.[22] The explanations for the annexation given in the ancient sources are the wrongs that the Carthaginians had inflicted on the crews of the ships sailing from Rome during the war against the mercenaries – which Polybius denies took place – and the belief that Sardinia was included in the treaty of Lutatius in 241.[23] Neither of these explanations is credible. Polybius condemns the annexation: 'it is impossible to discover any reasonable pretext or cause. In this case everyone would agree that the Carthaginians, contrary to all justice, and merely because the occasion permitted it, were forced to evacuate Sardinia and pay the additional sum.'[24]

Several possible motives have been put forward for the change in Roman policy. According to Piccard, Rome was concerned about Hamilcar Barca's rise to power in Carthage at the expense of Hanno and his faction and wanted to damage his reputation. Goldsworthy suggests that the ambitions of the consul of 238, Tiberius Sempronius Gracchus, to command during a war may have played a role and that he managed to persuade the senate to accept the mercenaries' offer. Hoyos believes that the Romans were determined to secure their grip on Sicily and thought that, if the Carthaginians under the leadership of Hamilcar Barca were allowed to take back Sardinia, they might then turn to Sicily. Harris sees the takeover as motivated by the more general aim of increasing Roman power and possessions.[25]

The situation shows the weakness of the Carthaginians, who could keep Sardinia only for as long as the Romans allowed them to do so. Before the First Punic War, Carthage had sought Rome's support for its ambitions in Sicily, as can be seen in the terms of the third and fourth treaties which closed Sicily to the Romans. It had then defeated the mercenaries, thanks to Rome's decision to impose a trade embargo on the rebels and allow mercenaries to be hired from Italy. Now, though, faced with the Romans' decision to annexe Sardinia, the Carthaginians had no means of resisting. Their fleet was capable of keeping watch on the African coast and transporting troops and supplies but it was not strong enough to take on the Romans in another sea battle. The Carthaginians could only land troops in Sardinia if they defeated the Roman fleet first and there was always the danger of a renewed attack on Carthaginian territory in Africa. Therefore the Carthaginians had to give way in Sardinia for the same reason that they had had to give way in Sicily: they were no longer able to support their forces on these islands because the enemy commanded the sea.

The Romans seized on this moment of Carthaginian weakness, especially as they knew that the indemnity the Carthaginians had been forced to pay would reduce their capacity for future shipbuilding. So the fleet that was sent out with the consul also seized Corsica, which must have been included in the senate's plan to extend Roman influence in this part of the Mediterranean. In addition, the Romans conquered the Ligurian seaboard and part of the Gallic seaboard between 240 and 237. In this way they commanded the important sailing route that ran along the Sardinian and Corsican coasts to Liguria. Several campaigns were required before the islands were fully under their control. According to Zonaras, the Carthaginians interfered, supporting uprisings by the local people and keeping ships in ports on the islands but the Romans threatened them with another war if they did not leave.[26] From 227 on, two *praetors* were assigned to Sicily and Sardinia as their *provincia*.

The Roman Campaign in Illyria

The Roman campaign in 229 against Illyria was about control of the Adriatic and the Romans established ties with the leading Greek maritime cities in the area. This was their first crossing to Illyria under arms.[27] The expedition can be seen as a continuation of their involvement in the Adriatic which had started in the 290s and 280s with the foundation of colonies there. The Romans were also taking control of territory in the Po valley in the 230s. So this campaign and its aftermath can be regarded as the beginning of the Roman conquest of Greece.[28]

According to Polybius, complaints about piracy presented to the senate by Italians sailing in the Adriatic caused a Roman embassy to be sent to Queen Teuta of Illyria in 230 and Appian states that the Greeks in Issa also pleaded to the Romans. The protests of the Italians were probably led by Tarentum and it is plausible that Syracuse was also involved. So Rome, which had to listen to and protect its allies, sent the embassy.[29] Both sources make it clear that the murder of the Roman ambassador led to the declaration of war.[30] The Romans dispatched both consuls with their armies and a fleet of 200 ships in 229. Gnaeus Fulvius Centumalus celebrated a naval triumph 'from the Illyrians'. This is the only one we know of after the First Punic War and before those in the 180s celebrating Roman victories over Antiochus' fleet.

Teuta had a fleet of more than 100 *lemboi* or small oared vessels. Detailed information about the operations of the Roman fleet has not come down to us but we do know that the Romans sailed to various ports, among them Corcyra, Epidamnus, Apollonia and Issa. Some of these ports were being besieged by the Illyrians, who escaped when they learned the Romans were approaching. Teuta finally fled to Rhizon with only a few followers. According to the peace treaty, she agreed to pay any tribute the Romans imposed and to relinquish Illyria except for a few places and she undertook not to sail beyond Lissus with more than two *lemboi*. Rome's interest in the area remained; envoys were sent to the Achaean and Aetolian Leagues, who were the opponents of the Illyrians, and to Athens and to Corinth to explain that the Romans were providing a service to Greeks with their intervention. Rome, or possibly just the Roman envoys, were admitted to the Isthmian Games at Corinth and to the Eleusinian Mysteries at Athens.[31] The Isthmian Games were a Panhellenic festival administered by Corinth; the Eleusinian Mysteries were one of the most important agonistic festivals at Athens.

The Romans had wiped out the enemy fleet and established their position in the Adriatic and the coast of western Greece. The Illyrian ships had no chance if the Romans sent quadriremes, quinqueremes and triremes to fight the *lemboi*. Limitations on naval movements and on the number of ships a defeated enemy was allowed to keep were common features of Roman peace treaties. They wanted to make sure that the enemy ceased to be a threat and to leave it without any opportunities for further action at sea.

Barcid Power in Spain

Subsequent actions by Carthage until the new war concentrated on the expansion of Carthaginian territory in Spain. The revival of Carthaginian wealth and military power took place under the leadership of Hamilcar Barca, his son-in-law Hasdrubal and son Hannibal.

The events in Spain ignited the Second Punic War. This is the area where we see the massive Roman takeover of claims to be 'in the right'. This is apparent both in the immediate causes and underlying reasons for the war that are offered in the ancient sources. To put things briefly, the wrath of the Barcids cannot have been the driving force in their relations with Rome as is claimed by Polybius; it was probably just another way of putting all the blame on Carthage. The idea that Hasdrubal had alienated the Carthaginian leaders at home is mostly a Roman invention, probably going back to Fabius Pictor, who had the agenda of freeing Rome of war guilt and so set up a dualism between the Barcids and Carthage. Hannibal's conquest of Saguntum in 219 was seen as a breach of a treaty: one in a long list of Punic treaty breaches that we can find in Roman authors. Yet, we do not know when Saguntum's relations with Rome began and what its status was. Moreover, the Romans did nothing concrete to help the city when it was attacked.[32]

To begin with, Carthage did not have any direct control of Spain. There were old Greek and Phoenician colonies on the coast. The local groupings of peoples included the Iberians, Celtiberians, Lusitanians, Cantabrians and Gallaecians, subdivided into smaller tribes. Many of them were prosperous. In politics and military matters, individual communities made their own decisions. The Carthaginians had hired mercenaries from Spain for centuries and used them together with soldiers from Libya to fight Syracuse.[33]

The Barcids never exercised any independent empire-building in Spain aimed at creating a Hellenistic state on their own but everything happened in cooperation with the government at home. Hamilcar Barca operated from 237 until his death in the winter of 229/8. He sailed along the African coast to the Straits of Gibraltar and landed at Gadir.[34] He operated in southern Spain, especially in the lower and middle valley of the river Baetis, modern Guadalquivir. It has been estimated that his expeditionary army consisted of about 20,000 men, 2,000 or 3,000 cavalry and elephants. He could rely on the support of the Phoenician towns and use them as allies and could also find allies from Iberian states, as their disunion and quarrelsomeness made them relatively easy targets in Punic expansion. We know only a few details of his campaign. Together with the Celts, he made war on the Iberians and Tartessians and cut their whole force to pieces. This had been an anti-Punic coalition defending the richest region in Spain; Hamilcar was obviously interested in the silver and copper mines along the Rio Tinto. He took over and enrolled in his own army 3,000 survivors. Next, he besieged a chieftain called Indortes, slaughtered most of his force of 50,000 men and had him crucified. Hamilcar released the rest of over 10,000 of Indortes' men that he had captured. It is not mentioned in our sources but we can estimate that, next, Hamilcar operated in the Baetis region, including Sierra Morena. The success of the campaign was becoming visible: Gadir began to issue a new, high-quality silver coinage and, according to Cornelius Nepos, horses, weapons, soldiers and money were sent to Africa.[35] There was another Numidian rebellion in Africa – we do not know the reason for it – that Hasdrubal was sent to deal with; he cut down 8,000 men and took 2,000 alive. Hamilcar founded a city on the east coast of Iberia called Acra Leuce, probably the modern Alicante, to be the new power centre of Carthaginian rule in the peninsula. The Carthaginians could also use the ports of Malaca, Abdera and Mastia and Hasdrubal served as a trierarch, a naval commander.[36] We do not know if the Punic fleet had to fight for its position at the Spanish coast or whether the office was mainly to take care of the links between Spain and Africa. Any land operation in a new area naturally required the support of the fleet. Hamilcar died when he was trying to subdue the hinterland of Acra Leuce while besieging the town of Helice, the location of which is not known to us.[37]

Hasdrubal was acclaimed general by both the army and the Carthaginians. This probably means that the citizen officers and troops in Spain made their decision and then referred it to the citizen body at Carthage for ratification in spring 228. According to Diodorus, Hasdrubal collected the army of 50,000 infantry, 6,000 cavalry and 200 elephants. He used part of this army to make war with the Orissi and avenge Hamilcar's death. Hasdrubal then married the daughter of an Iberian prince, which served to symbolize his commitment to the lands he ruled; an approach different from the policy of conquest and exploitation exercised by Hamilcar. Hannibal served as the commander of cavalry. We do not know how Hasdrubal arranged to be acclaimed supreme general, *strategos autokrator*, 'by all the Iberians', as Diodorus puts it, but this gesture was immediately recognizable beyond Spain since election as leader by an alliance was common in the Hellenistic world. Hasdrubal founded New Carthage, the modern Cartagena, on the site of the earlier Mastia, 100 kilometres south of Acra Leuce. The city was located on a peninsula facing the sea to the west and the south and had a good natural harbour facing southwards. It was surrounded by four hills; Hasdrubal's palace was built on the hill on the western side. Polybius calls the city Carthage and New City. In Punic 'new city' was one word – *qart-hadasht* – so Hasdrubal's new city was another Carthage. With this choice of name, Hasdrubal advertised to the world the renewed power of Carthage.[38]

The First Punic War had made Rome the most powerful state in the western Mediterranean. However, the expansion of the Punic empire in Spain, interacting with the Celtic pressure on Rome's northern frontier, changed the strategic balance to Rome's disadvantage.[39] The Romans were aware of Punic expansion; they had their old ally Massilia with its trade contacts and they traded with cities in North Africa and Spain, including Emporiae, a small Greek port in north-eastern Spain. The Romans had sent an envoy in 231 to meet Hamilcar and ask about the meaning of his operations in Spain.[40] The foundation of New Carthage did not only catch the attention of the Spaniards and the Carthaginians at home. The Romans sent an envoy to the city to meet with Hasdrubal and the Ebro treaty was concluded in 226, under which Carthage agreed not to cross the Ebro in arms. Some scholars see it as a reciprocal agreement, dividing Spain into the spheres of interest of Carthage and Rome, giving Carthage the territory south of the river and Rome the authority over the areas north of it. I follow Eckstein in seeing the treaty as a purely military one with the aim of limiting Punic military activity. Carthaginian commercial and diplomatic activity continued north of the Ebro.[41] On the one hand the Romans imposed a limit on Barcid expansion but on the other they recognized the future scenario that most of Spain would belong to Carthage. The treaty had a specific military function for Rome: it received a guarantee that the Carthaginians would not join forces with the Gauls from the north; an important fact in the impending Gallic War. As Loreto points out, the treaty created 'a separation zone between the Gauls and the Spanish Carthaginians'. If there were any military movements in this area, the Romans would know and have time to get ready.[42]

The Gauls were defeated in the war and the Romans continued to take Gallia Cisalpina. Polybius speaks of great and general alarm in Rome at the time of the Gallic attacks in 225, with the Romans ready to defend every part of their state. They had one legion in Tarentum and one in Sicily as reserve. They sent the consul Lucius Aemilius with his army to Ariminum to wait for the Gauls; the other consul, Gaius Atilius, with two legions was sent to Sardinia but he returned to Pisa when the hostilities with the Gauls began. This was the first time since 240 that a large number of troops had been located in Sicily and Tarentum. We do not know the number of Roman ships deployed. The arrangement of troops indicates that the Romans were concerned about a seaborne attack by Carthage while Rome's back was turned, fighting the Gauls.[43] We have no information of any Carthaginian naval activity against Rome's dominions; nevertheless, the Romans cannot have acted for no reason. We have a later example from 208, when the

Romans received intelligence that the Carthaginians were making plans to blockade the coasts of Italy, Sicily and Sardinia and Roman ships were relocated accordingly.[44] No Punic naval raid took place at that time. Perhaps there was some similar intelligence in 225 of which we do not know.

Rome minted dozens of coins depicting the prow of a boat; the first coins of this type have been dated to 225–217. We cannot date these coins to any specific event but they convey the general feeling of Rome's growing ambitions. In the Barcid coinage too, there is a series of coins with a ship's prow; not otherwise a common motif in Punic coins. These have been dated variously either to Hasdrubal's reign or generally to the period 237–209. Again, it shows the general direction of Punic ambitions.[45]

Hasdrubal was murdered in autumn 221. By then, the Carthaginians controlled almost half of the Iberian Peninsula; the area exceeded Punic territory at home. They continued to exploit mineral resources around the area of New Carthage and Sierra Morena.[46] Hannibal was elected general in the same way as Hasdrubal had been: the troops in Spain chose him as their commander and the general assembly ratified the decision at Carthage.[47] Thus Barcid rule continued. Hannibal had a Spanish wife and his brothers Hasdrubal and Mago had high-ranking positions in the army in Spain, as did his nephew Hanno. His brother-in-law Bomilcar was in Carthage; he was probably one of the people looking after the Barcid interests there and served as admiral in the Second Punic War.

It is hard to say what Hannibal's long-term strategy was. He carried out a campaign against the Olcades; he took their strongest city, Althia, and the rest of them surrendered. He exacted tribute from the towns and retired to New Carthage to spend the winter there. In 220, he attacked the Vaccaei and took Hermandica and Arbucala. He defeated the Carpetani, the fugitive Olcades and those who had escaped from Hermandica who had started a joint offensive.[48] He spent that winter in New Carthage too. The Saguntines had sent messages to Rome informing the Romans of the developments in Spain. The Romans sent legates, Publius Valerius Flaccus and Quintus Baebius Tamphilus, who met Hannibal at New Carthage in late 220. The facts about this embassy were probably later deliberately distorted in the Roman historical tradition. Polybius' version makes most sense. According to him, the Romans asked Hannibal to 'keep off Saguntum, which they

1. Carthaginian silver tetradrachm dated to 330–300 BC, a period of heavy Carthaginian-Syracusan confrontations over Sicily. This could be money minted to pay the soldiers. Obv: Head of Tanit with four dolphins around. Tanit was chief goddess of Carthage, equivalent to Astarte, chief deity of Tyre. Rev: Horse's head, palm tree. Legend: 'MMHNT', *ommachanat* in Punic, meaning 'in the camp or people of the camp', meaning army headquarters.

2. An example of Roman *aes signatum* or 'struck bronze' bars used in early Roman coinage, often drawing on military themes. From the decades before the First Punic War (also dated to 260–242 BC). Obv: Anchor. Rev: Tripod.

3. Ram of a Roman warship (Egadi 1). This is the first of the rams discovered at the Egadi Islands. This object was originally recovered by a fisherman and then recovered by the authorities from an antiquities dealer in Trapani in 2004. There is no information regarding its provenance but the discovery prompted investigation into the battle zone at the Egadi Islands, where more discoveries have since been made.

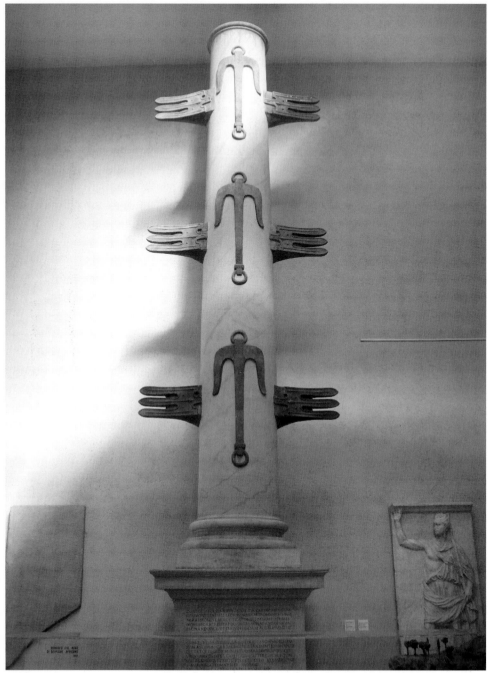

4. Reproduction of the Columna Rostrata C. Duilii for the victory at Mylae in 260 BC. This represents a marble column to which the prows of captured Carthaginian warships were attached.

5. Roman bronze triens from 225–217 BC. Obv: Head of Minerva with Corinthian helmet, four value marks. Rev: Prow, four value marks. The coin belongs to the first Roman prow series. There were many more to come. Ships' prows are a common motif on coins and war memorials in the Hellenistic world and Rome minted coins with the prow more than any other state. Minerva was the goddess of defence in Roman mythology, as well as the goddess of wisdom and a protector of the state.

6. Roman as, minted after 211 BC. Obv: Laureate head of Janus, value mark above. Rev: Prow, value mark above. Legend: ROMA. Janus was regarded as a warlike god in Rome. The gate called Janus Geminus in Rome, through which the armies passed, was ritually opened in times of war and kept closed in times of peace.

7. Syracusan silver litra from 274–216 BC. Hiero II was a long-time supporter of Rome, making the Roman war effort in Sicily possible. Obv: Portrait of Hiero diademed, bucranium. Rev: Nike driving a quadriga. Legend: BASILEOS/HIERONOS. Nike personified victory in Greek mythology, a quadriga was the chariot of the gods and an emblem of triumph. The coin follows the Hellenistic practice of using ruler portraits on coins, the ruler being depicted with upward gaze and diadem.

8. A rare representation of a Carthaginian warship. A Carthaginian shekel from Spain, where the Barcids rebuilt the state's wealth and military power after the First Punic War. Dated either to Hasdrubal's reign (228-221 BC) or generally to the period 237–209 BC. The Barcid ruler is depicted in the typical Hellenistic manner with upward gaze and diadem. The coin belongs to a series with a ship's prow, a motif otherwise unknown on Punic coins. It provides tangible evidence that the navy had a place in the general plan of Carthage; a fact also visible in the historical records as the Second Punic War became a full war at sea.

9. Silver denar from 125 BC. Obv: Helmeted head of Roma. Legend: ROMA. Rev: Jupiter crowned by flying Victory, driving a biga of elephants, holding thunderbolt in left hand and reins in right hand. Legend: C. METELLUS. The coin recalls the victory of Lucius Caecilius Metellus in 250 BC over Hasdrubal at Panormus and the capture of Hasdrubal's elephants.

10. Bronze coin minted in Etruria, 3rd century BC. Obv: Head of an African. Rev: Elephant. Legend: M. The motifs would refer to the Second Punic War, when Hannibal, Hasdrubal and Mago sought and received the support of the Etruscans against Rome.

said was under their protection, or crossing the Ebro, contrary to the treaty engagements entered into in Hasdrubal's time'.[49]

As Hoyos points out, these demands had a very different tone from that used in 226 when the Romans had, by 'petting and conciliating', made the treaty with Hasdrubal. The Romans did not receive Hannibal's compliance; he accused the Romans of having a short time previously, when there was a factional quarrel at Saguntum, unjustly put to death some of the leading men. This had probably taken place just before the envoys came to New Carthage and been carried out by the same envoys or their companions. The Saguntines had invited the Romans to settle a domestic political struggle that probably took place between the faction that wanted to make Saguntum a subordinate ally of the Punic empire and those who favoured Saguntum staying independent. Valerius and Baebius sailed over to Carthage to repeat their protest. We have no information of the discussions there.[50]

Hannibal started to besiege Saguntum in May 219 and took the city by storm eight months later, gaining a great booty of money, slaves and property. The Romans saw this as a breach of a treaty: it is one in a long list of Punic treaty breaches that we can find in works of Roman authors. In a fragment of Fabius Pictor the attack is labelled as an *adikia*, injustice, and the same view was adopted by other ancient writers including Polybius.[51] When the news of the fall of Saguntum reached the Romans they sent legates to Carthage, demanding that Hannibal and the members of his council must be given up to the Romans or war would be declared. The Carthaginians declined and the Roman envoys declared war.[52]

Still, the Romans did nothing to help Saguntum during the siege. This was covered up in later Roman histories: Livy's narrative shows traces of a tradition that put the siege of Saguntum and Hannibal's invasion of Italy within the same consular year, giving the impression that there was no time to help the Saguntines. Valerius' and Baebius' mission to Saguntum, which took place in late 220, was also redated to 219 – during the siege – to imply that the Romans did help the Saguntines.[53]

Only Polybius gives a credible explanation for not helping Saguntum. The Romans spent the summer of 219 fighting Demetrius in Illyria. Polybius states that the Romans wanted to secure their position in Illyria before the looming war with Carthage broke out. Demetrius was relying on support from Macedon and sacking and destroying the Illyrian cities subject to Rome. He had also broken the terms of the treaty by sailing beyond Lissus with fifty *lemboi* and pillaging many of the Cyclades. The consuls Lucius Aemilius Paullus and Marcus Livius Salinator were sent to Illyria. They besieged and took Dimale and defeated Demetrius at Pharos. Demetrius fled, sailing with some *lemboi*, and reached Philip of Macedon. The Romans took Pharos and razed it to the ground and subdued the rest of Illyria; both consuls celebrated a triumph. This was Polybius' first mention of Macedon as a major factor in Roman strategy. The Romans feared a regional Macedonian expansion towards the Adriatic, including an attack on Roman Illyria, which would have led to a war with Macedon at the same time as the Hannibalic war was impending.[54]

Being told to keep away from Saguntum gave Hannibal the chance to test how far the Romans were prepared to go; the possibility of a peaceful solution was lost as soon as the siege began. The Romans could not really have interfered in the situation to save the city without de facto starting a war with Carthage. Maybe the explanation for their passiveness lies in the fact that in 219 they were not yet prepared for a war; they only sent the embassy to Carthage in the following spring after preparations had been made.

Chapter 5

The Second Punic War, 218–201 BC:
Roles Reversed

T he Second Punic War was the world war of its time, with battles taking place in Italy, Spain, Africa, Sicily and Sardinia. Since Hannibal made an alliance with Philip of Macedon, Rome also became irreversibly involved in matters in the eastern Mediterranean in the First Macedonian War (211–205).

The main sources for this war are Polybius and Livy. Most of Polybius' text has been lost and we mainly rely on Livy. The two writers do not seem to have had much interest in war at sea but concentrate on war on land and the deeds of certain commanders such as Scipio Africanus. Hannibal is also in their focus; consequently, they do not give much attention to the other troop commanders that fought alongside him. This means that we do not have a full picture of the complex measures undertaken from Carthage to meet the demands of the war on all the fronts. Although Hannibal was able to make all the decisions concerning warfare in Italy himself, the overall conduct of war was decided by the Carthaginian government.[1]

This war was different from the first one in that there were very few big naval battles. Naval history cannot, however, be written based on sea battles and other spectacular events: the lack of battles does not make the navies insignificant. Warships were used for the same purpose as before: to transport the troops and supplies, to attack and ravage the enemy territory and for diplomacy. Fleets also fought their war at sea, trying to gain and keep control of the coastlines and harbours, thus enabling the armies to operate. This was decisive in terms of winning the war. We do not have information from all the coastal areas and islands for every year, so there are gaps in our knowledge; on the other hand, we have detailed information on some points, showing the intensity of warfare at sea. I will accept the ship numbers as they are presented in our sources. Both states still operated with large fleets, having over 200 quinqueremes in action in most of the years.[2] The fleets were divided into smaller units that at the same time operated on the coasts of Spain, Africa, Italy, Sicily and Sardinia. The Second Punic War became a full war at sea.

The Outbreak of the War

Finishing one war had cost the Carthaginians Sicily. Avoiding another war had cost them Sardinia. The demand to hand over Hannibal to the Romans was an impossible one and, generally, the reasons for indignation were many. Nonetheless, now the Carthaginians were ready for a revision of the power structure and did not need to accept any more demands. The new enterprises in Spain had brought in huge revenue. It has been estimated that the mining districts of southern Spain produced 46 tons of silver a year, the equivalent of 10 million denarii. The total cost of the 60,000-strong army in Spain just before the beginning of the war, including weapons, ships, war matériel, provisions and pay, was about 9.5 million denarii per year. Thus the mining income was sufficient to cover the maintenance costs of the armies in Spain and Italy. Any surplus was probably transferred to Carthage. Another important source of wealth was the rich agricultural resources in North Africa.[3]

Because of the political, financial and strategic reality, the Carthaginians probably intended to carry out a short efficient campaign against the Romans to change the balance of power and thus the obvious target was Italy. The Carthaginians had much to protect. They wanted to avoid operations on African soil as they knew the precarious situation with the indigenous people; another Roman campaign in Africa might start another rebellion, not to mention the damage it would cause to the landowners and their estates. The Spanish possessions had to be protected to guarantee the business activities that brought wealth to Carthage. The Carthaginians must have felt indignation at the loss of the islands and their abundant revenues. These are probably objectives shared by most Carthaginians.[4]

There were factors preventing transports going from Spain to Italy by sea: the Carthaginians needed safe ports on the way, which would have meant using the route by the Gallic and Ligurian coasts that were mostly under

Roman control; moreover, they would run the risk of confronting Roman ships and would have to pass Massilia and its fleet. If it was not possible to transport the troops by sea, then Hannibal would have to take the route over the Alps. Hannibal was not the first one in the ancient world to cross the Alps but he was the first to do so leading an entire organized army.[5] This famous story should not prevent us from seeing that the Carthaginians were also active at sea, using their fleet to support their army in Spain, where they had uninterrupted contact between Carthage and New Carthage. Furthermore, the fleet stationed in Carthage was active from the beginning, attacking ports in Sicily, Sardinia and the coast of Italy.

Hannibal arranged forces in Spain and Africa, sending soldiers from Africa to Spain and vice versa, thus binding the two provinces in reciprocal loyalty. Polybius bases this information on a bronze tablet that he found at the Lacinian promontory, the modern Capo Colonna near Croton on the south coast of Italy, where Hannibal set out his account in Punic and Greek at the temple of Hera Lacinia in the summer of 205. The inscription, which has not survived, stated that Hannibal sent to Africa 1,200 horse and 13,850 foot supplied by the Thersitae, Mastiani, Iberian Oretes and Olcades, as well as 870 Balearian slingers. The troops were stationed in Metagonia in Libya and some in Carthage itself. From the Metagonian towns he sent 4,000 foot soldiers to Carthage to serve both as a reinforcement and as hostages. In Spain, he left 50 quinqueremes, 2 quadriremes and 5 triremes with Hasdrubal, 32 of the quinqueremes and all of the triremes being fully manned. He gave as cavalry 450 Liby-Phoenicians and Libyans, 300 Ilergetes and 1,800 Numidians drawn from the Massyli, Masaesylii, Maccoei and Maurusi, and as infantry 11,850 Libyans, 300 Ligurians and 500 Balearians, as well as 21 elephants.[6] The list does not include everything: for example, the fleet at Carthage is not mentioned and in the Carthaginian territory in Africa there must also have been other troops defending it than just those sent by Hannibal. So we are seeing only one part of the Carthaginian total plan. Hasdrubal was supposed to follow from Spain soon afterwards, using the same route as Hannibal, and the army in Italy was supposed to receive reinforcements from Africa.

The chronology of the events in 218 goes as follows: the Romans declared war on the Carthaginians in March. Hannibal's voyage from New Carthage to northern Italy took five months. There are different opinions on when he left New Carthage: according to Sumner and Walbank, he set out at the end of April; according to Lazenby, this happened at the beginning of June. Hannibal's relatively late departure can be explained by the fact that he waited for the spring flooding of the Spanish rivers to subside and that he wanted to see the military dispositions of the Romans. He needed to know where the consuls were going to be sent and also to make sure that the Romans would not learn too early that he was going to Italy.[7]

As for the Roman plan, they were going to fight Hannibal in Spain and attack the Carthaginian territory in Africa with consular armies and a full fleet. The plan was based on the control of the landing-places needed on the way. No part of it worked as intended; instead the Romans had to rethink as soon as they saw the scale of Carthaginian operations.

The Romans Land in Spain: The Battle of Ebro

The consul Publius Cornelius Scipio was assigned Spain. He was given sixty quinqueremes and there must have been transport ships too. He sailed in five days from Pisa to the area of Massilia and came to anchor off the mouth of the Rhône. There he received the news that Hannibal had left Spain and was crossing the Pyrenees. Following Walbank's calculations, the consul must have started from Pisa in mid-August. This late start can be explained by the fact that the decision to declare war was taken late.[8] After failing to intercept Hannibal, the consul sent his brother, Gnaeus Cornelius Scipio, to Spain with a small army and returned to Italy, sailing with a small number of soldiers to Pisa.[9]

We have no figures on this but we can expect that most of the Roman fleet must have been sent to Spain to secure the safe landing of the army. Based on Livy's narrative, it seems that there was quite a demonstration of Roman sea power on the northern Spanish coast:

> Gnaeus Cornelius Scipio, who had been sent out to Spain with a fleet and an army, had set sail from the mouth of the Rhone and passing the Pyrenees had put into Emporiae. Landing his army there and beginning with the Laeetani, he had brought all that coast, as far as the

river Ebro, under Roman sway, partly by renewing old alliances and partly by forming new ones.[10]

There is no information about the Punic navy for this year. The Carthaginians did make an attempt to stop the Romans on land: Hanno lost a battle to Scipio and the Romans plundered Cissis and the camp close to it. Hasdrubal tried to expel the intruders near Tarraco, where they had gone on a raid:

> He came upon the soldiers of the fleet and the mariners, who were dispersed and wandering over the countryside ... and sending out his cavalry in all directions he drove them, with much slaughter and more confusion, to their ships ... Scipio ... after punishing a few of the ships' captains, left a garrison of moderate size in Tarraco and returned with the fleet to Emporiae.[11]

After more fighting on land, the Romans set their camp at Tarraco and spent the winter there. The fight for control of the Spanish coast took place at the mouth of the Ebro in the spring of 217 when the Romans and the Carthaginians departed from their winter quarters of Tarraco and New Carthage. Polybius states that during the winter Hasdrubal had repaired 30 ships left by Hannibal and had manned 10 additional ones and thus had a fleet of 40 ships. He appointed Hamilcar (Himilco, according to Livy) as his admiral and the two forces proceeded together; the fleet sailing close to the coast and Hasdrubal leading his army along the beach. Gnaeus Cornelius Scipio had thirty-five ships and the Romans also used two swift-sailing Massilian ships for intelligence. We do not have much information about the battle. Polybius states that after a short struggle the Carthaginians, having lost two ships with their crews and the oars and sailors of four others, ran their ships ashore when the Romans pressed on, and they took refuge with the troops on land: 'The covering military force on the beach did not benefit them so much by the confidence it inspired as it damaged them by ensuring an easy and safe retreat.'[12]

The Romans towed off twenty-five of the Carthaginian ships. Livy tells basically the same story. He states that the Roman ships were first detected from the Spanish watchtowers, which were used to protect the coast against pirates. From Livy we also get the idea that the Carthaginian sailors were badly prepared since they did not expect any fighting to take place that day. Both Polybius and Livy describe how the Romans in one easy battle had made themselves the masters of the sea (Polybius) or masters of all that coast (Livy).[13]

A fragment from Sosylus gives valid details which Polybius has omitted and generally conveys that it was a fierce battle and not just an occasion where the Punic navy immediately gave in. He gives the credit to the Massilians for stopping the Carthaginian *diekplous* attack with a two-line formation:

> They all fought outstandingly, but most of all the ships of the Massilians, who were the first to join battle and were wholly responsible for the success of the Romans ... The Carthaginians suffered a two-fold defeat, because the Massilians knew their particular style of fighting ... When they drew up their line, they ordered the front ships to face forwards, but to leave other ships waiting behind them at suitable intervals, which as soon as the first ships had been passed could take the opportunity to attack the enemy's ships as they were still advancing, without moving from their original formation. This is what Heracleides[14] did in past times, and as a result he was responsible for the victory. And now, as we said, the Massilians followed the description of this ancient event. As the Carthaginians advanced in the anticipated fashion ... they fought alongside ... the Carthaginians turned to flight.[15]

This battle was decisive, since as a consequence the Carthaginian navy lost its position on the Spanish coast. Had they won, they could perhaps have expelled the Romans from Tarraco or cut their supply line, making the Roman situation in Spain untenable. The Battle of Mylae in 260 had opened the north coast of Sicily for the Roman fleet; now the Romans could venture south of the Ebro, raiding along the coast with the fleet and troops. They landed at Honosca and took the city by storm. They then made for New Carthage, devastating the surrounding country and setting fire to the buildings alongside the wall and gates. The fleet, already filled with booty, arrived in Longuntica, where the Romans found a great quantity of *spartum*, esparto grass, which was used as material for rope and which Hasdrubal had collected for the use of his ships. The Romans took what they needed and burned the rest. They crossed to the island of Ebusus (Ibiza), where they tried in vain to take the city and devastated the countryside. They retired to their ships and ambassadors from the Balearic Islands came to Scipio to sue for peace. The Roman fleet then returned to the northern parts of the province, where the expedition resulted in other ambassadors coming to meet the Romans, giving hostages and coming under Roman rule. According to Livy, there were more than 120 ambassadors. Hasdrubal retired into Lusitania.[16] Therefore, the local communities' first recognition of Roman dominance was based on the showcasing of Roman sea power.

In 217, Publius Cornelius Scipio was sent as proconsul with twenty ships (according to Polybius, or thirty according to Livy) and 8,000 soldiers and supplies to join Gnaeus. He took the command of the navy, while Gnaeus commanded the army.[17] The use of proconsuls in campaigns was a new feature and enabled the Romans to develop long-term strategies as now the commanders operated on the same front for several years.

Roman control of the Spanish coast was, of course, not complete. Messengers sailed from Spain to Carthage and back, and new troops were sent to Spain. In 216, Hasdrubal received the order from Carthage that he should at the first opportunity lead his army to Italy. Livy states that the spreading of this news throughout Spain made nearly everyone incline to the side of the Romans. Accordingly, Hasdrubal sent a letter to Carthage demanding that they should send him a successor to hold his position with a strong army. The Carthaginian senate did not make any change in Hasdrubal's position but sent Himilco with a complete army and an enlarged fleet to hold and defend Spain by land and sea. We do not know where he landed but he beached his ships and reached Hasdrubal. Livy states that Hasdrubal did not trust either part of his force and stayed at a distance from the enemy. As he received the reinforcements, he wanted to take up a position closer to the enemy and told the navy to be prepared to protect the coast and the islands. At that point, however, the naval captains started a revolt. They had been punished after the Battle of Ebro for their cowardly behaviour and had since been loyal neither to their commander nor to the Carthaginian cause.[18]

This underlines the importance of the Battle of Ebro and the consequences it had for Punic warfare in Spain. As Thiel points out, if the officers were

Spanish, the rowers and sailors must have been Spanish as well.[19] Thus, Hasdrubal was facing trouble with mercenaries, or should we call them allies? The Spanish tribes had a tendency to support whichever side was winning in the war, just like the tribes in north Italy. Perhaps this explains why we do not have any further information on attempts to challenge the Roman navy and expel it from the Spanish coast. The Romans had an undisturbed supply route from Italy to Spain.

The Punic Fleet Targets Bases in Sicily and Sardinia: The Battle at Lilybaeum

There was a swift Punic attack on Sicily right at the beginning of the war. The island was defended by the *praetor* Marcus Aemilius and Hiero. The Carthaginians sent 20 quinqueremes to lay waste the coast of Italy: 9 of them reached Lipara, 8 the Isle of Vulcan south of Lipara and 3 of them were diverted by the current into the Straits. Hiero, who was in Messana at that time, captured them and brought them to the harbour. By interrogating the prisoners it emerged that thirty-five other quinqueremes had been sent to Sicily to meet with their old allies. In particular, their mission was to occupy Lilybaeum.[20]

Taking back naval bases must have been one of the top priorities for the Carthaginians: they needed ports to land troops in Sicily to win back the island, they could use them to open a route from Africa to Italy to assist Hannibal, and taking Lilybaeum was especially important to prevent the Romans from using it to launch another campaign against Punic territory in Africa.

Livy states that Hiero warned the *praetor* to garrison Lilybaeum strongly. The Romans manned watchtowers and crews at Lilybaeum were told to bring ten days' worth of cooked rations to their ships. The Carthaginian ships tried to sail in at night but were discovered in the moonlight:

The signal was at once displayed from the watchtowers, and in the town the call to arms was sounded and the ships were manned; some of the troops were at once on the walls or guarding the gates, some on the ships. And the Carthaginians, seeing that they should have to do with men who were not unprepared, stood off from the harbour until dawn and employed the time in taking down their masts and sails and putting the fleet in fighting trim. When the day broke, they withdrew into the open sea, to give room for the battle and to allow their enemy's ships a ready egress from the harbour. Nor did the Romans shun the encounter.[21]

According to Livy, the Romans wanted to pitch their strength against the enemy's at close quarters. The Carthaginians preferred to manoeuvre and to make it a contest of ships rather than of men and arms. Their fleet was well-equipped with rowers but was short of fighting men; when a Punic ship was grappled, the soldiers were greatly outnumbered by their enemies. Seven Punic ships were instantly cut out and captured and the rest took flight. There were 1,700 soldiers and sailors on the captured ships, including three Carthaginian nobles. The Roman fleet returned intact into the harbour: only one ship had been rammed and even this was brought safely in.[22]

The consular army and navy with 160 quinqueremes intended for the invasion of Africa arrived in Messana, unaware of the battle. We do not know if the consul Titus Sempronius Longus had collected ships from allies on the way as he sailed along the coast. Hiero put out with his navy to meet him as he was entering the Straits, giving him intelligence about the designs of the Carthaginians and reporting the danger that Lilybaeum and other cities of the coast were in. He promised to furnish grain and clothing for free to the legions and naval crews of the consul and with his fleet sailed with the consul to Lilybaeum.[23] The consul left the *praetor* to protect the coast and sailed to Malta, where the Punic garrison surrendered. Titus returned to Lilybaeum and sold the prisoners publicly. He made another short expedition to the Isle of Vulcan in search of the Punic fleet, which had already sailed to attack the Italian coast, threatening the town of Vibo. The attack was reported to the consul as he was returning to Sicily; he received the letter from the senate telling him about the passage of Hannibal into Italy and commanding him to bring assistance to his fellow consul as soon as possible.[24]

Our sources do not specify which other cities in Sicily were targeted by the Carthaginian fleets. The consul sent his army in ships to Ariminum and assigned the defence of the territory of Vibo and the coast of Italy to the legate

Sextus Pomponius with twenty-five warships. He made up a fleet of fifty ships for the *praetor* Marcus Aemilius and then sailed to Ariminum, whence he set out with his army for the river Trebia and joined his colleague.[25] The preparations for the invasion of Africa were interrupted at an early stage. The figure of 160 quinqueremes must reflect the number of Punic ships the Romans expected to face on the coast of Africa. As Sempronius was called back to Italy, he missed the opportunity of finding and defeating the Punic navy which, undefeated, continued to confront the Romans. The problems the Romans faced in the following years in the islands and the Italian coast all follow from this.

Polybius and Livy give basically the same information about the events in 217. The Carthaginians, after hearing about the defeat at Ebro, dispatched a fleet of seventy ships, regarding command of the sea as essential to all their projects. The ships touched first at Sardinia and then at Pisa in Italy, where the commander believed they would find Hannibal. This must be seen as part of the Carthaginian strategy led from Carthage. However, after the battle at Lake Trasimene, Hannibal had turned to the Adriatic. Off the port of Cosa, the Carthaginian navy captured transport ships that had been sent from Ostia to Spain. The Romans reacted strongly by sending a fleet of 120 quinqueremes from Rome, led by the consul Gnaeus Servilius. His task was to pursue the enemy and protect the coasts of Italy. The consul sailed around Corsica and Sardinia, taking hostages from both. The Carthaginians avoided encountering the Romans; they sailed back to Sardinia and returned to Carthage. The consul followed them but, being left a long way behind, gave up the chase. He put in at Lilybaeum and then sailed to the island of Cercina in the Syrtis Minor, where the inhabitants paid the Romans for not ravaging their territory. He moved on and landed the troops to pillage the countryside in Africa. The Romans were ambushed and forced to flee, suffering great losses. Gnaeus took Cossyra and the fleet returned to Lilybaeum.[26]

Thus, Carthage's strategy took the Romans by surprise, not only on land, but also at sea. It seems that the Romans only had control of the islands for as long as the Punic navy remained inactive; as soon as it appeared, they were in trouble. If the Carthaginians had held a harbour in the islands they could have opened a route between Africa and Italy, helping Hannibal with troops and supplies.

Why Did the Battle of Cannae Not End the War?

Hannibal based his strategy in Italy on disrupting Rome's alliance system and building a Punic one. He gained a series of victories, starting with a cavalry skirmish at the river Ticinus in 218, followed by the victory over the 40,000 men led by Tiberius Sempronius Longus and Publius Cornelius Scipio at the river Trebia at the end of 218.[27] Hannibal's army now numbered about 40,000 men. He kept increasing the number of troops by having the Gauls in northern Italy join his war effort. Their motivation was booty and the fact that invading the peninsula would avoid Romans attacking their homelands. After the winter break, Hannibal moved south with between 50,000 and 60,000 men.[28]

The Carthaginians defeated the consul Gaius Flaminius in Etruria, at Lake Trasimene in 217. Flaminius and 15,000 men were killed. Hannibal continued east to the Adriatic to rest his army. He also sent messengers to Carthage by sea to pass on the news; according to Polybius, this was the first time he had done so since invading Italy. Hannibal dismissed the idea of approaching Rome for the present.[29] The question of whether Hannibal ever intended to attack the city has been widely debated. From the naval point of view, I find it implausible. It would have required the cooperation of the army and the fleet. On land, Rome was not defenceless and to blockade it by sea, the Carthaginians would have needed to keep the fleet in a place for a long period of time. It was not the same as making a quick visit to the Italian coast, of which we have many examples. Moreover, the Carthaginians would have taken the risk of fighting the Roman fleet and there is no indication that they were prepared to do that. The Carthaginian fleet that had sailed to Pisa to find Hannibal had left as soon as the 120 quinqueremes arrived from Ostia.[30]

Quintus Fabius Maximus was appointed dictator and, as he avoided contact with Hannibal's army, was nicknamed *cunctator* – delayer. He based his strategy on following Hannibal with four legions and cutting off stragglers and making sure that Hannibal would not find supplies. Livy states:

> He also issued an edict that those who dwelt in unfortified towns and hamlets should remove to places of safety; and that all the inhabitants of that district where Hannibal was likely to be marching should abandon

their farms, first burning the buildings and destroying the crops, that there might be no supplies for him of any kind.[31]

There had been a general mobilization of forces in 225, when the Romans dealt with the Gauls and placed legions in Tarentum, Sardinia and Sicily. However, they had not had to fight in all these areas then. Now that Italy and the islands needed to be defended, there were many problems. The Romans were distressed by conscription, taxes, hunger and idleness due to the devastation of the fields.[32] In 216, the senate received letters from the *propraetors* of Sicily, Titus Otacilius Crassus, and Sardinia, Aulus Cornelius Mammula, who both complained that neither pay nor grain were being furnished to the soldiers and the crews at the proper time and that they had no means of doing so. The senate replied that there was nothing to send and ordered the *propraetors* to provide for their own fleets and armies. Otacilius sent legates to Hiero and received what money was needed and grain for six months. According to Livy, in Sardinia the allied states made generous contributions to Cornelius. These 'contributions' were one of the reasons for the rebellion the following year.[33] Hiero sent a fleet to Ostia with shipments that included 300,000 measures of wheat and 200,000 of barley; the Syracusans also promised to transport as much more as was needed to any port named. Hiero also sent a 220–pound golden statue of Victory and some bowmen and slingers. He advised that they needed to invade Africa, for that would mean that Hannibal had a war at home as well and Carthage would be less free to send him reinforcements. Consequently, twenty–five quinqueremes were added to the fleet of fifty ships that was under the command of Titus Otacilius in Sicily and he was given permission to sail across to Africa if he deemed it advantageous to the state.[34] According to Polybius' calculations of rations and size of legions, the 300,000 measures of wheat were enough to feed around two and a half Roman legions for six months.[35]

The option of relieving the pressure on Italy by an attack in Africa was discussed and naval resources were increased; nevertheless, the Romans decided to end the war with a battle in Italy. Hannibal had moved to Campania, where he gained vast amounts of booty, and then to Apulia, where he had spent the winter. In the summer of 216, his situation was becoming critical in terms of supplies and how to keep the Gauls and Spanish mercenaries involved in the campaign. He captured a large Roman store at Cannae. The Romans decided to put together a larger army than ever before – about 80,000 men – led by the consuls Lucius Aemilius Paullus and Gaius Terentius Varro. The battle at Cannae in August 216 was supposed to be the one in which they would finally be strong enough to fight and defeat Hannibal and make him leave Italy. Still, it ended in a dismal failure. Hannibal entrapped and defeated the Roman army with his 40,000 infantry and 10,000 cavalry. The figures of losses are confusing: Polybius' total number of 70,000 dead and 10,000 captured exceeds the number of troops at the beginning of the battle. According to Livy, 45,500 Roman and allied infantry and 2,700 cavalry were killed and 17,000 were taken prisoner. Lucius Aemilius Paullus was killed, as were twenty-nine of the forty-eight military tribunes. The Romans lost eighty senators and ex-magistrates. Hannibal's losses amounted to fewer than 6,000, of which 4,000 were Gauls.[36]

Hannibal had attacked Italy to win the war and now he had a large enough victory that he could start peace negotiations with the Roman senate. In all probability he did not intend to annihilate Rome but was looking to change the balance of power from the situation in 241 and 238.[37] He had thousands of captives, many of high rank. The terms on which the prisoners would be returned were an important feature in all peace treaties of the third century BC. As Goldsworthy puts it, 'the amount paid to redeem captives was as much a gauge of victory and defeat as the forfeiture of territory or the payment of an indemnity.'[38] Livy states that Hannibal had dismissed the allies of Rome without a ransom and given the captive Romans the liberty of ransoming themselves at the price of 500 denarii for a horseman, 300 for a foot soldier and 100 for a slave. Nevertheless, his envoy, which consisted of ten Romans and Carthalo, who was supposed to propose terms, was refused entry to the city.[39]

Once again the Carthaginians faced the resolute Roman approach to war and peace: negotiating only when they had the upper hand. Even in this situation they were by no means ready to give up. Everything the Romans did after Cannae shows the depth of the crisis. Fabius Pictor was sent to Delphi to consult the oracle.[40] Spoils were taken down from the temples and porticoes, 8,000 slaves were purchased at the public expense and armed.

Livy states: 'They preferred these slaves for soldiers, though they might have redeemed the prisoners of war at less expense.'[41]

Had the peace been concluded after Cannae and according to the Hellenistic principles, Rome would have lost a great deal. It had never had a very good grip on the islands and they would certainly have been one of the main objects in the negotiations. Carthage would have again become the leading state in the western Mediterranean. The Romans must have thought about the wider political situation as well: how could they secure the relations with Syracuse? What to do with Illyria, where Philip was extending his power, threatening local Roman interests? Accepting a defeat would have put Rome in a weak position in international politics. It would also have eroded Rome's position in Italy; we cannot be sure what kind of role Carthage would have had in the future development of the peninsula but if Rome lost its allies and they became linked to Carthage instead in one way or another, Rome would lose the source for manpower, timber and money that formed the basis of its expansion.

Intensified Carthaginian Efforts at Sea After Cannae

Hannibal had achieved all his victories in Italy without the help of the Punic navy. For the Carthaginian government the refusal to negotiate meant that they had to find new ways of putting more pressure on the Romans. Hannibal tried to find allies and build up an Italian front against the Romans. After Cannae, many towns in Apulia, Lucania, Bruttium and Samnium changed sides and started to support him. In Campania, he won the support of Capua, the second most important city in Italy. Capua hoped to play a leading role in the protectorate that Carthage was expected to form in southern Italy.[42] Livy records Capua's treaty with Carthage: 'That no general or magistrate of the Carthaginians should have any authority over a Campanian citizen, and that no Campanian citizen should be a soldier or perform any service against his will: that Capua should have its own laws, its own magistrates.'[43]

The Carthaginians made huge efforts to open a supply route to Italy. Hannibal took control of several ports in Italy, while the Punic fleet tried to take over the ports on the islands that were needed as landing-places. Right after Cannae, Titus Otacilius Crassus asked for more ships and reported that a Carthaginian fleet was doing serious damage to the dominions of Hiero and that a second Punic fleet was lying fully equipped and ready for action at the Egadi Islands, waiting to attack Lilybaeum and the rest of Roman territory there as soon as Otacilius turned his attention to protecting the Syracusan coast.[44]

Hannibal sent his brother Mago to Carthage to give a report on their success at Cannae and Capua, and to ask for reinforcements, money and grain.[45] Troops were sent in three separate fleets. The Romans had taken hostages in Sardinia to keep the people on their side but the Sardinians were in a rebellious mood. Livy states that a secret embassy sent by the nobles in Sardinia arrived in Carthage to say that the Sardinians were tired of Roman rule, which during the last year had been exercised with particular severity and rapacity. The people were weighed down with heavy taxes and demands for an excessive contribution of grain. All that was required was a leader for a revolt.[46] The Carthaginians sent 12,000 foot soldiers, 1,500 horsemen, 20 elephants and 60 warships to Sardinia. Livy states that, as the Punic fleet was sailing towards Sardinia, it was blown off course and ended up in the Balearic Islands. Hasdrubal Calvus, who was leading the fleet, repaired the damage, sailed back to Sardinia, landed with his army, joined the Sardinian rebels and fought with them against the Romans but he was defeated by Titus Manlius Torquatus, who had been awarded a triumph over Sardinia in 235. Manlius punished the Sardinian cities by demanding tribute and grain in proportion to the resources of each place and its relative guilt. He sailed from Carales back to Rome with the tribute and the grain. As the Punic fleet was returning to Africa, it encountered a Roman fleet led by Titus Otacilius Crassus that had crossed from Lilybaeum to the African coast to pillage the country around Carthage. The Romans had then sailed for Sardinia. Livy describes a slight engagement; seven Carthaginian ships were captured and the rest of the ships broke formation and fled.[47]

The Carthaginians made great efforts to get the Greek cities in the south to join them. The Bruttians had allied themselves with the Carthaginians and assisted and guided them in the operation: Livy states that this cooperation made the cities more disposed to continue in their alliance with the Romans, because they feared and hated the Bruttians. The attempt to make Rhegium join the Carthaginians failed but Locri made a pact after much persuasion in the summer of 215.[48] Livy recorded its terms as follows: 'They were to live in freedom under their own laws, the city to be open to the Carthaginians, the harbour in the power of the Locrians ... the Carthaginian should help the Locrian and the Locrian the Carthaginian, in peace and in war.'[49]

The port was used at once; the Punic fleet landed in Locri and 4,000 Numidian cavalry, forty elephants, money and provisions were transported to Hannibal; Bomilcar was in charge. This is the one and only time we know of when the Carthaginians actually succeeded in sending help to Hannibal in Italy. It took place while the battle for Sardinia was under way. Bomilcar left immediately, before Appius Claudius arrived from Messana, to join Hanno in Bruttium.[50]

Consequently, the Romans put more ships on guard on the Italian coast. The *praetor urbanus* Quintus Fulvius Flaccus was given twenty-five ships. His mission was to secure the coast around Rome. The *praetor peregrinus* Marcus Valerius Laevinus was given another twenty-five ships with which he was supposed to defend the coast between Brundisium and Tarentum.[51]

The third Carthaginian shipment in 215 was also intended to go to Italy. It included 12,000 foot soldiers, 1,500 horsemen, 20 elephants and 60 warships. Mago was making preparations for this in Carthage but he was sent to Spain instead, since Hasdrubal had suffered a great defeat at the Battle of Ibera in 215 and almost all the Spanish tribes had revolted to Rome; hence it was necessary to change plans.[52] The Carthaginian strategy thus demonstrates that they had the resources and means of sending troops and supplies to different war zones, with which they communicated by sea. In particular, they were looking for ways to link up with Hannibal. The Punic navy was active and taking the initiative; a feature that had been missing in the First Punic War.

Hannibal's Treaty with Philip of Macedon in 215 BC

After Cannae, Philip of Macedon saw the possibility of increasing his power through an alliance with Carthage. The story of how he contacted Hannibal in Italy and how the Romans learned about the treaty shows the effort they put in to guarding the coast but despite this it was not completely under their control.

According to Livy, Philip's ambassadors avoided the ports of Brundisium and Tarentum as they were guarded by Roman ships. They landed at the temple of Hera Lacinia near Croton and continued by land to Capua, where they met Hannibal. A treaty was made and the Macedonian ambassadors, accompanied by Carthaginian ambassadors Gisco, Bostar and Mago returned to the temple where the ship lay in hidden anchorage.[53] When they had set out and reached open sea, they were spotted by the Roman fleet, which was guarding the coasts of Calabria. *Praefectus classis* Publius Valerius Flaccus sent *kerkouroi* that pursued and caught the ship. The ambassadors, with a letter from Hannibal to Philip, were sent to Rome with five fast ships, commanded by Lucius Valerius Antias. At Cumae, the ships were stopped by the consul Titus Sempronius Gracchus and his fleet, since, as Livy states, it was uncertain whether the ships were friendly or not. The prisoners were brought before the consul. He sent the papers under seal by land to the senate and ordered the ambassadors to be taken on board to Rome where they were questioned by the senators.[54]

Our knowledge of the treaty is based on Polybius. The text contains expressions that are recognizable in Phoenician diplomacy, hence it has been deduced that it is probably a transcription of the Punic section of the agreement.[55] The treaty contains paragraphs of mutual support to the other party and its allies, including Carthage's allies in Italy, until the Romans are defeated. Philip's interests would be included in the peace treaty that the Carthaginians would make with Rome:

> As soon as the gods have given us the victory in the war against the Romans and their allies, if the Romans ask us to come to terms of peace, we will make such a peace as will comprise you too, and on the following conditions: that the Romans may never make war upon you; that the Romans shall no longer be masters of Corcyra, Apollonia, Epidamnus, Pharos, Dimale, Parthini, or Atitania: and that they shall return to Demetrius of Pharos all his friends who are in the dominions of Rome.[56]

As Walbank points out, the vagueness of the treaty was deliberate and required a quick Carthaginian victory for it to be significant. For Hannibal, it offered a convenient second front on which to embarrass the Romans and it had a considerable propaganda value among the Greeks in southern Italy without really binding him to anything.[57] It would also guarantee Philip the areas he was conquering. It is unlikely that Philip was going to invade Italy with his army; the treaty nevertheless put more pressure on the Romans, because with it the Carthaginians could have secured a naval base in Illyria, thus gaining access to Italy.[58] The shortest route across the Adriatic from Corcyra to Cape Iapygia is only about 70 kilometres.[59] The Romans responded by adding twenty-five ships to Publius Valerius Flaccus' fleet; thirty ships, including the five that had been used to transport the prisoners, sailed from Ostia to Tarentum. Publius Valerius Flaccus was ordered not merely to defend the coast of Italy but to get information regarding the Macedonian War.[60]

Syracuse Makes an Alliance with Carthage in 215 BC: The Roman Siege of Syracuse

Hiero of Syracuse died in the spring or early summer of 215 and the city's allegiance to Rome was replaced by an alliance with Carthage. The events leading to the change of policy are somewhat obscure; we do not know whether Hiero's son Gelo, who died before him, went over to the Carthaginians after the Battle of Cannae, or whether the initiative was made by the young Hieronymus who followed Hiero to the throne. What is known is that Hieronymus sent ambassadors to Italy to meet Hannibal and after negotiations Hannibal sent them back with three Carthaginians: Hippocrates and his brother Epicydes, who were natives of Carthage and had fought in his army in Spain and Italy and whose grandfather was an exile from Syracuse, and a trierarch called Hannibal. Our sources do not record where the ambassadors met Hannibal but it is obvious that the Romans only learned about this when the envoys had returned to Syracuse. The *praetor* at Lilybaeum, Appius Claudius Pulcher, sent envoys to Hieronymus to renew the Roman–Syracusan alliance but he treated them rudely and sent ambassadors to Carthage to make a treaty in accordance with the alliance arranged with Hannibal. The clauses explained by Polybius and Livy show the intended division of power whereby the Carthaginians were supposed to assist Hieronymus on land and at sea to expel the Romans from Sicily; thereafter the river Himera would be the line dividing the island into the Carthaginian part in the west and the Syracusan part in the east. Because they needed to detach him from the Romans, the Carthaginians even agreed to Hieronymus's increased demands for the whole island, with him promising to assist the Carthaginians in their Italian campaign.[61]

Hannibal's campaign needed a boost. Hasdrubal and Mago, who were supposed to come over to Italy with more troops, were tied up in Spain. Through an aggressive policy Hannibal could get local support from various communities in southern Italy, yet once they had become his allies he would have to protect them from the Romans, who had adopted the tactics of encircling his army rather than attacking it directly. Moreover, he had to move around and constantly find new sources of supplies for his army. Having the fleet link up with the army would open new possibilities in military operations. Ports were needed; Hannibal had laid siege to Naples and taken over the ports in southern Italy, including Caulonia, Croton and Locri where Bomilcar landed. Now the alliance with Syracuse offered the potential for a supply route between Africa and Italy. For the Romans, in contrast, the new alliance meant that they risked losing the rest of the island and faced the threat of increased Punic naval activity on the Italian coast. Moreover, it would put an end to Syracusan provisions for the Roman troops on the island and to the shipments to Italy. From this point onwards, warfare on the island made agriculture difficult and the Roman armies in Italy were largely dependent on the resources of the peninsula.[62]

Direct hostilities between Rome and Syracuse did not begin immediately: there were further failed negotiations in Syracuse as well as complicated internal events in which Hieronymus and later the rest of the royal family were murdered. All-out war broke out over the possession of Sicily. Most of the fighting concerned Syracuse but cities in other parts of the island also defected and began to support the Carthaginians.

In 214, Rome built 100 new ships, of which 30 were sent to Syracuse. Following a decree from the senate, the sailors were furnished by wealthy individuals, according to their property. The Romans appointed Appius Claudius Pulcher as *propraetor* to command the land forces and they put the fleet under the command of Marcus Claudius Marcellus. The fleet started the blockade of Syracuse's harbour and in 213 they tried to take the city by storm. Syracuse was defended very efficiently, however, with the machines invented by Archimedes. The Romans had to give up the idea; consequently they continued to besiege the city by land and by sea, cutting off the supplies needed in the city. Appius remained with the siege and Marcus took one-third of the troops and made raids on the parts of Sicily which favoured the Carthaginians. He obviously used the fleet to the north and south of Syracuse when he forced Helorus and Herbesus to surrender and demolished and plundered Megara. The Carthaginians sent an army led by Himilco to relieve the Roman siege. He landed 25,000 infantry, 3,000 horse and 12 elephants at Heraclea Minoa. He retook Heraclea, and a few days later Agrigentum, which was then used as winter quarters by Himilco and Hippocrates. Bomilcar sailed into the large harbour in Syracuse with fifty-five warships. The Roman army with thirty quinqueremes landed a legion at Panormus and continued from there, escorted by the fleet, until they joined Appius Claudius. Himilco tried to engage Marcellus in a land battle but when that failed he started to take possession of Roman garrisons. At Murgantia, the modern Morgantina, the Roman garrison was betrayed by the inhabitants themselves and Himilco received a great quantity of grain and provisions of every kind that the Romans had stored. The revolt became widespread: Livy does not give all the names but states that the Roman garrisons were now either driven out of the citadels or treacherously given up and overpowered. At Enna, the Romans slaughtered the people as an example to other cities that considered joining the Carthaginians.[63]

In Italy, Hannibal's grip on the ports was increased: by 212 he held Thurii, Heraclea, Metapontum and also Tarentum, except for the harbour and the citadel around it. One reason for his success was that the Romans had no fleets in this area in those years, since from 214 onwards Laevinus's fleet was operating on the Illyrian and Greek coasts and the fleet in Sicily was preoccupied with the siege of Syracuse. Again, the Carthaginians had noticed a gap in Roman defence and taken advantage of it. Even so, there is no information of any Carthaginian shipments landing in Italy in these years. At Syracuse, the Roman fleet intercepted a Spartan called Damippus who had been sent from Syracuse to King Philip.

In 212, Marcellus used the intelligence that the Syracusans were celebrating the three-day festival of Artemis and stormed the city, taking it except for the harbour.[64] The Romans continued to blockade it. The support the Carthaginians could give to Syracuse was now hanging on the trips Bomilcar made between Carthage and Syracuse. Livy states:

> Bomilcar, favoured by such a night that on account of a violent storm the Roman fleet could not ride at anchor in open water, came out of the harbour of Syracuse with thirty-five ships, and with no enemy to prevent, put to sea, leaving fifty-five ships to Epicydes and the Syracusans. And after informing the Carthaginians how critical was the situation at Syracuse, he returned after a few days with a hundred ships.[65]

There was a joint attack by the Carthaginian army and fleet on the Roman positions but it failed; from Livy's short description we cannot say why. There was a plague that spread among the Carthaginians in particular but it also affected the Romans.[66] Bomilcar returned to Carthage to collect new troops. He also planned to besiege Syracuse. We cannot be sure how many trips he made but Livy records the last one, when something went wrong. Bomilcar returned from Carthage with 130 warships and 700 transport ships. However, an easterly wind prevented him from doubling Cape Pachynus. Epicydes sailed from Syracuse to discuss the situation with Bomilcar,

> who was keeping his fleet in a roadstead facing Africa. He feared a naval battle, not so much because he was inferior in his forces and the number of his ships - in fact he had even more – as because the winds then blowing were more favourable to the Roman fleet than to his own. Nevertheless, Epicydes gained his consent to try the fortune of a naval engagement.[67]

So far the Romans had not tried to fight the Punic fleet, which had managed to sneak in and out by night and in rough weather and generally by using the fact that maintaining a blockade in the open sea was not easy. Now, Marcus Claudius Marcellus was informed of the situation and he sailed south to stop the Carthaginian navy from reaching Syracuse. After the easterly wind began to subside, Bomilcar was the first to move. According to Livy:

> At first his fleet appeared to be heading out to sea, the more readily to round the promontory. But on seeing that the Roman ships were steering towards him, Bomilcar, alarmed by something unforeseen, made sail for open water, and after sending messengers to Heraclea, to command the transports to return thence to Africa, he himself sailed along the coast of Sicily and made for Tarentum.[68]

There was no sea battle and no Carthaginian siege of Syracuse. Epicydes fled and sailed to Agrigentum. The Romans took the whole city under their control and it was given up to be plundered by the soldiers; in the general confusion Archimedes was killed. The victors and vanquished in Syracuse were fed with the grain Titus Otacilius Crassus had just captured in the harbour of Utica. He had crossed over from Lilybaeum with eighty quinqueremes, also ravaging the area around Utica and collecting all kinds of booty in the ships.[69]

Thiel sees Bomilcar as 'one of the most inferior admirals Carthage ever possessed.'[70] Nonetheless, he had previously landed in Locri and kept the Carthaginian operations going in Syracuse for years, bringing in more ships, troops and supplies. Unfortunately, we do not have Polybius on this and we do not know the nature of the unexpected occurrence to which Livy refers. At Tarentum, Bomilcar achieved nothing. The large fleet ran out of supplies and became a burden to the Tarentines and the Romans kept their position in the citadel. Livy gives no names but says:

> A Carthaginian fleet was summoned from Sicily to Tarentum to cut off the supplies of the Roman garrison which was in the citadel of Tarentum, and it had indeed closed every approach to the citadel from the sea, but by lying there for a long time it was making the grain supply more limited for their allies than for the enemy. For it was impossible for such a quantity of grain to be brought to the townspeople by way of the peaceful shores and open harbours, under the protection of the Carthaginian ships, as the fleet itself was consuming, with its swarming

crews, including men of every race. The result was that, while the garrison of the citadel, as being few in number, could be supported from previous stores without importation, for the Tarentines and the fleet even the imported grain was insufficient. In the end the departure of the fleet was more welcome than had been its coming.[71]

Polybius states:

Bomilcar, the Carthaginian admiral, came with a very large force to its help, and finding himself unable to render any assistance to those in the town, as the Roman camp was so securely defended, he used up his supplies before he was well aware of it. He had been forced to come by urgent entreaties and large promises, and he was now compelled to sail off at the earnest request of the inhabitants.[72]

So, despite the fact that Hannibal had taken cities in the Gulf of Tarentum, and that there was a vacuum in the defence of the coast of Italy that enabled Bomilcar to sail there with up to 130 warships, this period did not give the expected breakthrough by which the Carthaginians could have sent substantial supplies to Italy and built a proper partnership between army and fleet. The port of Tarentum and the citadel around it remained in Roman control. It would seem that the previously discussed possibility of a Carthaginian blockade of Rome by sea would have faced similar difficulties.

The question of Sicily was finally decided in Agrigentum, which Hanno and Epicydes still held. Hannibal had followed the situation and from Italy had sent a Liby-Phoenician called Muttines to take command of the Numidian cavalry. Muttines was successful and, inspired by his success, Epicydes and Hanno crossed the river Himera and challenged Marcellus' army but lost the battle. The Carthaginians sent over 8,000 infantry and 3,000 cavalry. Livy does not say where they landed but the Murgantian territories revolted to these forces and Hybla, Macella and other towns followed their defection. In late 210, the consul Marcus Valerius Laevinus arrived in Sicily; he arranged the matters of Syracuse and then marched his army to Agrigentum. The military operations of Muttines were going well; too well if we can trust Livy, who states that because the fame of Muttines began to eclipse the fame of the commander-in-chief, Hanno replaced him with his own son. Consequently, Muttines betrayed Agrigentum to the Romans. Hanno and Epicydes fled the town in a small vessel and crossed over to Africa. The remaining Carthaginians and Sicilians were cut to pieces. The consul took slaves and booty and sold them and sent the money to Rome. The fate of Agrigentum made the states in Sicily change their allegiance and they turned to the Romans.[73]

Muttines and others who had done service to the Roman people were brought into the senate and rewarded with Roman citizenship and land.[74] The huge booty taken from Syracuse was displayed in Marcellus' ovation:

> In his ovation he caused a great amount of booty to be carried before him into the city. Together with a representation of captured Syracuse were carried catapults and ballistae and all the other engines of war, and the adornments of a long peace and of royal wealth, a quantity of silverware and bronze ware, other furnishings and costly fabrics, and many notable statues, with which Syracuse had been adorned more highly than most cities of Greece. As a sign of triumph over Carthaginians as well, eight elephants were in the procession.[75]

Marcellus used the art of Syracuse to adorn Rome, especially in decorating the temple of Honos and Virtus at the Porta Capena. There had been Greek art in Rome before but in 211 the Romans saw for the first time a large number of first-class Greek statuary in bronze and marble as well as high-quality Greek paintings. As McDonnell puts it, Marcellus found a new way to represent military success. The subsequent conquerors of Greek cities followed his example.[76]

The booty from Syracuse also started a new period in Roman finances. There was a big difference in the First and Second Punic Wars in that in the first war the Romans had soon made the treaty with Hiero, receiving annual payments as well as grain and other supplies; there had also been a constant flow of booty from successful battles. Now, there had been no military success that could have been used to pay the enormous expenses and the support from Syracuse had ceased. Consequently, the Romans had used credit to finance operations and by the end of 214, silver coinage was debased. The conquest of Syracuse marked the turning-point; from 212 onwards metal became available. The new resources of revenue made it possible to create the denarius system in 212 or 211. The capture of many other cities in the following years further increased Roman wealth and stabilized the economy.[77]

The First Macedonian War, 211–205 BC

Events in the east are outside the scope of this book but the First Macedonian War needs to be briefly discussed because it was an offspring of the Second Punic War and opened the road for the Roman conquest of the eastern Mediterranean.[78]

The war took place in Greece and in the Aegean; the Roman fleet was involved but we also have information that some Punic ships were sent to help Philip. As these fleets sailed to the east, there were moments when the balance of power on the Italian coast changed. Hannibal's treaty with Philip was the obvious reason that brought about the conflict; nevertheless, it is plausible that even without the treaty Philip's operations in Illyria would have made the Romans react. Philip had had a naval base at Oeniadae on the west coast of Aetolia since 219. He had built 100 *lemboi* in the winter of 217/16, using Illyrian shipwrights.[79] Polybius states his motives: 'Philip took into consideration that for his enterprise he would require ships and crews to man them, not it is true with the idea of fighting at sea – for he never thought he would be capable of offering battle to the Roman fleet – but to transport his troops, land where he wished, and take the enemy by surprise.'[80]

The limited range of Philip's fleet became apparent when in 216 and 214 he attacked Apollonia and Oricum on the Illyrian coast. In 216, the news that ten quinqueremes from the fleet in Lilybaeum had been sighted off Rhegium made him flee with the fleet in total disorder.[81] In 214, he made an attack with 120 *lemboi* and biremes but the arrival of the Romans made him flee by land after he had either hauled on shore or burned his ships.[82] In 213 and 212 he conquered more territory and in 212/11 he took Lissus, thus gaining a base on the coast, but he did not use his fleet for this. There is some evidence that he started to build a war fleet at Lissus.[83] Consequently, he was able to challenge the Roman possession of Illyria.

As in any other overseas operation, the Roman campaign depended on shipments and it was important to defeat the enemy fleet and to take control of the coast. The Romans based their operation in Greece on the alliance made with the Aetolians in 211 and their other allies, including Elis, Sparta, King Attalus of Pergamum and King Scerdilaidas of Illyria, with his son Pleuratos. The Aetolians had bases such as Naupactus on the Gulf of Corinth, Heraclea on the Malian Gulf and garrisons in Lysimacheia and Cius.[84] Attalus's fleet of thirty-five quinqueremes worked alongside the twenty-five Roman quinqueremes. In the division of booty, the Romans got the people and the movable property and Attalus the cities.[85]

The deficiencies in Philip's shipbuilding also became Macedon's downfall – he fought the Romans with his infantry and cavalry but his fleet was never a match for the Romans and their allies. The Roman navy established itself in Greece without battle and Rome and its allies sailed freely and attacked Macedonian bases. Philip had no resources to stop this and he tried to build a coalition based on Achaean, Bithynian and Carthaginian ships to challenge the Romans to a sea battle. The reciprocal help that Hannibal and Philip could give each other had been expressed in their treaty and there is information on Carthaginian fleets in the east in 209 and 208. Livy briefly states that in 209 a Carthaginian fleet was sent to Corcyra.[86] We have no information that it did anything there but it is an important and interesting move because the Punic fleet left the Italian coast and Tarentum unprotected, which enabled the Romans to recover Tarentum. In 208, Philip sent for the Carthaginian fleet to be at Aegium and he sent some quinqueremes and more than twenty *lemboi* into the Gulf of Corinth to be added to the Carthaginian force. The Punic fleet was in the area but something went wrong. The Carthaginians had crossed to the Oxean Islands opposite Cephallenia, yet the Punic fleet never entered the gulf to meet Philip and sailed to Acarnanian ports instead. According to Livy, they did so because they had heard that Attalus and the Romans had left Oreus and they were afraid of being overpowered in the Gulf of Corinth.[87] The Punic fleets could have made a great difference to Philip, given how much trouble they had caused the Romans in the Second Punic War.

The presence of the Romans finally forced Philip to change his strategy in shipbuilding and build a fleet that would match the combined fleets of

Rome and its allies. At the end of 207, he started a shipbuilding project at Cassandrea and laid down the keels of 100 warships and recruited a large number of shipbuilders to carry out the work.[88] However, this fleet was not finished by the end of the war. The Romans had already achieved their goal: they had stopped Philip from increasing his power and made sure that the Punic fleets could not use the Illyrian or Greek harbours to attack Italy, while at the same time they had significantly improved their position in the war against Hannibal. In the peace treaty of 205, the Romans gained areas in western Greece: Parthini, Dimallum, Bargyllum and Eugenium. Lissus, the Macedonian fleet or the situation in the Aegean Sea were not mentioned in the treaty.[89] The Romans finished the war by securing the western coast of Greece and a Roman embassy visited Delphi on its way to meet with Attalus.[90]

Spain in 215–206 BC: The Romans Take New Carthage

The Scipios defeated Hasdrubal at the Battle of Ibera in 215, making sure he could not leave Spain to assist Hannibal; consequently, the forces that were supposed to be sent to Italy were directed to Spain instead. As for Roman supplies, the Scipios sent a letter in 215, stating the magnitude and success of their operations in Spain and asking for money, clothing and corn; their crews needed everything.[91] The Romans used credit to have the money and supplies sent; the task was given to contractors on the condition that they would be the first to be paid as soon as there was money in the treasury and that they would be exempt from military duty and that the state should accept all risks from tempest or enemy action to goods sent by sea. Livy praises the patriotic sentiment and the honesty and generosity with which the contracts were carried out.[92] We also have some information on fraud in the operation. A few years later, Marcus Postumius Pyrgensis and Titus Pomponius Veientanus were charged for reporting imaginary shipwrecks.[93] Livy states:

> These men, since the state assumed the risk from violent storms in the case of shipments to the armies, had falsely reported imaginary shipwrecks, and even those which they had correctly reported had been

brought about by their own trickery, not by accident. They would put small cargoes of little value on old, battered vessels, sink them at sea, after taking off the crews in small boats that were in readiness, and then falsely declare that the shipments were far more valuable.[94]

The Scipios operated with extended *imperium*, first conquering the areas north of the Ebro and then continuing southwards. They also became involved in the affairs of Numidia, making an alliance with Syphax, king of the western Masaesylii, who had revolted from Carthage. In the following conflict in 214/13, the Carthaginians were supported by Gala, king of the eastern Massyli. Hasdrubal and a part of his army were recalled to Africa to deal with the revolt.[95] While this took place, the Romans were able to increase their power in southern Spain and in 212, they captured Saguntum. A major crisis occurred in 211, when the Scipios changed the strategy and divided their army to take control of the whole peninsula but were killed in two separate operations, one against Hasdrubal, son of Gisco and Mago Barca, and one against Hasdrubal Barca.[96] The Romans needed to keep the Spanish front active because it tied up a substantial amount of Carthaginian energy and resources. To compensate for the losses, the senate sent Gaius Claudius Nero with 6,000 infantry and 300 cavalry and from the Latin allies the same number of infantry and 800 cavalry. Nero embarked the army at Puteoli and arrived at Tarraco and disembarked his troops, beached the ships and armed even the crews to increase his numbers.[97]

Next, the proconsul Publius Cornelius Scipio arrived in the autumn of 210 with reinforcements. He sailed with thirty quinqueremes from Ostia and landed his troops at Emporiae. He ordered his ships to follow him and marched by land to Tarraco, where he ordered the ships to be hauled on shore and held a congress of deputies from all the allies. Four triremes of the Massilians had come to him from their home. Scipio continued the work of his father and uncle with a new plan. The total size of the army in Spain was 28,000 infantry and 3,000 cavalry and, as Goldsworthy puts it, it was barely equal to any one of the three Carthaginian armies.[98] Scipio changed strategy: he gave out the false information that he was planning to attack the three Carthaginian armies but instead made an attack against New Carthage with the navy and army. Only *praefectus classis* Gaius Laelius was told about the plan.

Polybius represents the young Scipio as the calm aristocratic general who carefully analysed the strategic situation in Spain and the causes of the Roman defeat. The story of the conquest of New Carthage, as it is told by Polybius, probably does not do justice to Mago, the commander of New Carthage, as Polybius deliberately contrasts the disorder of Mago's battle with the orderliness and perfect timing of Scipio.[99] New Carthage contained the hostages of all the important kings and peoples in Spain, money, arms and war matériel and it also made an important harbour. The idea of attacking the city was not new. Gnaeus Cornelius Scipio had made a raid on the coast after the Battle of Ebro, also targeting the area of New Carthage, and devastating the surrounding country. We cannot be sure whether it was on their agenda then to take the city. The Punic army in southern Spain had been strong but now, as the Carthaginian armies were out in the field, only 1,000 soldiers and 2,000 armed citizens were present to defend the city. Scipio marched with 25,000 infantry and 2,500 cavalry and blockaded the city from land and sea. The Punic ships were blockaded in the harbour and were unable to do anything to protect the city. After futile attempts to cross the wall, Scipio used the intelligence that it was possible to make an easy crossing on foot through shallow water in the lagoon and up to the wall. The Romans entered the city. Scipio ordered the slaughter of the civilian population and then the city was looted in an organized manner. Some 10,000 men were captured; citizens of New Carthage were released as well as the hostages. The 2,000 artisans that were not citizens were announced to be public slaves of the Roman people, with the promise of freedom if they cooperated in providing the equipment for war. Young non-citizens and strong slaves Scipio incorporated into his fleet as oarsmen. According to Livy, he captured eight ships; eighteen if we follow Polybius. The Romans obtained catapults and other throwing weapons, gold and silver, and wheat and barley. They also took 113 cargo ships in the harbour, some of them with their cargoes of grain and arms, as well as brass, iron, sails, esparto grass and other naval materials.[100] Scipio gave the *corona muralis*, the award for being first over the city wall, to a soldier in the army and to a sailor in the navy. Gaius Laelius was given a *corona aurea* and thirty bulls.[101] Polybius describes how Scipio exercised and refitted his army and fleet after the victory before returning to Tarraco with the hostages.[102]

The capital of Punic Spain had been captured and the Iberians deserted the Carthaginian cause. From 209 on, the ouput of the Spanish mines became available to the Romans. In 208, Scipio defeated Hasdrubal at Baecula; however, he could not prevent him from leaving Spain. Hasdrubal crossed the Alps and started his journey to Italy, where he arrived in 207, about ten years later than planned.[103] The last major battle between the Carthaginians and the Romans in Spain took place at Ilipa in southern Spain in 206. Polybius states that Hasdrubal, the son of Gisco, had 70,000 infantry, 4,000 cavalry and 32 elephants. Scipio's army consisted of 45,000 foot and 3,000 cavalry. The battle ended in the wholesale escape of the Carthaginian army; Scipio had driven the Carthaginians out of Spain.[104]

Hasdrubal sailed to North Africa, as did the Numidian prince Masinissa after defecting to the Romans and promising support to Scipio's campaign in Africa. Mago escaped to Gadir. There was nothing to keep the army together any longer and the soldiers were dispersed through the neighbouring states. Scipio suppressed a mutiny in the Roman camp at Sucro and had the ringleaders executed.[105]

Livy reports a sea battle in 206 when the Romans were trying to take the city of Gadir with help from deserters from the city. A small Roman fleet – seven triremes and one quinquereme – led by Gaius Laelius met one Punic quinquereme and eight triremes. Livy's description of the battle is not very clear; it seems that the navies had great difficulty in fighting the weather and the tide. Adherbal escaped to Africa and Laelius, the victor, returned to Carteia.[106] Mago received orders from the Carthaginian senate to take the fleet he had in Gadir over to Italy. There he was supposed to hire Gauls and Ligurians to join Hannibal. For this purpose money was sent from Carthage and he also plundered the town and the temples in Gadir. As he was sailing along the coast of Spain, he made an unsuccessful attack on New Carthage by landing the soldiers on the shore by night, attacking the city wall in the same place where the Romans had breached it. The Romans, however, opened the gate and rushed out, and in the following confusion the Carthaginians escaped to their ships.[107] Mago sailed to the Balearic Islands, where he spent the winter.

The Islands and Italy, 210–207 BC: The Romans Defeat the Carthaginian Fleet

Marcus Valerius Laevinus sailed to Rome in 210 to report that the war for Sicily was over and that a deserted land was again in cultivation. However, it is obvious that the Carthaginians had not given up and that the Romans still had to defend the islands. The consul sent *praefectus classis* Marcus Valerius Messalla to Africa to make a plundering and espionage expedition. He approached the coast with fifty ships before daybreak and made an unexpected landing on the territory of Utica. He ravaged it far and wide, captured many people and much booty, returned to his ships and sailed back to Lilybaeum. Livy does not relate any Carthaginian resistance during this two-week operation, so it seems that the Romans were able to sail without being stopped. The captives were interrogated and the information was reported to Laevinus:

> That five thousand Numidians were at Carthage under Masinissa, son of Gala and a most impetuous young man; and that other soldiers were being hired everywhere in Africa, to be sent over to Hasdrubal in Spain, so that he should cross over into Italy with the largest possible army as soon as he could and join Hannibal; ... furthermore that a very large fleet was being made ready, for the purpose of recovering Sicily.[108]

Consequently, Quintus Fulvius Flaccus was appointed dictator to hold the elections and Marcus Valerius Laevinus continued in Sicily as proconsul.[109] The Carthaginian naval attack on Sicily never took place. Nevertheless, the Carthaginians attacked Sardinia with a fleet of forty ships. First they laid waste to the region of Olbia; then, after the *praetor* Publius Manlius Vulso appeared there with the army, the Carthaginian fleet sailed to the other side of the island and ravaged the territory of Carales. The fleet returned to Africa with a large amount of booty.[110]

In 210, the Tarentines intercepted the Roman convoy that was sailing from Sicily along the Italian coast to bring supplies to the garrison in Tarentum. Democrates defeated Decimus Quinctius' fleet of about twenty ships with an equal number of ships at Sapriportis, about 22 kilometres west of Tarentum. The transport ships escaped to the sea. The Romans prevailed on land and kept the citadel.[111] Here we have some rare information about how ships were collected from the cities that were under obligation to supply them. To begin with, Decimus' fleet at Rhegium consisted of triremes and smaller ships and some quinqueremes. Livy states: 'By personally demanding from the allies and from Rhegium and Velia and Paestum the ships due under the treaty, he [Decimus Quinctius] formed a fleet of twenty ships … in the neighbourhood of Croton and Sybaris he had fully manned the ships with oarsmen, and had a fleet remarkably equipped and armed considering the size of the ships.'[112]

In 209, the Romans took advantage of the absence of the Carthaginian fleet as it had sailed to the Greek coast and recovered Tarentum. Quintus Fabius Maximus pitched his camp in the mouth of the harbour to besiege the city. Here we see a plan to use some of the ships as a naval siege unit, carrying artillery for shooting missiles at a long range:

> Of the ships which Laevinus had had to protect his supplies, the consul loaded some with devices and equipment for attacking city walls, while some of them he fitted out with artillery and stones and every kind of missile weapon. And so also with the merchantmen, not merely those propelled by oars, in order that some crews should carry engines and ladders up to the walls, and others from ships at long range should wound the defenders of the walls. These ships were equipped and made ready to attack the city from the open sea. And the sea was unmolested by the Punic fleet, which had been sent over to Corcyra, since Philip was preparing to attack the Aetolians.[113]

As this was taking place, the city was betrayed to the Romans by the commander of the group of Bruttians that Hannibal had put in place to protect the city. The Romans took a huge amount of booty and 30,000 slaves. Hannibal marched to Tarentum but realized that nothing could be done and retired to Metapontum; his plot to make Fabius follow him there failed.[114]

Lack of resources became an issue in the same year when twelve Latin colonies informed that they were no longer able to send soldiers or money to support the war effort. The senate could do nothing to change their refusal but made sure that the remaining eighteen colonies fulfilled their duty.[115]

In 208, there was another report of naval preparations being made at Carthage with the intention of blockading the whole coast of Italy, Sicily and Sardinia with 200 ships. We cannot pay too much attention to the number of ships, which we have from one source only; what matters is the fact that the Carthaginians could have put pressure on the ports and interrupted shipments, a problem the Romans had faced since the beginning of the war. Consequently, the Romans repositioned their ships. Publius Scipio was ordered to send over to Sardinia for the defence of the island fifty of the eighty ships that he had either brought with him from Italy or captured at New Carthage. The *imperium* of Marcus Valerius Laevinus was continued in Sicily and the seventy Roman ships there were increased with the addition of the thirty ships that had been stationed at Tarentum the preceding year. With this fleet he was to cross over into Africa and collect booty, if he thought the time was suitable. The *praetor urbanus* was given the task of preparing the thirty old warships that were in Ostia and of manning twenty new ships with crews, so that he could defend the coast near Rome.[116]

The building of the fleet shows the serious intention of the Carthaginian government to continue the struggle for the islands. It should be seen as a reaction to the loss of New Carthage and Tarentum. There is no information of any Carthaginian attack taking place, apparently because the Romans did not give them any opportunity. Livy gives a frustratingly short description of what became the biggest sea battle in the Second Punic War:

> The same summer Marcus Valerius crossed over from Sicily to Africa with a fleet of a hundred ships, and making a landing at the city of Clupea [Aspis], he ravaged the country far and wide, meeting hardly any armed men. Then the foragers were hurriedly brought back to the ships, because suddenly came the report that a Carthaginian fleet was approaching. There were eighty-three ships. With these the Roman fought with success not far from Clupea. After capturing eighteen ships and putting the rest to flight, he returned to Lilybaeum with a great quantity of booty from the land and from the ships.[117]

Livy states that the Roman fleet ravaged the African coast again the following year. Despite the many similarities in stories from 208 and 207, they are not duplicates of the same event.[118] Marcus Valerius Laevinus was leading the fleet that sailed from Sicily and laid waste the territory of Utica and Carthage. When the Roman fleet was returning to Sicily, a Carthaginian fleet with seventy warships met them. Again, Livy does not give any details but only states that seventeen Carthaginian ships were captured, four sunk at sea and the rest of the fleet routed and put to flight. We do not know the size of the Roman fleet. It returned to Lilybaeum with much booty. Livy adds that thereafter, since the enemy ships had been expelled from the seas, large supplies of grain were brought to Rome.[119]

This information looks like any other story of raids on the enemy territory but the significance is that now there was a Punic fleet confronting the Romans and that it suffered serious losses. Consequently, the possibility of attacking the islands and the coast of Italy was lost. The Romans had taken the edge off the new Punic campaign before the fleet had had the chance to do anything. Now we see the Romans implementing the strategy they had in mind at the beginning of the war, when Titus Sempronius Longus was sent to Lilybaeum with the mission to prepare for the invasion of Africa. Because of the failure to defeat the Punic fleet then, the Romans had to defend the islands for a decade more but these two battles made the turning-point in the war and now the Romans could go back to their original plan. The Carthaginian losses probably explain why there was no attempt to stop Scipio from crossing to Africa in 204.

The Romans awaited the approach of Hasdrubal in Italy in 207 with great anxiety. The sea route from Spain to Italy was still unusable for the Punic fleet, as it had been in 218, and Hasdrubal took the same route that Hannibal had used. However, the Roman situation was now different from 218. The Romans had had experience and time to get ready. They were informed by the Massilians that Hasdrubal had passed over into Gaul. Once in Italy, Hadsrubal sent messengers to find Hannibal and give him instructions to link up with Hasdrubal's army in Umbria. The Romans, however, caught the messengers – four Gauls and two Numidian horsemen – who had come all the way to Metapontum to find Hannibal.[120] Livy's narrative is difficult to follow and we cannot be sure of all the routes Hannibal took but he moved around southern Italy to break away from the Romans.[121] The Romans made sure that the brothers could not meet. Livy explains the Roman strategy:

For they felt that Hasdrubal must be met as he came down from the
Alps, to prevent his stirring up the Cisalpine Gauls or Etruria, which
was already aroused to the hope of rebellion, and likewise that Hannibal
must be kept busy with a war of his own, that he might not be able to
leave the country of the Bruttii and go to meet his brother.[122]

The pressure from the Punic fleet had eased and the Romans could prepare
for Hasdrubal's arrival by transporting troops from several fronts. Livy
refers to some unnamed authors and states that Scipio sent 8,000 Spaniards
and Gauls, 2,000 legionary soldiers and 1,000 cavalry of Numidians and
Spaniards. Marcus Lucretius brought these in ships. Gaius Mamilius
sent 4,000 archers and slingers from Sicily. Slave volunteers were recalled
to their standards. The senate gave the consuls Gaius Claudius Nero and
Marcus Livius Salinator unrestricted freedom to fill up their numbers from
whatever source they pleased, of selecting men from whichever army they
liked and of exchanging and removing men from one province to another.
They also resorted to a resource so far unused: the settlers on the sea coast,
who had been exempt from service. Alsium, Anxur, Minturnae, Sinuessa and
Sena Gallica were compelled to furnish soldiers. Antium and Ostia were still
exempt.[123] The number of soldiers thus enrolled did of course not change
the total significantly but all this shows the need to use exceptional methods
to find men. The consuls destroyed Hasdrubal and his army in the Battle of
the Metaurus in northern Italy in June 207. Livius celebrated a triumph and
Nero an ovation.[124] After the defeat, Hannibal withdrew to Bruttium.

The Roman Invasion of Africa, 204–201 BC

The war was now turning to Rome's advantage. The Carthaginians had lost
control over Spain, there was no longer any way they could take the islands
and the territory in which Hannibal could operate in Italy continued to shrink.
Carthage's grand design had worked in the sense that it had been able to wage
war and challenge Rome in all those areas and had even got Philip involved;
nevertheless, this pressure was not enough to make the Romans agree to peace
terms that would change the power balance in the western Mediterranean in
Carthage's favour. The task of keeping the fronts supplied with resources sent

by sea was manageable for Spain and the islands, and the Carthaginians were able to get help through their alliances in every area. The loss of Syracuse, Capua, Tarentum and New Carthage and the mines in Spain, however, eroded the Carthaginian war economy. The Romans recovered from their difficult start and prevented the Barcids linking up in Italy and also made sure that the Punic fleet was never able to begin proper cooperation with the Punic armies in Italy. With booty from conquests and the introduction of the denarius, the Roman financial situation kept improving.

Publius Cornelius Scipio returned from Spain with much booty in 205 and was elected consul. His colleague was pontifex maximus Publius Licinius Crassus.[125] Scipio wanted Africa as his province to finish the war there but the idea did not go unopposed in the senate. Livy explains the concerns that were raised by old Quintus Fabius Maximus especially; they concerned the need to keep securing Italy both on land and at sea and the senator felt that this was not the right time to take any risks in enemy territory. Hannibal's army must first be defeated in Italy before the Romans went to besiege Carthage. Mago had left the Balearic Islands and was sailing along the coast of Liguria. The danger that he might join up with Hannibal had to be taken as seriously as that concerning Hasdrubal. Moreover, Fabius pointed out that the treasury was not able to maintain two different armies, one in Italy and one in Africa, and there was nothing left from which to equip fleets or to furnish provisions.[126] Finally, it was decided that Scipio would be given command of Sicily and thirty warships; he was also permitted to cross to Africa if he saw it as being in the state's interest – *permissumque ut in Africam, si id e re publica esse censeret, traiceret*. Publius Licinius was assigned Bruttium and the war with Hannibal. The senate granted Scipio permission to celebrate the games, which he had vowed during the mutiny in Spain, and defray the cost out of the money which he had brought into the treasury. The legates Marcus Pomponius Matho and Quintus Catius were sent to Delphi to convey a present from the spoils taken from Hasdrubal, a 200-pound golden crown and 1,000 pounds of silver providing a good illustration of the spoils.[127]

Livy gives very little information about the debates on policy in this war and of course we cannot be sure how far his account of the speech is authentic. Nevertheless, it is true that there were many things to consider, as the Romans were maintaining an army of at least twenty legions for the tenth year, they were in the process of quelling a Spanish revolt, four legions in Bruttium were watching Hannibal, two were probably in Tarentum and one at Capua. One legion with the allied troops was taken to Greece. Furthermore, Mago's landing in Liguria created the need to move forces from Etruria to Gallia Cisalpina and these had to be replaced by the *legiones urbanae* that had been used to protect Rome.[128] The Romans continued the policy of preventing the brothers from meeting. Mago sailed from Minorca to Italy with about thirty warships and a great number of transport ships, bringing 12,000 infantry and about 2,000 cavalry. He took Genua, where there were no troops employed in protecting the coast, and beached his fleet on the Ligurian coast. He kept ten warships and sent the rest of them to Carthage to defend the coast.[129] The distance between the brothers was 900 kilometres. Mago could not land further south, closer to Bruttium, as he would have to sail along the Italian coast guarded by the Romans. Supplies were sent from Carthage; Livy states that the *praetor* Gnaeus Octavius captured eighty Carthaginian transport ships near Sardinia.[130] According to Appian, Hannibal was awaiting new forces from Carthage. He was sent 100 merchant ships full of supplies, soldiers and money but there were not enough rowers and the ships were driven to Sardinia by the wind. The *praetor* attacked them with his warships, sinking twenty of them and capturing sixty. The remainder escaped to Carthage.[131]

Scipio executed both parts of the original Roman strategy: he took New Carthage, marking the turning-point in the war in Spain, and invaded Africa, as had been the plan in 218. Had the Romans kept control of the islands throughout this time, they would probably have invaded Africa years earlier. We can only guess at the reasoning in 216 – Livy does not give any details – when the Romans followed Hiero's advice to attack Africa, giving Titus Otacilius permission to cross to Africa – if he saw it as being in the state's interest – and increasing the size of his fleet. Livy uses the above-quoted wording of the senate's authorization in 216 and 205.[132] In 216, in the execution of that year's strategy, the idea that priority should be given to defeating Hannibal in Italy prevailed, with disastrous consequences.

Credit financing seems to have disappeared thanks to the booty coming from Syracuse and other conquered areas but in 205 the Romans used it again.[133] Political reasons perhaps dictated that Scipio did not receive permission to levy troops but was given the right to take volunteers. The fleet was not paid for by the state but Scipio was to receive the money and materials supplied by the allies for building fresh ships. Livy gives the most detailed list that we have of the assistance given by allies:

> The men of Caere promised grain for the crews and supplies of every kind, the men of Populonium iron, Tarquinii linen for sails, Volaterrae the interior fittings of ships, also grain. Arretium promised three thousand shields, an equal number of helmets; and that they would furnish a total of fifty thousand javelins, short spears and lances, with an equal proportion of each type; also axes, shovels, sickles, baskets and hand-mills, as many as were needed for forty war-ships; a hundred and twenty thousand pecks of wheat also; and that they would contribute allowances for petty officers and oarsmen. Perusia, Clusium and Rusellae promised fir for shipbuilding and a great quantity of grain. He used fir also from forests belonging to the state. The communities of Umbria and in addition Nursia and Reate and Amiternum and the whole Sabine district promised soldiers. Marsians, Paelignians and Marrucini in large numbers gave in their names as volunteers for the fleet. Camerinum, although it treated with the Romans on an equal footing, sent an armed cohort of six hundred men.[134]

Scipio built twenty quinqueremes and ten quadriremes; the ships were launched forty-five days after the materials were taken from the woods. As to the nature of this support, there is no reason to think that it was voluntary but a punishment for rebelling.[135] The arrival of Hasdrubal had had the effect that the Etruscans in particular took the Carthaginian side and in 206 Marcus Livius Salinator had been sent by the senate to Etruria to investigate the depth of the rebellion.[136] The arrival of Mago had a similar effect; the consul Marcus Cornelius Cethegus punished traitors in Etruria who had negotiated with the Carthaginian.[137]

Scipio and the *praefectus classis* Gaius Laelius went to Sicily in 205. The preparations for the actual invasion included training cavalry, in which Scipio got the Sicilians involved. He distributed his army through the towns and ordered the Sicilian states to furnish grain, to spare that which had been brought from Italy. He hauled the new ships on shore at Panormus for the winter, to allow the timber to dry. He repaired his old ships and sent Gaius Laelius with them to plunder the African coast. He reached Hippo Regius by night and led out his soldiers and marines at daybreak to lay waste to the countryside. With no proper information, the Carthaginians panicked and at first thought that Scipio had arrived.[138] They also started military preparations; according to Livy, they sent embassies to Syphax and the other petty princes to strengthen their alliances. They sent envoys to Philip to persuade him to cross to Sicily or Italy and they informed their commanders in Italy that they should keep Scipio at home by harassing the enemy in every way they could. Mago received 25 warships, 6,000 infantry, 800 horse and 7 elephants, besides a large sum of money to be employed in hiring auxiliaries. The aim was to move closer to Rome and join forces with Hannibal. In Africa, Hasdrubal, the son of Gisco, was sent to hunt elephants. On his return he levied 6,000 infantry and 600 cavalry from both the Carthaginian and the African population and bought 5,000 slaves as oarsmen for the ships. He also obtained 2,000 horse from the Numidians and hired mercenaries and exercised them all in a camp 200 stades from Carthage.[139]

The last political obstacle before the invasion could begin concerned the Roman takeover of Locri. The city had defected to the Carthaginians in 215. Late in 205, some Locrian prisoners who had been captured by Roman raiding parties from Rhegium offered to betray Locri to the Romans. Scipio recaptured the city but later had to answer questions for failing to impose proper discipline on his soldiers, led by the legatus Quintus Pleminius. The charges against their brutal action included accusations of plundering houses and temples and that the garrison had been divided into two rival bands, which fought each other. The Locrians had made a complaint to Scipio but he had left Pleminius in charge. Then the Locrians sent envoys to Rome to complain. At the senate, Fabius Maximus was again Scipio's loudest opponent. Ten commissioners were sent to Locri and Sicily to investigate the matter. The episode threatened Scipio's career but he turned the situation to his advantage in a meeting at Syracuse, where he had gathered his land and naval forces, drilling the soldiers and the fleet likewise manoeuvring as if in a naval battle in the harbour. The *praetor* and the legates were conducted on a tour of inspection of arsenals and magazines and other equipment for war. They were impressed and the senate voted that the crossing to Africa should take place at the earliest possible moment.[140]

The invasion of Africa was launched in 204 from Lilybaeum with the traditional ceremony where Scipio himself threw the entrails of the sacrificed animal into the sea. We do not know the exact number of forces taken to Africa. The army probably consisted of two legions and the allied fighting forces. Livy refers to unnamed sources and gives figures of 10,000 to 35,000 infantry and 200 to 1,600 cavalry; 35,000 being the maximum total of all the forces. Appian states that there were 16,000 infantry and 1,600 cavalry. Lazenby estimates the number as 28,200, consisting of 10,000 Roman infantry, 600 Roman cavalry, 16,000 allied infantry and 1,600 allied cavalry; Goldsworthy estimates about 25,000–30,000 men.[141]

The Romans sailed across with 40 warships and 400 cargo ships. After sighting Cape Bon they sailed westwards and landed at Cap Farina at the northernmost point of the Bay of Carthage. There is no information of any movement by the Carthaginian navy to stop them.[142] The local people escaped to cities and the gates to Carthage were closed and soldiers posted on the walls. The Carthaginians sent 500 horsemen to the coast to investigate and to break up the disembarkation but the Romans were already moving southwards towards Utica and defeated them. They plundered the countryside and sent booty and slaves to Sicily. Masinissa, who was at this point at war with Syphax over the throne of the Numidians, joined the Roman campaign bringing with him either 200 or 2,000 cavalry; Livy gives both figures.[143] Masinissa and the Romans defeated another cavalry force of 4,000 men sent by the Carthaginians at the city of Salaeca, about 22 kilometres from the Roman camp. Roman transport ships, which had taken the booty to Sicily, returned with supplies and were again loaded with booty. Scipio laid siege to Utica from land and sea. The Carthaginians had by then mobilized their army, led by Hasdrubal Gisco, and Syphax arrived with his army. They stayed in two camps through the winter, watching the Romans, who had established their camp at a site named *Castra Cornelia* on a peninsula east of Utica which functioned as the headquarters of Rome's operations. The figures given by both sources – 30,000 infantry and 3,000 cavalry for Hasdrubal Gisco and 50,000 infantry and 10,000 cavalry for

Syphax – are probably too high, considering the difficulties of feeding such a crowd throughout the winter.[144] The plan was to besiege the Romans from land and sea. Livy states that the Punic fleet had been launched and was ready and equipped to intercept the supplies. Yet Scipio broke out from the position before the Carthaginians could act. During the winter, Scipio had started discussions with Syphax that led to an offer to mediate between Rome and Carthage. In fact, Scipio was buying time to make preparations and early in the spring gave out the false information that he was going to intensify the siege of Utica; in reality he made a night attack on both camps, setting them on fire and making the few survivors flee. The supply route continued uninterrupted and Scipio received provisions from Sardinia, Spain and Sicily; getting grain, clothes, arms and all kinds of supplies, and sending the booty home.[145] The Romans kept defending the islands; this was important to make sure that the Carthaginians could not land in Italy and also to secure the supply transports. They had 160 ships in service in 204, including 40 ships in Sicily and another 40 assigned to protect the coast of Sardinia; they also continued to guard the Italian coast.[146]

In 203, the Punic army suffered a defeat in the Battle of the Great Plains near Bulla in the Bagradas valley. Consequently, Hannibal was ordered to return to Africa. Scipio occupied Tunis, which its garrison had abandoned. While he was there, the Carthaginian navy attacked the Romans in Utica; they tried to challenge the Romans to a proper sea battle but that was not possible as the Roman ships were involved in the siege and unprepared for a naval action. Scipio saved the fleet by anchoring the ships in line and positioning the transport ships around them. He held the transport ships together by placing masts and yards crosswise from ship to ship. In addition, he laid down planks to make a gangway the whole length of the ships. Beneath these bridges he left openings where scouting vessels could sally out against the enemy. The Carthaginians attacked this assembly of ships and after the battle towed away about sixty Roman transport ships to Carthage.[147]

Scipio sent Laelius and Masinissa with the Roman and Numidian cavalry and the light infantry to pursue Syphax and Hasdrubal. Syphax was captured and Laelius took Syphax's capital Cirta. Scipio declared Masinissa the king of his tribe, which was confirmed in the Roman senate.[148] Peace negotiations were started in 203 at the Carthaginian initiative. The terms included the withdrawal of armies from Italy and Gallia Cisalpina, the Carthaginians were to give up all claim to Spain, retire from all the islands between Italy and Africa and hand over their navy except for twenty ships. According to Polybius, the treaty was approved in Rome. Livy, on the other hand, states that the negotiations in Rome broke up because the ambassadors asked for the continuation of the Catulus treaty and the Romans thought the Carthaginians were only negotiating because they were waiting for Mago and Hannibal to return in order to proceed with war.[149]

Hannibal left Italy in the autumn of 203 and landed in Leptis Minor. According to Livy, he had pre-empted the order to return and had already put ships in readiness so he could leave soon. Appian, however, says that Hannibal built a fleet, for which Italy supplied abundant timber.[150] Mago's troops returned from the Ligurian coast. Mago had been recruiting troops since his arrival and in 203 he was heavily defeated in a battle against the Romans in the territory of the Insubres. On his way to Carthage he died from the wounds he had received in the battle, and a number of Carthaginian ships, which were scattered on the open sea, were captured by the Roman fleet off Sardinia.[151]

It seems that the Roman supply transports worked without any problems. During the truce, the *praetor* Lentulus sent 100 transports from Sardinia with stores, under a convoy of 20 warships. The shipment coming from Sicily, however, containing 200 transports and 30 warships, was caught and scattered by the south-westerly wind on the African coast. Many of the transports were driven to the Bay of Carthage. Some heated discussions ensued in Carthage, involving the senate and the popular assembly, raising the obligation imposed on Carthage in having solicited peace and the restraint required by the existence of a truce as well as their own shortage of food. Finally the decision was made that Hasdrubal should cross with fifty ships and he picked up the transports and towed them to Carthage.[152] Scipio sent legates to Carthage to protest. The Romans accused the Carthaginians of breaching the treaty. They received no proper answer from the Carthaginians and on their way back to camp their ship was attacked, which started the war again.[153] In 202 Scipio continued with an extended *imperium*. Now he was more ruthless in his dealings with the conquered African towns, taking slaves even from towns that surrendered voluntarily. The cavalry played an important part in the victory won by Scipio over Hannibal in Zama, in the south-west, five days' march from Carthage. We do not know the exact numbers of the armies. Following Polybius' figures, Hannibal had about 36,000 infantry, 4,000 cavalry and 80 elephants; Scipio had around 29,000 infantry and 6,100 cavalry.[154]

Polybius records the conditions of the peace treaty as follows:

Carthage was to retain all the cities it formerly possessed in Africa before entering on the last war with Rome ... They were to be governed by their own laws and customs and to receive no garrison ... Prisoners of war and deserters who had fallen into their hands at any date were to be delivered up. They were to surrender their ships of war with the exception of ten triremes, and all their elephants. They were not to make war at all on any nation outside Africa and on no nation in Africa without consulting Rome. They were to restore to King Masinissa, within the boundaries that should subsequently be assigned, all houses, lands, and cities, and other property which had belonged to him or to his ancestors. They were to furnish the Roman army with sufficient corn for three months and pay the soldiers until a reply arrived from Rome regarding the treaty. They were to contribute ten thousand talents in fifty years, paying two hundred Euboean talents each year. Finally they were to give as surety a hundred hostages chosen by the Roman general from among their young men between the age of fourteen and thirty. [155]

Carthage could not regain its position as the leading state in the western Mediterranean. The treaty left it in a subordinate position to Rome, without an independent foreign policy. The open clause concerning the boundaries of Masinissa's territory and his alliance with Rome gave him the freedom to deal with Carthage as he pleased; Carthage could not quarrel with its neighbour without the Romans becoming involved. Rome was now the master of the western Mediterranean and the Punic ships were put to sea and burned. Livy states: 'The ships Scipio ordered to be put to sea and to be burned. Some historians relate that there were five hundred of them – every type of vessel propelled by oars; and that when the Carthaginians suddenly caught sight of the fire it was as doleful for them as if Carthage itself were in flames.'[156]

Chapter 6

Rome and Carthage after the Second Punic War: The Last Fifty Years of the Punic State

C arthage and Rome were no longer equals. The following decades meant continuous warfare for Rome in both west and east, whereas Carthage was reduced to being a city-state on the coast of Africa. The final fifty years of Punic Carthage should be seen in the context of how Rome's expansion progressed in general.

Rome's Expansion

In the west, the Romans continued campaigns against the Gauls in Gallia Cisalpina. The project that had been interrupted by the Second Punic War came to an end in 191 with the defeat of the most powerful tribe, the Boii. In 187, the Via Aemilia was built from Placentia to Ariminum. Thereafter, the Romans fought tribes in Liguria and the northern Apennines. They took Istria in 178–177. Spain was divided into two provinces, Hispania Ulterior and Hispania Citerior. The harsh measures taken by the Romans, which included heavy looting of Spain, caused a revolt in 197. The war ended in 179, when Titus Sempronius Gracchus as *propraetor* achieved important victories over the Celtiberians and made treaties with them. The Romans fought the Lusitanians in 154–138 and the Celtiberians in 153–151. These wars turned out to be extremely difficult for the Romans, as they suffered losses and had problems finding men who would be willing to fight in Spain. The Spaniards were subjected to many atrocities. The third war against the Celtiberians was fought from 143 to 133, when Scipio Aemilianus destroyed Numantia. The natives in Sardinia revolted in 181–176 and in Corsica in 181 and 166–163.

In the western Mediterranean the Romans had no important navies to fight but in the east the competition for thalassocracy in the Aegean continued. The First Macedonian War had already meant a rearrangement of sea power: Attalus had used the situation to increase his influence in the Aegean, to the dismay of Rhodes and Egypt. Philip had started a new and very expensive shipbuilding project that he might not have undertaken in other circumstances. In all their later campaigns in the east, the Romans used the system of safe harbours, allies, shipments and the whole organization needed in overseas warfare that they had created in the First Macedonian War.

Rome's return to the east took place during a major power transition in the state system of the Greek east. While the Romans were finishing off the war with Hannibal, the situation in the Aegean kept changing: both Philip and Antiochus extended their power, while that of Egypt was diminishing. Philip started an aggressive expansion with his newly-finished fleet, aspiring to thalassocracy in the Aegean and threatening the Rhodian and Pergamene possessions. They tried to stop this development in the battles of Chios and Lade in 201 but their fleets were not strong enough. Ptolemaic Egypt had previously held a stabilizing role in the Aegean but could not now help as Philip and Antiochus were attacking its possessions. Rhodes and Pergamum called for help from the Romans.[1]

The Second Macedonian War in 200–197 progressed very much as had the first.[2] There were no sea battles; the Romans settled in and gave an ultimatum whereby they made themselves the protectors of Greece.[3] Philip was unable to do anything to stop the Roman shipments or warfare in general and he lost his position in the Aegean to the Rhodian and Pergamene fleets, which were lesser sea powers and could never have gained such a position without the presence of the Romans. At the end of the war, Philip had to surrender his fleet: all his decked ships except for five and the royal galley, which was a sixteen. He was allowed to have a maximum of 5,000 soldiers and no elephants. He was to wage no war outside Macedon without the permission of the senate, to pay an indemnity and evacuate and leave free areas listed in the treaty.[4]

The Romans were concerned about the Seleucid expansion, which during the Second Macedonian War had been extended to the coast of Asia Minor. Antiochus tried to conquer areas on both sides of the Aegean in the same way that Philip had done before him. The Romans delayed their withdrawal from Greece after the proclamation of freedom at the Isthmian Games in 196.[5] Assisted by the Pergamene and Rhodian fleets, they fought two campaigns against Nabis, king of Sparta, in 195 and 192. Nabis was forced to give up his fleet. He was not allowed to have any ship except for two *lemboi* propelled by no more than sixteen oars.[6]

In the war with Antiochus in 191–188 the Romans defeated him both on land and at sea.[7] In this the Romans entered the coast of Asia Minor for the first time. The fleet had the task of securing the crossing over the Hellespont and defeating the Seleucid fleet. There were several sea battles and Hannibal, who had escaped to Antiochus' court after he had been forced to flee from Carthage in 195, served as a commander of part of the Seleucid fleet. The fleet could not stop the Romans from entering the Aegean and joining forces with Pergamum and Rhodes or change the fact that the Romans used Chios as a depot. As it had with Philip, the coming of the Romans forced Antiochus to increase the numbers of his fleet, which he might not have done otherwise. Hannibal was sent to obtain ships from the Phoenicians and the fleet was built in Cilicia. However, the Rhodians defeated Hannibal and the new fleet, ensuring that the Seleucid fleets could not join forces, so Antiochus was never able to gather a large fleet to meet the Romans, exactly like Philip's failure in naval warfare.[8] In the Battle of Myonnesus in 190, the ship numbers were about the same as those of the largest battles in the Second Punic War: there were eighty ships in the Roman coalition and eighty-nine ships in the Seleucid fleet. The *praetor* Lucius Aemilius Regillus was awarded a naval triumph 'From Asia over King Antiochus', as was the *praetor* Quintus Fabius Labeo in the following year.[9]

According to the peace treaty of Apamea in 188, Antiochus had to surrender his warships and their rigging and he was not allowed to have more than ten decked ships. His ships were not permitted to sail beyond the river Calycadnus and the Sarpedonian promontory unless they were conveying tribute, envoys or hostages.[10] Yet another seafaring state had been forced to surrender its fleet and Rome was now the master of the Aegean. Pergamum and Rhodes were rewarded for their support of the Roman war effort and were expected to continue that support.

The success of Roman military operations was based on several factors: the legions that were sent had all the knowledge and experience they had gained in the Second Punic War and for this reason they were markedly superior to their professional opponents in the east.[11] Moreover, they had experience of waging wars overseas where operations were based on the control of coasts and harbours. They started a new war by securing landing-places on the west coast of Greece and always finished the war by securing the coast as they withdrew back to Italy. The road to Greece was always kept open. Therefore, when we consider the larger question of whether there was a greater plan in the Roman conquests in the east or whether we should see each of these wars as separate incidents, it is clear that the system of safe ports, landing-places and shipments and keeping the west coast of Greece secured for a quick landing whenever needed were all elements that had been established in the First Macedonian War and remained in use in all the following campaigns. As to supplies, the Romans used the resources of Sicily and Sardinia for grain as they had done in the Second Punic War. Grain was shipped to Rome and to the armies in the east. Masinissa also sent grain.

After the peace of Apamea, Rome became increasingly involved in Greece. Numerous embassies visited Rome as individuals and groups sought Rome's support for their own purposes. The combination of Roman orders and Rome's adherents seeking the support or approval of Rome in their internal strifes gradually eroded Greek independence.[12]

In the war with King Perseus of Macedon in 171–168, the Romans used the complaints by King Eumenes of Pergamum as a pretext for the war, intending to place Greece under more firm control.[13] They tricked Perseus into continuing negotiations and into believing that the war could be avoided but in fact they were already proceeding in Greece by the time Perseus learned that the discussions had failed in Rome. The Roman army was at Gomphi, looking for Perseus's army, and the fleet was stationed at Chalcis, the maritime gateway to Greece. The Romans made preparations as in any other war but fought it without military allies. They sent home the large coalition of allied ships that had gathered in Chalcis; these included ships from Carthage, Heraclea Pontica, Chalcedon, Samos and Rhodes, with the explanation that there was no great naval threat from Perseus and no need for the fleets.[14] Only the help of Eumenes was enlisted. Macedon was divided into four separate republics. A thousand leading members of the Achaean League were deported to Italy, among them Polybius. It was forbidden for the Macedonians to cut timber for shipbuilding or to let anyone else do so.[15] The consul Lucius Aemilius Paullus celebrated a triumph 'from Macedon and King Perseus' and the *praetor* Gnaeus Octavius celebrated a naval triumph 'from Macedon and King Perseus'.[16] Macedon was thoroughly plundered, as Livy states:

> The spectators were not more interested in the scenic representations and the athletic contests and chariot races than they were in the display of the spoils from Macedon. These were all laid out to view – statues, pictures, woven fabrics, articles in gold, silver, bronze and ivory wrought with consummate care, all of which had been found in the palace, where they had not been intended, like those which filled the palace at Alexandria, for a moment's ornament but for constant and lasting use. They were all placed on board the fleet under the charge of Gnaeus Octavius to be transported to Rome.[17]
>
> A few days later [Lucius Aemilius] Paullus himself sailed up the Tiber to the city in the king's ship, a vessel of enormous size propelled by sixteen banks of oars and adorned with the spoils of Macedon in the shape of glittering armour and embroidered fabrics which belonged to the king [Philip]. The river banks were crowded with multitudes who had streamed out to greet his arrival.[18]

The value of the booty is reported by Livy as more than 30,000,000 denarii, subsequently, *tributum*, property tax was suspended from the Roman citizens.[19] In 150, the Romans interfered in the business of Greece again, to subdue an uprising in Macedon led by Andriscus, and as a result Macedon became a province of Rome in 148. Attalus provided a fleet for this war and sent troops to the Achaean War, when the Achaean League revolted and was crushed in 146. Lucius Mummius occupied Corinth without a fight and then destroyed and plundered it. The abundant booty was on display in the triumph in Rome and afterwards distributed elsewhere in Italy and in Spain.[20]

The role of Rome's allies was not easy. Quartering Roman troops and furnishing them with supplies was a major burden. The difficulty of accommodating the Roman fleet was the reason why Eumenes had decided to turn down Antiochus's first offer of peace; he reasoned that if they made peace before the consul arrived, the Roman forces would stay in Asia over the winter while they waited for the reaction from Rome and their allies would be exhausted again from furnishing supplies.[21] There were many problems in the war with Perseus: after the allies had been sent home, the Roman fleet stayed idle at Chalcis. Envoys from Chalcis went to Rome, stating that it would have been better if they had never let the Romans in. Among other complaints, it was said that free people had been sold into slavery and temples looted and that the *praetor* Gaius Lucretius Gallus had transported the looted temple adornments in his ships to Antium. He stayed there in the middle of the campaign and used the money from the booty to construct water canals there and decorated the temple of Aesculapius with paintings. His successor, Lucius Hortensius, continued the practice of quartering the sailors in private houses, both in summer and winter. He took and robbed the city of Abdera where the Romans had gone to demand grain and sold its inhabitants into slavery. The senate disapproved of what had happened; Roman envoys were sent to Abdera and to the commanders in charge.[22]

The first signs of the decline of Roman military competence became visible in this war; it was the last war in which soldiers with experience from the Second Punic War participated.[23] The ineffectiveness of the Roman army and navy were a great concern: in the legates' report from 168 the envoys claimed that the Roman army had been led to Macedon taking unnecessary risks; they had heard that some of the sailors had been lost to disease and others, especially the Sicilians, had gone home, with the result that the ships were short of crews. Those who remained had not received money or clothes. Eumenes and his fleet had come and gone as they pleased. The loyalty of Eumenes was questioned; Attalus, on the other hand, received a good report.[24]

The Romans needed the connections and local knowledge of the situation in the Aegean, which they received from Pergamum and Rhodes. Willingly or not, the Romans also became the protectors of the ambitions of these states as they tried to increase their power in the Aegean. However, after the war with Perseus, the Romans withdrew their support and began to support others instead, such as King Prusias of Bithynia and the Galatians. They would not allow these people to become too powerful, as Rome's intervention in the war between Prusias and Pergamum shows. Rhodes' badly-timed attempt to mediate a settlement between Perseus and Rome made the Romans see it as an enemy and through a series of decisions they subsequently made sure that the Rhodians lost their possessions in Asia Minor, lost the leadership of the Nesiotic League and were financially weakened.

Carthage Subordinate

Due to the scarcity of sources, we have very little information about post-war Carthage and the reasons leading to the Third Punic War; therefore, we can speculate but draw very few conclusions. Archaeological evidence shows that Carthage had wide cultural and commercial contacts. Trade with Spain continued, as did trade with the islands and Italy. In the east Rhodes was an important partner in trade. Furthermore, the Numidian people were well-integrated in the Hellenistic world.[25]

The clauses of the oppressive peace treaty had removed any possibility of independent Carthaginian foreign policy. The Romans now had constant business in Africa. They sent envoys to Carthage in 200 to complain about a commander called Hamilcar, who had been left in Gaul either with a part of the army formerly commanded by Hasdrubal, or with that of Mago; he had called on the armies of the Gauls and Ligurians to rise up against the Romans. The envoys also demanded the return of all the deserters; a great many of them were said to be living openly in Carthage. Rome needed Masinissa's cavalry in the war with Philip and he was openly supported in African affairs: Roman envoys were sent congratulating him and bringing him lavish gifts for having extended his territory by taking parts of Syphax's territories. They also promised future support, as Livy states: 'The ambassadors were directed to promise him that if he pointed out anything he needed to strengthen and enlarge his kingdom, the Roman people would make every effort to secure it for him, in recognition of his services to them.' The request from the ambassadors from Vermina, the son of Syphax, to be given the title of king, friend and ally was turned down.[26]

Hannibal urged the Carthaginians to accept the peace treaty and he gave up the generalship in 199. The two-year gap between the end of the war and his resignation was because of the need to discharge the soldiers in an orderly fashion, avoiding the chaos of 241.[27] Hannibal became a *suffete*, chief magistrate, in 196 by popular vote. Livy reports that there was corruption in the use of state funds by the leading elite, which threatened Carthage's ability to pay the indemnities; private citizens were at risk of having to pay a heavy tribute to cover the missing funds.[28] The problem was probably an old one. As long as there had been plenty of revenues it was perhaps not such an issue but now that the sources of income had greatly diminished, such a loss of state funds was no longer acceptable, especially as it had the consequence of attracting Rome's attention once again. Hannibal intervened and caused an outcry among the people that were involved in the embezzlement. Livy reports:

> When Hannibal had investigated the revenues, how much was collected as taxes on land and as duty at the ports, for what purposes it was spent, how much the ordinary expenses of the state required, and how much embezzlement took from the treasury, he asserted in the assembly that the state would be rich enough, if it collected the revenues not otherwise used and omitted the assessment on individual citizens, to pay its debt to the Romans, and this assertion he was able to make good.[29]

The case of Hannibal shows that the Carthaginians were eroding their independence in the same way as the Greeks. The people whose fortunes were under threat instigated the Romans to turn against Hannibal. In Rome, Scipio Africanus long opposed the sending of envoys to take part in the animosity against Hannibal, yet in the end the point was carried that an embassy should be sent to Carthage to represent to the senate there that Hannibal, in concert with King Antiochus, was planning to start a war. Hannibal's enemies had arranged this. The pretext for the embassy was that they came to mediate in the disputes between the Carthaginians and Masinissa. Livy states that this pretext was generally believed. Yet Hannibal knew that the Romans were after him and fled Africa. He sailed to Tyre, where Livy states he was received by the founders of Carthage as coming from a second homeland; Tyre was then part of the Seleucid empire and Hannibal then continued to Antioch and Ephesus, where he met the king.[30] The accusation that Hannibal and Antiochus cooperated to wage war against

Rome cannot be true. As Hoyos explains, there is no sound evidence that the king was looking for a Roman war in 196 or before and when Antiochus's relations with Rome worsened, it was only by 193 that he treated Hannibal as a serious adviser. Hannibal was a *suffete* and one of the leading citizens in Carthage and naturally had connections in Africa to the Numidians and abroad. Carthage as a state had contacts with the mother–city Tyre and many other places. Hannibal held social events, including regular morning meetings for a large number of people, including visitors from elsewhere. This kind of aristocratic lifestyle could be used against him to start rumours.[31] The Roman envoys had come to Carthage in 218 to demand the surrender of Hannibal and the members of his council or else there would be a war. The Carthaginians had refused. Now, in 195, Hannibal's adversaries arranged for the Romans to come and take action against Hannibal.[32]

The total change in Carthage's international position is best illustrated by the fact that the former enemy, which had been forced to surrender its fleet, now supported the Roman war effort. Carthage sent grain to Rome and to the army in Macedon in 200 and again in 191 when Rome was at war with Antiochus. In 191, the Carthaginians offered to pay all the remaining indemnities at once but the Romans declined. Carthage also sent its few remaining warships to fight in the Roman navy against Antiochus and against Perseus. At the same time, Hannibal worked on the opposing side as an adviser and naval commander of the Seleucid navy.[33]

There are many possible explanations for the development of the situation leading to the final conflict with Rome. The official reason was that Carthage violated the peace treaty by waging war against Masinissa. The peace treaty had given Masinissa unrestricted possibilities to expand his territory. He not only took the lands that could reasonably be described as belonging to Numidia before the Punic Wars but also entered lands that clearly were Carthaginian possessions. These included the entire Emporia region and the region of the Great Plains and Theveste region. Carthage's Libyan territories were reduced to the size they had been 300 years earlier and, as Hoyos estimates, the conquests probably halved their agricultural and tax resources. The Carthaginians sent envoys to Rome to make appeals that Rome should intervene and put a stop to the raids, yet Rome continued to support Masinissa.[34] The Carthaginians had to endure it, until they raised an army which in winter 151–150, led by Hasdrubal, suffered a defeat by Masinissa at the city of Oroscopa.[35] This became the formal reason for the war. Polybius states that the idea of destroying Carthage had originated a long time ago and that the Romans 'were looking for a suitable opportunity and a pretext that would appeal to foreign nations ... their disputes with each other about the effect on foreign opinion very nearly made them desist from going to war.'[36]

In Roman politics there was nothing new about finding a suitable reason and a suitable war: in 192 they had been looking for a reason to stay in Greece and the Roman envoys who had been sent to explore the situation stated that there was no sufficiently good reason for war except against Nabis; however, the war was started.[37] In 152, after having visited Carthage as a member of a committee sent to arbitrate in a dispute, Cato the Elder started to finish every speech he made in the senate by stating that Carthage must be destroyed. In 149 he presented in the senate with a fig and said that the country where it grew was only three days' sail from Rome. For a long time Cato was opposed by Scipio Nasica, who held that Carthage ought to be spared so that Roman discipline, which was already lapsing, might be preserved through fear of the Carthaginians. The aspect of fear is also visible in Appian's account of how the Romans celebrated the destruction of Carthage: as being delivered from some great fear and being assured of the permanence of their own city.[38]

So why destroy Carthage? Morrison and Coates see maritime rivalry as the cause for the war: that the Romans saw Carthage as a commercial threat. They also point out the possibility that Carthage, with ship-sheds for 220 warships, could have been a naval threat.[39] Yet, considering that Carthage had no war fleet to speak of and had just been defeated in its first military engagement since the Second Punic War, I do not see any Punic military threat as real. When we look at what happened in the four years before the final destruction of Carthage, there are no signs of any kind of naval threat. The Romans were badly prepared and that is why it took four years to defeat the Carthaginians; it was not that the Carthaginians had a chance of withstanding the Romans. The two lavish harbours that have been dated to the period after the Second Punic War were probably built with the intention of giving Carthage defended harbours. As Hurst sees it, enclosing the fleet within the city walls implies an excessively defensive mentality rather than aggressive inclinations. The new construction was unnecessary in the sense that naval power had been achieved without it; that it was presumably built shortly before the Third Punic War can be seen as a 'last gesture of a power which had lost the belief as well as capacity to defend itself conventionally'.[40] In 153, the envoys sent to negotiate between the Carthaginians and Masinissa said they had seen a great deal of timber in Carthage. [41] This timber could, of course, be used for any kind of building project and we cannot connect it to the building of the harbour or ships or anything specific but again it shows that the Romans were watching everything that took place in Carthage.

As Le Bohec points out, lack of evidence makes it hard to accept the political thesis that the senate would have wanted to change Rome's attitude to Carthage and opt for direct control of the defeated state, or that democratic movements that started to flourish in Africa, Greece and Spain were seen as a threat to the Roman government and had to be quashed. Second, the economic thesis is not credible because Carthage, despite its financial upswing – which is hard to measure – had lost control of its empire, thus it was probably not the best target for booty. The psychological thesis – that the key factor was Roman fear of the Carthaginians, combined with ignorance of the true situation – is important because the trauma of Hannibal's war basically followed on from the Romans' fear of the Gauls.[42]

There is no overall reason that explains Rome's action but keeping in mind Roman expansion generally, the fate of Carthage is in no way different from other areas that Rome had already conquered and in which a military uprising was started. So why would they have treated Carthage any differently?

The Roman Siege of Carthage: The Third Punic War, 149–146 BC

The conflict is traditionally called the Third Punic War but the siege of Carthage might be a more accurate name, since there was only one military operation, the siege of the Punic capital.[43] The Romans had started the war with Perseus having made him believe that war could be avoided through negotiations but in fact they were already proceeding in Greece. This strategy was repeated with Carthage. The Romans began making demands. The consuls that had arrived in Sicily in 149 with 80,000 infantry, 4,000 cavalry, 50 quinqueremes and 100 *hemiolia* – fast, two-banked galleys – delivered the declaration of war in Carthage by messenger. The Carthaginians sent an envoy to Rome to settle the difficulty by any terms they could. The senate stated that the freedom and autonomy of Carthage should be preserved and Carthage would retain its lands in Africa if it handed over to the consuls in Lilybaeum 300 children from the leading families as hostages. The captives were sent and taken to Rome in a sixteen. Yet the consuls sailed to Utica, which had defected to them, and set the camp on the *Castra Cornelia*; the fleet stayed in the harbour at Utica. The following meetings took place at Utica. Now the consuls demanded that the Carthaginian arsenal was handed over. It included complete armour for 200,000 men, innumerable javelins and darts and 2,000 catapults for throwing pointed missiles and stones. The demand included Carthaginian ships. When this had been fulfilled, lastly, the Romans demanded that the Carthaginians must evacuate the city and the citizens settle in countryside about 20 kilometres inland. Free access to temples and tombs was granted but the rest of the city was going to be destroyed. The Carthaginians were not allowed to send an embassy to Rome but the envoys returned to Carthage to discuss the demands at the senate. Appian's account tells about the anger and frustration of the people; envoys were lynched and so were the senators who had spoken for accepting the Roman demands for hostages and arms. Some Italians who happened to be in Carthage were also maltreated.[44] The senate declared war on Rome. Preparations began, as Appian states:

All the sacred places, the temples, and every other unoccupied space, were turned into workshops, where men and women worked together day and night without pause, taking their food by turns on a fixed schedule. Each day they made 100 shields, 300 swords, 1000 missiles for catapults, 500 darts and javelins, and as many catapults as they could. For strings to bend them the women cut off their hair for want of other fibres.[45]

The Carthaginians had two armies defending their city: one outside at Nepheris, 25 kilometres south of Carthage, led by the Hasdrubal who had been defeated by Masinissa, and one in the city, led by another commander called Hasdrubal. The army outside also arranged for supplies to be sent from the countryside to Carthage.[46] The consuls began the siege of Carthage but because of vigorous Carthaginian defence the Romans did not achieve much in 149 or 148. They were defeated in their attempts to overcome the army at Nepheris and to take Hippo Acra. They attacked Aspis by land and sea and were repulsed. They made a failed attempt to besiege the city of Hippagreta, located between Carthage and Utica, because it intercepted the Roman supply ships.[47] In 147, Publius Cornelius Scipio Aemilianus was elected consul although he was only 38 years old – the minimum age for consulship was 42 – and sent to continue operations in Africa. He started by returning discipline to the army. The problems reported by Appian – the idleness and greed of the soldiers resulting in unauthorized plundering expeditions and quarrels about how the booty should be shared – were basically the same issues of an idle army that the Romans had to deal with in the war with Perseus.[48]

Carthage was mostly depending on supplies coming from land but some supplies by sea also got through because the blockade of the Roman fleet stationed outside Carthage was not complete. In his depiction of the situation, Appian describes all the typical difficulties of a sea blockade: the Romans were not able to keep their positions as they had no shelter and the sea was full of reefs; they were not able to anchor near the city itself, with the Carthaginians standing on the walls and the sea pounding on the rocks there. Some merchants, watching for a strong and favourable wind, spread their sails and ran the blockade with the Roman galleys unable to pursue them as they sailed before the wind.[49] Scipio made the soldiers carry out works that would cut Carthage off from supplies coming from Africa. This caused a shortage of food in Carthage. He also installed a mole to prevent the entry to the two harbours that Appian describes as follows:

> The harbours had communication with each other, and a common entrance from the sea seventy feet wide, which could be closed with iron chains. The first port was for merchant vessels, and here were collected all kinds of ships' tackle. Within the second port was an island which, together with the port itself, was enclosed by high embankments. These

embankments were full of shipyards which had capacity for 220 vessels. Above them were magazines for their tackle and furniture.[50]

Archaeological excavations have proved the description to be substantially correct.[51] The Carthaginians began a carefully-hidden operation from inside the harbour to excavate another entrance at another part of the harbour in mid-sea. The women and children helped in the digging. At the same time they built triremes and quinqueremes from old material and launched fifty triremes and smaller ships from the new entrance. These were defeated, however, by the Romans in two sea battles outside the harbour, so their last attempt to take charge of the situation failed.[52] Finally, the Roman troops stormed the city and started to take it in stages in street fights, starting from the lower city and ending in the upper. After a week of horror that would be recognizable in any modern footage covering street fights in the middle of a civilian population, the surviving citizens were sold for slavery and the city was razed to the ground. Scipio gave the soldiers a certain number of days for plunder, preserving the gold, silver and temple gifts. The Romans declared that the city of Carthage should be left uninhabited and gave the territory of Carthage to the Uticans as a reward. Scipio celebrated a triumph splendid with gold and overflowing with the statues and votive offerings that the Carthaginians had gathered from all parts of the world over many eras; the fruits of their countless victories. In the following year the Romans celebrated the triumph of Lucius Mummius from Achaea and Corinth, another helpless city that had been sacked.[53]

The naval rivalry between Rome and Carthage that started in the fourth century BC had ceased in 201. Rome had challenged – and beaten – the Carthaginians, Macedonians and Seleucids in a shipbuilding arms race. In this competition Carthage fared best, while the Macedonian and Seleucid resources turned out to be very limited. All these states would have had a chance of gaining supremacy in the Mediterranean if the Romans had not been involved. Rome's success can be explained by good planning, determination to succeed and a large pool of resources in Italy, including finance, manpower and timber. Allies played important roles in the conflict. The Romans could not have taken and kept Sicily without support from

Syracuse; the Massilian fleet helped the Romans on the Spanish coast; and, in the eastern Mediterranean, the Romans benefited from assistance given by the Aetolians and by Pergamum and Rhodes, gaining access to ports and advice on the local conditions. None of Rome's opponents had similar support from its allies and none of them could draw on resources of the same scale. As a result, Rome overcame all its enemies in the Mediterranean, in the west and in the east, and was master of the sea.

Glossary of Ancient Nautical Terms

akatia: an oar-propelled boat using thirty to fifty rowers.

bireme, biremis, *dieres*: a ship with two banks of oars ranging fore and aft on each side of the ship. Each oar was operated by a single oarsman.

corvus, boarding-bridge: a device used in the Roman ships in the First Punic War to invade Carthaginian ships.

diekplous: battle manoeuvre in which ships were arranged in a column in front of the enemy, where they tried to break through the line of enemy ships and, by using the ram, damage the hulls and oars of the enemy ships.

duoviri navales: two naval commissioners in Rome in charge of equipping and refitting the fleet.

hemiolia: light, fast, two-banked galley.

kataphract ship, *navis tecta, navis constrata, naus kataphraktos*: a decked ship, a ship with a deck ranging fore and aft.

kerkouroi, cercurus: oared auxiliary ship, not equipped with ram.

lembos, lembus: a term that covers a variety of small oared ships, probably originally used for piracy, known for speed and agility.

longship, *navis longa, naus makra*: a warship, propelled by oars and sails. The oars were used in battle; the smaller foresail could be raised in battle. The principal armament was a bronze ram.

pentecontor, *pentekontoros*: a fifty-oared ship, with twenty-five oarsmen on each side on one or two levels.

periplous: battle manoeuvre in which the attacking ships tried to sail around or outflank the enemy ships and, by using the ram, damage the rear of the hulls and oars of the enemy ships.

quadrireme, a four, *quadriremis, tetreres*: a warship with four rows of oarsmen ranging fore and aft on each side of the ship, arranged in such a way that more than one man sat at an oar.

quinquereme, a five, *quinqueremis, penteres*: a warship with five rows of oarsmen ranging fore and aft on each side of the ship, arranged in such a way that more than one man sat at an oar.

six, *hexeres*: a warship with six rows of oarsmen ranging fore and aft on each side of the ship, arranged in such a way that more than one man sat at an oar.

socius navalis: a term used for a city under contract to supply ships, equipment and crew for the Roman navy. Also used for citizens and Italians serving as seamen and oarsmen in the Roman fleet.

triacontor, *triakontoros*: a thirty-oared ship with fifteen oarsmen a side at one or two levels.

trireme, a three, *triremis*, *trieres*: a warship with three banks of oars ranging fore and aft on each side of the ship. Each oar was operated by a single oarsman.

This glossary was originally published in C. Steinby, *The Roman Republican Navy*, pp.216–17, and is reprinted with some changes, with the publisher's permission.

Notes

Chapter 1: Introduction

1. All the dates in this book are BC unless otherwise stated.
2. See J.H. Thiel, *Studies on the History of Roman Sea-Power in Republican Times* (Amsterdam, 1946); J.H. Thiel, *A History of Roman Sea-Power before the Second Punic War* (Amsterdam, 1954). Thiel's studies have been used as the standard reference works on Roman seafaring; the idea that the Romans were not interested in seafaring and that the Roman naval capability developed virtually from nothing in the First Punic War is more or less visible for instance in H.D.L. Viereck, *Die Römische Flotte* (Herford, 1975); B. Caven, *The Punic Wars* (New York, 1980); J. Briscoe, 'The Second Punic War', *CAH* VIII, 2nd ed. (Cambridge, 1989), pp.44–80; H.H. Scullard, 'Carthage and Rome', *CAH* VII, part 2, 2nd ed. (Cambridge, 1989), pp.486–569; L. Casson, *The Ancient Mariners*, 2nd ed. (Princeton, New Jersey, 1991); S. Lancel, *Carthage: A History* (Oxford, 1995); S. Hornblower in *OCD* (3rd ed., Oxford, 1996) on Greek and Roman sea power; J.F. Lazenby, *The First Punic War* (London, 1996); J.S. Morrison and J.F. Coates, *Greek and Roman Oared Warships 399–30 BC*, (Oxford, 1996); A. Goldsworthy, *The Punic Wars* (London, 2000); C.J. Dart and F.J. Vervaet, 'The Significance of the Naval Triumph in Roman History (260–29 BC)' *ZPE* 176 (2011), pp.267–280, to mention just a few.
3. *The Athlit Ram*, eds L. Casson and J.R. Steffy, (Texas University Press, 1991); C. Buccellato and S. Tusa, 'Il Rostro', *Il Museo Regionale 'A. Pepoli' di Trapani, Le collezioni archeologiche*, ed. M.L. Famá, (Bari, 2009), pp.333–334.
4. Polybius, 1.1.5, 3.32, 6.2.3.
5. Diodorus, 1.4.6, 5.1.4.
6. M. Crawford, *Roman Republican Coinage* (Cambridge, 1974), nos 10, 11 and 12. See C. Steinby, 'Early Roman coins with naval types', *RIN* 106 (2005), pp.39–45.
7. My thanks to Philip de Souza for discussing this with me.
8. See B. Rankov, 'The Second Punic War at Sea', *The Second Punic War: A Reappraisal*, eds T. Cornell, B. Rankov and P. Sabin (London, 1996), pp.49–57.
9. See P. de Souza, 'Naval battles and sieges', *The Cambridge History of Greek and Roman Warfare*, eds P. Sabin, H. van Wees and M. Whitby (Cambridge, 2007), pp.434–460.

10. C. Steinby, *The Roman Republican Navy, From the Sixth Century to 167 BC* (Helsinki, 2007), pp.143–170.
11. R. Meiggs, *Trees and Timber in the Ancient Mediterranean World* (Oxford, 1982), p.141.
12. S.C. Humphreys, *Anthropology and the Greeks* (London, 1978), pp.166–167; L.-M. Günther, 'Die karthagische Aristokratie und ihre Überseepolitik im 6. und 5. Jh. v. Chr.', *Klio* 75 (1993), pp.76–84; M. Cristofani, *Gli Etruschi del Mare* (Milan, 1983), pp.7–10; V. Gabrielsen, *Financing the Athenian Fleet, Public Taxation and Social Relations* (London, 1994), pp.24–25.
13. Triremes are not mentioned in the Battle of Alalia in c. 540; however, this does not prove anything as the battle was not fought over state concerns about trade but must be seen as a local conflict.
14. See Pliny, *The Natural History* 7.207; Diodorus, 14.41.3, 14.42.2, 14.44.7; Aelian, *Various History* 6.12.
15. See D. Feeney, *Caesar's Calendar, Ancient Time and the Beginnings of History* (University of California Press, 2007), pp.44–52.
16. In 315, Antigonus possessed a fleet in which in addition to quadriremes and quinqueremes nines and tens were also included. Diodorus, 19.62.8. At the Battle of Salamis off Cyprus in 306, Demetrius had a fleet which included sixes and sevens, while in Ptolemy's fleet, the largest ships were quinqueremes. Diodorus, 20.49.2, 20.50.3. By 301, Demetrius had a fleet which included eights, nines, tens, an eleven and a thirteen. Plutarch, *Demetrius* 31.1. In 288, he launched a fifteen and a sixteen. Plutarch, *Demetrius* 43.4–5. Ptolemy II had a fleet that included a twenty and two thirties. Athenaeus, 5.203d. Ptolemy IV built a forty. Plutarch, *Demetrius* 43.5.
17. For ancient shipbuilding and warfare at sea, see L. Casson, *Ships and Seamanship in the Ancient World* (New Jersey, 1971); L. Casson and E. Linder, 'The evolution in shape of the ancient ram', *The Athlit Ram*, pp.67–71; J. Morton, *The Role of the Physical Environment in Ancient Greek Seafaring, Mnemosyne Supplementum* (Leiden, 2001); J.S. Morrison, J.F. Coates and N.B. Rankov, *The Athenian Trireme*, 2nd ed. (Cambridge, 2000); W.M. Murray, *The Age of Titans: The Rise and Fall of the Great Hellenistic Navies* (Oxford University Press, 2012).
18. For the archaeological evidence showing Phoenician and Greek trading activity in the west in the preceding centuries, see S. Moscati, 'La colonizzazione mediterranea', *I Fenici*, ed. S. Moscati (Milan, 1988), p.48; L. Vagnetti, 'The First Contacts between the Minoan-Mycenaean and the Western Mediterranean Worlds', pp.109–116 and D. Ridgway, 'Relations between Cyprus and the West in the Precolonial Period', pp.117–120, *The Western Greeks, Classical Civilization in the Western Mediterranean*, ed. G. Pugliese Carratelli (London, 1996).

19. J-P. Morel, 'Early Rome and Italy', *The Cambridge Economic History of the Greco-Roman World*, eds W. Scheidel, I. Morris and R. Saller (Cambridge, 2007), pp.489–490; M. Pallottino, *A History of Earliest Italy* (London, 1991), pp.63–64.

20. See Lancel, *Carthage: A History*, p.83. However, it is sometimes difficult to say which of the colonies in the west were founded in the Phoenician period and which later during the Carthaginian hegemony. See S. Moscati, 'La colonizzazione mediterranea', pp.47–56. For details concerning the sites in Sicily and Sardinia, see V. Tusa, 'Sicilia', pp.231–250 and E. Acquaro, 'Sardegna', pp.259–276, *I Fenici*; M. Aubet, *The Phoenicians and the West, Politics, Colonies and Trade*, 2nd ed. (Cambridge, 2001), pp.231–243.

21. For the history of the research and the problems in combining archaeological information and textual indications, see Lancel, *Carthage: A History*, pp.1–32.

22. Aubet, *The Phoenicians and the West*, pp.226–227. See W. Huss, *Geschichte der Karthager* (Munich, 1985), for the founding and the topography of Carthage, pp.39–51.

23. Aubet, *The Phoenicians and the West*, pp.150–157.

24. For the religion of the Carthaginians, see Lancel, *Carthage: A History*, pp.193–256; D. Hoyos, *The Carthaginians* (Routledge, 2010), pp.23–24.

25. G. Pugliese Carratelli, 'An Outline of the Political History of the Greeks in the West', *The Western Greeks*, pp.145–146.

26. See Pugliese Carratelli, 'An Outline of the Political History of the Greeks in the West', pp.141–155.

27. Morel, 'Early Rome and Italy', pp.489–492.

28. Pallottino, *A History of Earliest Italy*, pp.87–91.

29. Pallottino, *A History of Earliest Italy*, pp.66–71.

30. M. Dietler, 'The iron age in the western Mediterranean', *The Cambridge Economic History of the Greco-Roman World*, pp.249–250, 267–270. See M. Lejeune, J. Pouilloux and Y. Solier, 'Étrusque et ionien archaïques sur un plomb de Pech Maho (Aude)', *Revue Archéologique de Narbonnaise* 21 (1988), pp.19–59. The Greek text dated to 475–450 records the purchase of an *akatia* in Emporia by a Greek merchant.

31. There were other archaic temples: the Capitoline temple in Rome from the late sixth century as well as the temple of Castor from the early fifth century. Similarly, the remains of archaic temples from the late sixth to the early fifth have been found at Veii, Orvieto, Lanuvium, Ardea and Satricum. T.J. Cornell, *The Beginnings of Rome: Italy and Rome from the Bronze Age to the Punic Wars (c. 1000–264 BC)* (London, 1995), pp.108–113. M. Torelli, 'Archaic Rome between Latium and Etruria', *CAH* VII, part 2, pp.48–51.

32. For the archaeological evidence on settlements in Rome and Latium, see Cornell, *The Beginnings of Rome*, pp.48–57 and 57–80 for the founding legends

concerning Romulus and Aeneas, which cannot be considered historical. For *Portus Tiberinus*, see C. Buzzetti, *LTUR* vol. IV (Rome, 1999), pp.155–156.

33. R.R. Holloway, *The Archaeology of Early Rome and Latium* (London, 1994), pp.166–173.

34. Pallottino, *A History of Earliest Italy*, pp.76–77, 87.

Chapter 2: Carthaginian and Roman Seafaring Before the First Punic War

1. For the Assyrian pressure on Tyre, see Aubet, *The Phoenicians and the West*, pp.54–60; M. Van De Mieroop, *A History of the Ancient Near East ca. 3000–323 BC*, 2nd ed. (Blackwell, 2007), pp.248–252, 276–277. A.M. Eckstein, *Mediterranean Anarchy, Interstate War, and the Rise of Rome* (University of California Press, 2006), p.159.

2. Diodorus (5.16.2–3) records the foundation of a Carthaginian colony in Ibiza in 654/653 BC. It was probably a Phoenician colony, created by the Phoenicians of the west. Lancel, *Carthage: A History*, pp.81–82.

3. Aubet, *The Phoenicians and the West*, pp.341–346.

4. Lancel, *Carthage: A History*, pp.83–84; Pallottino, *A History of Earliest Italy*, pp.81–82; G. Garbini, 'The Phoenicians in the Western Mediterranean', *The Western Greeks*, p.128.

5. Thucydides, 1.13.6. For the treaty between Carthage and Massilia, see Justin, 43.5.2. B. Scardigli, *I trattati Romano-Cartaginesi* (Pisa, 1991), p.22.

6. Herodotus, 1.163–167; Diodorus, 5.13. The Caeretans got the crews of the disabled ships and stoned them to death. Consequently, they sent a penitential embassy to Delphi.

7. Dietler, 'The iron age in the western Mediterranean', p.250.

8. Pugliese Carratelli, 'An Outline of the Political History of the Greeks in the West', pp.154–155.

9. See S. Mazzarino, *Il pensiero storico classico*, vol. I (Bari, 1966), p.196; M. Torelli, 'Colonizazzioni etrusche e latine di età archaica', *Gli Etruschi e Roma* (Rome, 1981), p.72; F. Coarelli, *Il Campo Marzio dalle origini alla fine della Repubblica* (Rome, 1997), p.347.

10. Aristotle, *Politics* 1280 a 36. Translation, H. Rackham.

11. Cornell, *The Beginnings of Rome*, p.212.

12. D. Asheri, 'Carthaginians and Greeks', *CAH* IV, 2nd ed. (Cambridge, 1988), p.750.

13. P.C. Schmitz, 'The Phoenician text from the Etruscan sanctuary at Pyrgi', *JAOS* 115 (1995), pp.559–575; T.J. Cornell, 'Rome and Latium to 390 BC', *CAH* VII, part 2, pp.256–257; Scardigli, *I trattati Romano-Cartaginesi*, pp.22–23.

14. Lancel, *Carthage: A History*, pp.85–86.

15. Scardigli, *I trattati Romano-Cartaginesi*, p.23.

16. See F. Coarelli, *Il Foro Boario* (Rome, 1988), pp.113–139; Cornell, *The Beginnings of Rome*, pp.108–112.

17. Cornell, *The Beginnings of Rome*, pp.204–208.

18. M. Frederiksen, *Campania* (Rome, 1984), p.166.

19. Cornell, *The Beginnings of Rome*, pp.237–238.

20. Polybius, 3.22. Translation, C. Habicht.

21. Polybius, 3.26.1.

22. See F.W. Walbank, *A Historical Commentary on Polybius*, vol. I (Oxford, 1957), pp.341–345; Cornell, *The Beginnings of Rome*, pp.210–214; Scullard, 'Carthage and Rome', pp.524–526. Thiel, *A History of Roman Sea-Power before the Second Punic War*, p.6, speaks of Rome as a little land power and Carthage as a great sea power; Scardigli, *I trattati Romano-Cartaginesi*, pp.47–53, 65–66.

23. Aubet, *The Phoenicians and the West*, p.226.

24. Dionysius of Halicarnassus, *Roman Antiquities*, 7.3–4.

25. Pallottino, *A History of Earliest Italy*, pp.83–91.

26. Walbank, *A Historical Commentary on Polybius*, I, pp.344–345.

27. Eckstein, *Mediterranean Anarchy, Interstate War, and the Rise of Rome*, p.159.

28. See Polybius, 3.23. R.L. Beaumont, 'The date of the first treaty between Rome and Carthage', *JRS* 29 (1939), p.79; Lancel, *Carthage: A History*, pp.86–87. For differing opinions about Fair Promontory and the area closed to the Romans, see Walbank, *A Historical Commentary on Polybius*, I, pp.341–342; Scardigli, *I trattati Romano-Cartaginesi*, pp.66–71.

29. Pallottino, *A History of Earliest Italy*, pp.85–99.

30. P. Garnsey, *Famine and Food Supply in the Graeco-Roman World: Responses to Risk and Crisis* (Cambridge, 1988), pp.137–141, 144–148, 150–151, 154–164.

31. *SEG* IX 2; *Greek Historical Inscriptions 404–323 BC*, eds P.J. Rhodes and R. Osborne (Oxford, 2003), pp.486–493. P. Horden and N. Purcell, *The Corrupting Sea: A Study of Mediterranean History* (Oxford, 2000), p.73. A. Bresson, 'Grain from Cyrene', *The Economies of Hellenistic Societies, Third to First Centuries BC*, eds Z.H. Archibald, J.K. Davies and V. Gabrielsen (Oxford, 2011), pp.66–95.

32. See R.M. Ogilvie, *A Commentary on Livy, Books 1–5* (Oxford, 1965), pp.256–257; Garnsey, *Famine and Food Supply in the Graeco-Roman World*, pp.168–181; Cornell, *The Beginnings of Rome*, p.268; R. Meiggs, *Roman Ostia*, 2nd ed. (Oxford, 1997), p.481 and Frederiksen, *Campania*, p.166.

33. Livy, 2.9–14; Dionysius of Halicarnassus, *Roman Antiquities*, 5.21–27, 5.32, 5.65. Ogilvie, *A Commentary on Livy*, pp.256–257.

34. Dionysius of Halicarnassus, *Roman Antiquities*, 6.17.2–4; 6.94.

35. Ogilvie, *A Commentary on Livy*, p.321; Garnsey, *Famine and Food Supply in the Graeco-Roman World*, p.169.

36. Livy, 2.34.2–7; Dionysius of Halicarnassus, *Roman Antiquities*, 7.1–2, 7.12–15; Plutarch, *Coriolanus* 16; Cassius Dio, 5.18.4. Dionysius mentions the existence of some independent, probably Greek sources, which knew about the embassy to Sicily and assigned it an Olympian date. See Garnsey, *Famine and Food Supply in the Graeco-Roman World*, p.169.

37. For the Carthaginian origin, see Meiggs, *Roman Ostia*, p.18; for the Greek origin, see Pugliese Carratelli, 'An Outline of the Political History of the Greeks in the West', p.162.

38. Livy, 2.41.8.

39. Livy, 2.51.2, 2.52.1; Dionysius of Halicarnassus, *Roman Antiquities*, 9.25.

40. Livy, 3.31.1, 3.32.2.

41. Livy, 4.12. There was also a private transport of grain by Spurius Maelius. Livy, 4.13–16; Dionysius of Halicarnassus, *Roman Antiquities*, 12.1–4. Garnsey, *Famine and Food Supply in the Graeco-Roman World*, pp.170–171.

42. Livy, 4.25.2.

43. Livy, 4.52.5–8.

44. Thucydides, 6.88.6. Ogilvie, *A Commentary on Livy*, p.614. Athens was soon to negotiate a treaty with Carthage.

45. For shortages in 399, see Livy, 5.13.4; compare 5.14.3; Augustine, *The City of God*, 3.17. For shortages in 392, see Livy, 5.31.5; Dionysius of Halicarnassus, *Roman Antiquities*, 13.4. For shortages in 390, see Livy, 5.39–48; Plutarch, *Camillus*, 23.1; Orosius, 2.19.8. For shortages in 384, see Livy, 6.20.15, 6.21.1–6.

46. See Huss, *Geschichte der Karthager*, p.67.

47. Diodorus, 1.20–26; Herodotus, 7.167.

48. Hoyos, *The Carthaginians*, p.16; Lancel, *Carthage: A History*, pp.273–279; D. Asheri, 'Sicily, 478–431', *CAH* V, 2nd ed. (Cambridge, 1992), pp.147–151.

49. Diodorus, 11.55.

50. Diodorus, 11.88.4–5.

51. For the intertwined destinies of Syracuse, Athens and Carthage, see Feeney, *Caesar's Calendar*, p.52.

52. Livy, 3.31.8; see also Gellius, *Attic Nights*, 20.1.4; Tacitus, *Annals*, 3.27. Ogilvie sees the embassy as a fiction of the early first century. Ogilvie, *A Commentary on Livy*, pp.449–450.

53. Pallottino, *A History of Earliest Italy*, pp.114–115. Campaign: D. Kagan, *The Peace of Nicias and the Sicilian Expedition* (1981, Cornell University Press); P. Green, *Armada from Athens* (London, 1971); A. Andrewes, 'The peace of Nicias and the Sicilian expedition', *CAH* V, pp.446–463.

54. Pausanias, 10.16.7; Thucydides, 3.88; Diodorus, 14.56.2.

55. Livy, 4.33–34.

56. Dart and Vervaet see the episode of the fleet as unreliable. 'The Significance of the Naval Triumph in Roman History (260–29 BCE)', p.268.

57. Meiggs, *Roman Ostia*, pp.19–23, 479–482, also discussing the tradition of a colony under Ancus Marcius' period. F. Zevi, in *Roma medio repubblicana, Aspetti culturali di Roma e del Lazio nei secoli IV e III a.C* (Rome, 1973), pp.343–363; F. Zevi, 'Appunti per una storia di Ostia repubblicana', *MEFR* 114.1 (2002), p.15.

58. For the voyage in 398, see Livy, 5.15.3, 5.16.8; for the voyage in 394, see Livy, 5.28.1–5; Diodorus, 14.93; Plutarch, *Camillus*, 8.3; Appian, *Italy*, 8.

59. Justin, 43.5.10.

60. R.M. Ogilvie, *Early Rome and the Etruscans* (London, 1983), pp.154–157.

61. Livy, 5.13; Dionysius of Halicarnassus, *Roman Antiquities*, 12.9.

62. For interpretations that this episode shows the weakness of the Roman navy, see Dart and Vervaet, 'The Significance of the Naval Triumph in Roman History (260–29 BCE)', p.268; Thiel, *A History of Roman Sea-Power before the Second Punic War*, pp.6–7.

63. B. Jordan, *The Athenian Navy in the Classical Period: A Study of Athenian Naval Administration and Military Organization in the Fifth and Fourth Centuries BC* (Berkeley, University of California Press, University of California Publications, Classical Studies), vol. 13 (1975), pp.153–156, 160–164. G. Daux, 'Un Règlement cultuel d'Andros', *Hesperia* 18 (1949), pp.58–72.

64. Diodorus, 13.54–62, 13.96.

65. Diodorus, 13.114.1. Translation, C.H. Oldfather.

66. Diodorus, 14.47.4–14.53, 14.56.1, 14.77–78.

67. Diodorus, 14.103.

68. Diodorus, 15.14; Strabo, 5.226; Servius, *Commentary on the Aeneid*, 10.184.

69. Diodorus, 15.27.4. See Torelli, 'Colonizazzioni etrusche e latine di età archaica', p.72, accepting the story; Thiel rejecting, *A History of Roman Sea-Power before the Second Punic War*, pp.54–56.

70. Livy, 7.16.3, 7.28.1–3, 7.28.6.

71. Cornell, *The Beginnings of Rome*, p.325.

72. Livy, 7.27.2. We get the date for this treaty from Livy and Diodorus, who calls it the first treaty. Diodorus, 16.69.1. See Walbank, *A Historical Commentary on Polybius*, I, pp.345–346; Cornell, *The Beginnings of Rome*, pp.325–326; Scardigli, *I trattati Romano-Cartaginesi*, p.112.

73. Polybius, 3.24. Translation, C. Habicht. The treaty also forbids both parties from abusing provisioning they have received from any place under the rule of the other party. The clauses that refer to piracy and raids make it clear that if the Carthaginians take captives in Latium, they cannot bring them in their ships into Roman harbours but if they do so, and a Roman lay hold of the captive, he shall be set free. The Romans were to follow the same rules in regard to Punic ports.

74. Eckstein, *Mediterranean Anarchy, Interstate War, and the Rise of Rome*, p.161.

75. See Cornell, *The Beginnings of Rome*, pp.212, 321. E. Bispham, '*Coloniam deducere*: How Roman was Roman colonization during the middle republic?', *Greek and Roman Colonization*, eds G. Bradley and J-P. Wilson (Cardiff, 2006), p.123.

76. Walbank, *A Historical Commentary on Polybius*, I, pp.347–348; D. Hoyos, *Hannibal's Dynasty, Power and Politics in the Western Mediterranean, 247–183 BC* (Routledge, 2003), p.45. P. Moret, 'Mastia Tarseion y el problema geográfico del segundo tratado entre Cartago y Roma', *Mainake* 24 (2002), pp.257–276. *Non vidi*. Moret sees the identification of Mastia Tarseion with Cartagena as an anachronism and that Mastia and Tarseion must be considered as two distinct places. My thanks to Pascal Arnaud for this reference.

77. See Eckstein, *Mediterranean Anarchy, Interstate War, and the Rise of Rome*, pp.118–121, 128–129. For the additions to Roman territory classified as *ager publicus* before the First Punic War, see S.T. Roselaar, *Public Land in the Roman Republic: A Social and Economic History of Ager Publicus in Italy, 396–89 BC* (Oxford, 2010), pp.298–320. As to Roman colonies, the normative categories of Ancient Latin colonies, Latin colonies and Maritime colonies are possibly the inventions of the late republic or the Augustan period. We do not know how the Romans saw colonization and its development in the fourth and third centuries and whether there was any single normative ideology making it happen. Bispham, '*Coloniam deducere*: How Roman was Roman colonization during the middle republic?', p.81.

78. Livy, 7.25.4, 7.26.11, 7.26.13. Translation, B.O. Foster.

79. Livy, 7.26.15.

80. So Frederiksen, *Campania*, pp.168, 209; E. Lepore, *Storia di Napoli* (Naples, 1967), p.224.

81. So for instance Thiel, *A History of Roman Sea-Power before the Second Punic War*, pp.7–8; Viereck, *Die Römische Flotte*, p.168.

82. Livy, 10.2.1. Translation, B.O. Foster.

83. Livy, 10.2.

84. Livy, 8.13.12; *Fasti triumphales*.

85. Livy, 8.14.12, 8.14.8. Translation, B.O. Foster. For the *Rostra*, see F. Coarelli, *LTUR* IV, pp.212–214. The *Navalia*, see F. Coarelli, *LTUR* III (Rome, 1996), pp.339–340; P.L. Tucci, '*Navalia*', *Archaeologia Classica* 57, n.s. 7 (2006), pp.175–202.

86. Pliny, *The Natural History*, 34.11.

87. Cornell, *The Beginnings of Rome*, pp.188–189, 362–365; Pallottino, *A History of Earliest Italy*, pp.132–133. For interpretations that there was no naval action at sea, see Thiel, *A History of Roman Sea-Power before the Second Punic War*, p.8; Dart and Vervaet 'The Significance of the Naval Triumph in Roman History (260–29 BCE)', pp.268–9.

88. J.K. Davies, 'Cultural, social and economic features of the Hellenistic world', *CAH* VII, part 1, 2nd ed. (Cambridge, 1984), p.285.
89. Diodorus, 16.5.3; *IG* II2, 1629, lines 217–233.
90. Livy, 9.38.2. Translation, B.O. Foster.
91. Livy, 9.38.3–4.
92. Livy, 9.41.3; Diodorus, 19.65.7.
93. See N. Purcell, 'South Italy in the fourth century BC', in *CAH* VI, 2nd ed. (Cambridge, 1994), p.388.
94. For the details of the war, see T.J. Cornell, 'The conquest of Italy', in *CAH* VII, part 2, pp.368–377.
95. Livy, 8.25.8, 35.16.3; Cicero, *Balbus*, 8.21; Polybius, 6.14.8. See H.H. Schmitt, *Die Staatsverträge des Altertums*, vol. III (Munich, 1969), pp.22–23.
96. Livy, 8.22.6, 8.26.1–2; Dionysius of Halicarnassus, *Roman Antiquities*, 15.5.3.
97. Livy, 9.28.7; Diodorus, 19.101.3.
98. Livy, 9.30.3. Translation, B.O. Foster.
99. Gabrielsen, *Financing the Athenian Fleet*, p.28.
100. For the idea of the *duoviri* commanding small squadrons of ten ships each, see M.M. Sage, *The Republican Roman Army, A Sourcebook* (Routledge, 2008), p.284. However, there is no direct evidence to say that the *duoviri* actually commanded ships in action before 181–176, when the Romans fought pirates along the Ligurian and Illyrian coasts and we cannot use it to make any conclusions from the earlier period.
101. See J-P. Morel, 'L'atelier des petites estampilles', *MEFR* 81 (1969), pp.59–117; J-P. Morel, 'La Ceramica di Roma nei secoli IV e III A.C.', *Roma medio repubblicana, Aspetti culturali di Roma e del Lazio nei secoli IV e III a.C.* (Rome, 1973), pp.43–48; J-P. Morel, 'The Transformation of Italy, 300–133 BC, The Evidence of Archaeology', *CAH* VIII, pp.479–480; Morel, 'Early Rome and Italy', p.499; Cornell, *The Beginnings of Rome*, pp.385–390.
102. Theophrastus, *Enquiry into Plants*, 5.8.1–2. Translation, A.F. Hort.
103. R.E. Mitchell, 'Roman–Carthaginian treaties: 306 and 279/8 BC', *Historia* 20 (1971), pp.640–641.
104. Eckstein, *Mediterranean Anarchy, Interstate War, and the Rise of Rome*, p.161. See Lancel, *Carthage: A History*, pp.269–273.
105. Diodorus, 20.61–62. Quote 20.62.1. Translation, R.M. Geer.
106. Diodorus, 19.106, 20.44.7.
107. See K. Meister, 'Agathocles', *CAH* VII, part 1, pp.384–411. For the treaty see Diodorus, 20.79.5; Justin, 22.8.15.
108. Livy, 9.43.26; Diodorus, 22.7.5; Servius, *Commentary on the Aeneid*, 4.628; Valerius Maximus, 3.7.10; Justin, 18.2. According to Servius, it was agreed that the Romans were not allowed to come to the Carthaginian coast and the Carthaginians were not allowed to come to the Roman coast. Corsica became a no-man's-land. Servius is the only source mentioning Corsica.

109. Polybius, 3.26. Translation, C. Habicht.
110. Mitchell, 'Roman-Carthaginian treaties', pp.643–644; Meister, 'Agathocles', p.404; F. Russo, 'Rodi e Roma tra IV e III secolo a.C.', *Considerazioni di storia ed archeologia* (2010), pp.51–52, W.V. Harris, 'Quando e come l'Italia divenne per la prima volta Italia? Un saggio sulla politica dell'identità', *Studi Storici* 48 (2007), p.314. Thiel, *A History of Roman Sea-Power before the Second Punic War*, p.13.
111. Walbank, *A Historical Commentary on Polybius*, I, p.354; A.M. Eckstein, *Senate and General; Individual Decision-Making and Roman Foreign Relations, 264–194 BC* (Berkeley, University of California Press, 1987), pp.77–79; Eckstein, *Mediterranean Anarchy, Interstate War, and the Rise of Rome*, pp.165–166. B.D. Hoyos, *Unplanned Wars: The Origins of the First and Second Punic Wars* (Berlin, 1998), p.10; Hoyos, *The Carthaginians*, p.180.
112. Polybius, 30.5.6. Translation, W.R. Paton.
113. The new information includes the new interpretation of *SEG* 33 (1983), no. 637, originally edited by V. Kontorini, 'Rome et Rhodes au tournant du IIIe siècle av. J.-C. d'après une inscription inédite de Rhodes', *JRS* 103 (1983), pp.24–32. See Harris, 'Quando e come l'Italia divenne per la prima volta Italia? Un saggio sulla politica dell'identità', pp.315–318; Russo, 'Rodi e Roma tra IV e III secolo a.C.', pp.48–72. Accepting the Roman-Rhodian relations: H.H. Schmitt, *Rom und Rhodos* (Munich, 1957), pp.13, 44; P.R. Franke, 'Pyrrhus' *CAH* VII, part 2, p.457; F. Càssola, *I gruppi politici Romani nel III secolo A.C.* (Trieste, 1962), pp.28ff, 41ff; Mitchell, 'Roman-Carthaginian treaties', p.642. Against: M. Holleaux, *Rome, la Grèce et les monarchies hellenistiques au IIIe siècle avant J.-C. (273–205)* (Paris, 1921), pp.30–46, F.W. Walbank, *A Historical Commentary on Polybius*, vol. III (Oxford, 1979), pp.423–426.
114. P. de Souza, *Piracy in the Graeco-Roman World* (Cambridge, 1999), pp.48–53.
115. See V. Gabrielsen, 'Piracy and the Slave-Trade', *A Companion to the Hellenistic World*, ed. A. Erskine (Oxford, 2003), p.396; P. de Souza, 'Rome's contribution to the development of piracy', *The Maritime World of Ancient Rome*, ed. R.L. Hohlfelder (Ann Arbor, Michigan, 2008), pp.71–96.
116. Strabo, 6.3. Eckstein, *Mediterranean Anarchy, Interstate War, and the Rise of Rome*, pp.147–154.
117. Dionysius of Halicarnassus, *Roman Antiquities*, 15.5.3; Diodorus, 19.70.8, 71.6.
118. Livy, 9.14.1–5.
119. See N. Purcell, 'South Italy in the fourth century BC', pp.387–388, 393; J.H.C. Williams and A. Burnett, 'Alexander the Great and the Coinages of Western Greece', *Studies in Greek Numismatics in Memory of Martin Jessop Price* (London, 1998), pp.388–389; Eckstein, *Mediterranean Anarchy, Interstate War, and the Rise of Rome*, pp.147, 152–154.
120. Appian, *Samnite History*, 7.1. Translation, H. White.

121. See Purcell, 'South Italy in the fourth century BC', pp.387–388.
122. Other suggestions range from 338 to 302. For 338, see M. Pitassi, *The Navies of Rome* (Boydell Press, 2009), p.20. For 332, see Mitchell, 'Roman-Carthaginian treaties', p.638; M. Cary, 'The early treaties with Tarentum and Rhodes', *Journal of Philology* 35 (1920), pp.165–173. For 302, see Eckstein, *Mediterranean Anarchy, Interstate War, and the Rise of Rome*, p.155; Schmitt, *Die Staatsverträge des Altertums*, pp.60–61; Càssola, *I gruppi politici Romani nel III secolo A.C.*, p.38.
123. Franke, 'Pyrrhus', p.456.
124. My thanks to David Blackman and Boris Rankov for discussing this with me.
125. Appian, *Samnite History*, 7.2–3; Polybius, 1.6.5.
126. Franke, 'Pyrrhus', pp.459, 463.
127. Plutarch, *Pyrrhus*, 15.1.
128. Valerius Maximus, 3.7.10; Justin, 18.2; Livy, *Summary*, 13; Diodorus, 22.7.5.
129. Polybius, 3.25.1–5. Translation, C. Habicht.
130. See Schmitt, *Die Staatsverträge des Altertums*, pp.106–109; Mitchell, 'Roman-Carthaginian treaties', pp.644–646.
131. Thiel, *A History of Roman Sea-Power before the Second Punic War*, pp.13ff, 48ff, 63; J.P. Roth, *The Logistics of the Roman Army at War (264 BC–AD 235)* (Leiden, 1999), p.158.
132. J. Beloch, 'Zur Geschichte des pyrrhischen Krieges', *Klio* 1 (1901), p.285.
133. For the story that the Carthaginian fleet was present at Tarentum in 272, see Livy, *Summary*, 14, 21.10.8; Orosius, 4.3.1–2; Zonaras, 8.6.12–13. Livy and Orosius treat this as an act that violated the treaty; i.e., the Philinus treaty. Thus the Carthaginians would have broken it before the Romans went to Messana in 264.
134. Diodorus, 22.7.5. Translation, F.R. Walton. The Carthaginians probably destroyed the timber in Locri, not in Rhegium. Beloch, 'Zur Geschichte des pyrrhischen Krieges', p.285; Thiel, *A History of Roman Sea-Power before the Second Punic War*, p.30.
135. Diodorus, 21.16.1, 22.8.
136. Appian, *Samnite History*, 12. Translation, H. White.
137. Livy, *Summary*, 15, 35.16.3. See Schmitt, *Die Staatsverträge des Altertums*, pp.128–129.
138. Lycophron, *Alexandra* 1226–1235, see A. Momigliano, 'Terra Marique', *JRS* 32 (1942), pp.53–64.
139. Justin, 18.2.9; Dionysius of Halicarnassus, *Roman Antiquities*, 20.14; Livy, *Summary*, 14; Eutropius, 2.15; Dio, frg. 41 = Zonaras, 8.6. W.V. Harris, *War and Imperialism in Republican Rome 327–70 BC* (Oxford, 1979), p.183, n. 4.
140. E. Badian, *Foreign Clientelae (264–70 BC)* (Oxford, 1958), p.44; Harris, *War and Imperialism in Republican Rome*, pp.183–184; Appian, *Sicily*, 1.1; L.H.

Neatby, 'Romano-Egyptian Relations During the Third Century BC', *TAPA* 81 (1950), pp.89–98.

141. See Crawford, *Roman Republican Coinage*, no. 22.

142. Dionysius of Halicarnassus, *Roman Antiquities*, 20.15. Harris, *War and Imperialism in Republican Rome*, pp.183–184.

143. Johannes Lydus, 1.27; Livy, *Summary*, 15; Tacitus, *Annals*, 11.22.8.

144. Thiel, *A History of Roman Sea-Power before the Second Punic War*, pp.32–34; Sage, *The Republican Roman Army*, p.284; Boris Rankov, communication by email; E.S. Staveley, 'Rome and Italy in the early third century', *CAH* VII, part 2, p.438. Harris argues that only two new quaestors were added. W.V. Harris, 'The Development of the quaestorship, 267–81 BC', *CQ* 26 (1976), pp.92–106.

145. According to Dionysius of Halicarnassus, *Roman Antiquities*, (20.4) the garrison was sent to protect the city against the Bruttians, Lucanians and Tarentines in 282. According to Polybius (1.7.6), it was sent to protect the city from Pyrrhus.

146. Polybius, 1.7–8; Zonaras, 6.8.14.

Chapter 3: The First Punic War, 264–241 BC: Arms Race at Sea

1. Polybius, 1.20.8. Translation, C. Habicht.

2. Polybius, 4.2.1–3.

3. Thucydides, 1.13.2, 1.14.1–3; Herodotus, 7.144.1–2. H. van Wees, '"Those who sail are to receive a wage": Naval warfare and finance in Archaic Eretria', *New Perspectives on Ancient Warfare*, eds G.G. Fagan and M. Trundle (Brill, 2010), pp.205–226.

4. See Thiel, *Studies on the History of Roman Sea-Power in Republican Times*, p.70; Thiel, *A History of Roman Sea-Power before the Second Punic War*, p.46.

5. For reduced fleet numbers, see W.W. Tarn, 'The Fleets of the first Punic war', *JHS* 27 (1907), pp.48–60; G. de Sanctis, *Storia dei Romani*, vol. III (Rome, 1916), pp.137–138; Thiel, *A History of Roman Sea-Power before the Second Punic War*, pp83–96; Walbank, *A Historical Commentary on Polybius*, I, p.83. Accepting the figures: G.K. Tipps, 'The battle of Ecnomus', *Historia* 34/4 (1985), pp.432–465; Goldsworthy, *The Punic Wars*, pp.110–111; Lazenby, *The First Punic War*, pp.108–109; Hoyos, *The Carthaginians*, p.150 and B. Rankov, 'A War of Phases: Strategies and Stalemates 264–241 BC', *A Companion to the Punic Wars*, ed. D. Hoyos (Blackwell, 2011), p.155.

6. Polybius, 1.9. For the date of the battle, suggestions range from 270/269 to 265. See Lazenby, *The First Punic War*, p.36; Goldsworthy, *The Punic Wars*, p.67.

7. Polybius, 1.10.1–2.

8. Diodorus, 22.13.

9. Polybius, 1.10.3–9.

10. Walbank, *A Historical Commentary on Polybius*, I, pp.57–60; Lazenby, *The First Punic War*, pp.37–38; Goldsworthy, *The Punic Wars*, p.68.

11. Polybius, 1.11.1–3. Translation, C. Habicht.

12. Thiel, *A History of Roman Sea-Power before the Second Punic War*, pp.136–137; J. Heurgon, *The Rise of Rome to 264 BC* (London, 1973), pp.217–218; G. Clemente, *Guida alla storia Romana* (Mondadori, 1977), p.142; S. Lancel, *Hannibal* (Oxford, 1998), p.4; Lazenby, *The First Punic War*, p.40; Harris, *War and Imperialism in Republican Rome*, pp.182–183; B. Bleckmann, 'Roman Politics in the First Punic War', *A Companion to the Punic Wars*, pp.168–171.

13. Goldsworthy, *The Punic Wars*, p.69; G. Forsythe, 'The Army and Centuriate Organization in Early Rome', *A Companion to the Roman Army*, ed. P. Erdkamp (Blackwell Publishing, 2007), pp.29–33.

14. Walbank, *A Historical Commentary on Polybius*, I, p.61; Lazenby, *The First Punic War*, p.39.

15. Diodorus, 14.56.1. Translation, C.H. Oldfather.

16. Diodorus, 23.2; Dio, 11. fr. 43; Zonaras, 8.8–9; Polybius, 1.11.4–6. Lazenby, *The First Punic War*, pp.43–46; Thiel, *A History of Roman Sea-Power before the Second Punic War*, pp.149–151.

17. Polybius, 1.20.15. Polybius has here probably followed Fabius Pictor. Walbank, *A Historical Commentary on Polybius*, I, p.74.

18. Polybius, 1.20.13–14. Translation, C. Habicht (with some adaptations by the author).

19. Diodorus, 23.1.2. Translation, F.R. Walton. Polybius, 1.11.7. Translation, C. Habicht.

20. Polybius, 1.11.9–12.4, 1.14–15; Zonaras, 8.9.

21. See *OCD*.

22. Polybius, 1.16; Diodorus, 23.4. Eutropius, 2.19.2 and Orosius, 4.7.3 speak of 200 talents. Hiero ruled over a substantial area in eastern Sicily including Acrae, Leontini, Megara, Helorum, Neetum and Tauromenium. See Lazenby, *The First Punic War*, pp.53–54.

23. Eckstein, *Mediterranean Anarchy, Interstate War, and the Rise of Rome*, p.167.

24. Polybius, 1.17.1–6.

25. Polybius, 1.17.7–1.19; Diodorus, 23.8–9. Lazenby, *The First Punic War*, p.59.

26. Polybius, 1.20.1–7. Translation, C. Habicht.

27. Walbank, *A Historical Commentary on Polybius*, I, p.73; Lazenby, *The First Punic War*, p.59.

28. Zonaras, 8.10; Orosius, 4.7.7.

29. *Ined. Vat.* 4. Goldsworthy, *The Punic Wars*, p.97; Lazenby, *The First Punic War*, p.54.

30. Pliny, *The Natural History*, 16.192. Florus, 1.18.7; Orosius, 4.7.8.

31. Polybius, 1.20.9–16. Translation, C. Habicht.

32. Diodorus, 14.41.3. Translation, C.H. Oldfather.

33. Polybius, 1.21.1–3. Translation, C. Habicht.
34. The long stroke described implies oar-manning no more than double. See Morrison and Coates, *Greek and Roman Oared Warships 399–30 BC*, pp.353–354.
35. For Rome and Ostia, see Lazenby, *The First Punic War*, p.64; Meiggs, *Trees and Timber in the Ancient Mediterranean World*, p.141; Caven, *The Punic Wars*, p.28; Casson, *The Ancient Mariners*, pp.145–146. For the Greek cities in the south, see L. Richardson Jr, *Pompeii, An Architectural History* (Baltimore and London, 1988), pp.7–8. Frank and Thiel suggest that the project was partly conducted in the Greek cities and partly in Rome and Ostia so that the Greeks and Etruscans were hired to lead the work. T. Frank, *An Economic Survey of Ancient Rome*, vol. I (New Jersey, 1959), p.62; Thiel, *A History of Roman Sea-Power before the Second Punic War*, pp.46–47, 67–68.
36. Zonaras, 8.11; Orosius, 4.7.12.
37. Polybius, 1.21.4.
38. Polybius, 1.21.5–8. Pliny, *The Natural History*, 8.169. There is also another version in which Scipio looks like the victim of treachery. Polybius, 8.35.9; Livy, *Summary*, 17; Florus, 1.18.11; Eutropius, 2.20.2. This is perhaps the Roman version. See Lazenby, *The First Punic War*, pp.66–67; Bleckmann, 'Roman Politics in the First Punic War', p.173.
39. Polybius, 1.21.9–11; Zonaras, 8.11. See Lazenby, *The First Punic War*, p.67; Walbank, *A Historical Commentary on Polybius*, I, p.77.
40. Polybius, 1.22.1, 1.23.1; Zonaras, 8.11.
41. Polybius, 1.22.2–3; Zonaras, 8.11.
42. Polybius, 1.22; H. T. Wallinga, *The Boarding-Bridge of the Romans; Its Construction and its Function in the Naval Tactics of the First Punic War* (Groningen, 1956), pp.69–78.
43. Polybius, 1.23.6. See Thiel, *A History of Roman Sea-Power before the Second Punic War*, p.128; Wallinga, *The Boarding-Bridge of the Romans*, pp.88–90.
44. See Thucydides, 7.60–71. J.S. Morrison and R.T. Williams, *Greek Oared Ships 900–322 BC* (Cambridge, 1968), pp.317–320.
45. Polybius, 1.23.3–6. Translation, C. Habicht.
46. Polybius, 1.23.7–10.
47. Diodorus, 23.10.1.
48. Wallinga, *The Boarding-Bridge of the Romans*, p.70.
49. *Fasti Triumphales*.
50. Pliny, *The Natural History*, 34.11; Quintilian, *Institutes of Oratory*, 1.7.12; Livy, *Summary*, 17.
51. *Inscr. Ital.* 13:3, no. 69 p.46. We have the text preserved as a restored version that was probably made in 150 BC and later by Augustus. Augustus built a new *Rostra* and four *columnae rostratae* on the Forum to celebrate his victory at Actium. See D. Palombi, *LTUR* I (Rome, 1993), p.308; P. Zanker, *Augustus und die Macht der Bilder*, 2nd ed. (Munich, 1990), pp.86–87. See L. Pietilä-

Castrén, *Magnificentia Publica: The Victory Monuments of the Roman Generals in the Era of the Punic Wars* (Helsinki, 1987), pp.29–34.

52. Translation E. Kondratieff, 'The Column and Coinage of C. Duilius: Innovations in Iconography in Large and Small Media in the Middle Republic', *Scripta Israelica Classica* vol. XXIII (2004), p.15.
53. Polybius, 1.24.1–2.
54. *Fasti Triumphales*. Polybius, 1.24.8; Diodorus, 23.9.4. Lazenby, *The First Punic War*, pp.74–75.
55. Polybius, 1.24.7.
56. *Fasti Triumphales*. Eutropius, 2.20.3.
57. See Livy, *Summary*, 17; Zonaras, 8.11.
58. *CIL* I, 2, 9, lines 5 and 6. Translation, R.W. Browne. Ovid, *Fasti* 6, 193–194. See Pietilä-Castrén, *Magnificentia Publica: The Victory Monuments of the Roman Generals in the Era of the Punic Wars*, pp.35–38.
59. Polybius, 1.24.5–7; Zonaras, 8.12; Orosius, 4.8.4; Livy, *Summary*, 17.
60. *Fasti Triumphales*. Dio, fr. 43.32.
61. Polybius, 1.24.9–13; Diodorus, 23.9.4. According to Polybius, both consuls operated in Sicily but this must be a misunderstanding. See Lazenby, *The First Punic War*, p.75.
62. *Fasti Triumphales*. Pietilä-Castrén, *Magnificentia Publica: The Victory Monuments of the Roman Generals in the Era of the Punic Wars*, pp.38–44.
63. Polybius, 1.25.1–4; Naevius, fr. 37 Buechner; Orosius, 4.8.4; Zonaras, 8.12; Polyainos, 8.20. See Lazenby, *The First Punic War*, pp.78–79.
64. Rankov, 'A War of Phases: Strategies and Stalemates 264–241 BC', p.156.
65. Diodorus, 20.3.3. Translation, R.M. Geer.
66. Diodorus, 20.5–20.9.1–2.
67. Diodorus, 20.3.3, 20.17; Polybius, 1.26.2–3.
68. Polybius, 1.26.1. Translation, C. Habicht.
69. Polybius, 1.25.7–9.
70. Zonaras, 8.12. Rankov, 'A War of Phases: Strategies and Stalemates 264–241 BC', pp.155–156; Walbank, *A Historical Commentary on Polybius*, I, pp.84–88.
71. Polybius, 1.26.7–9.
72. Tipps, 'The battle of Ecnomus', p.436.
73. The consul suffectus replaced a consul who had died in office and served the remainder of the term.
74. Polybius, 1.26.10–16. The legion in battle formation was deployed in three lines: the *hastati*, the *principes* and the *triarii*. Following this tradition, the last squadron in the fleet formation was called *triarii* because of their station in the rear of the formation. Polybius must have used a Roman source for this detail. Tipps, 'The battle of Ecnomus', p.447.
75. Polybius, 1.27.8–10. Translation, C. Habicht.

76. Polybius, 1.27–28. See also Livy, *Summary*, 18; Dio, fr. 43.20; Zonaras, 8.12; Eutropius, 2.21; Orosius, 4.8.
77. De Sanctis, *Storia dei Romani*, pp.140–141; W.W. Tarn, *Hellenistic Military and Naval Developments* (Cambridge, 1930), p.151; Thiel, *A History of Roman Sea-Power before the Second Punic War*, p.119.
78. Tipps, 'The battle of Ecnomus', p.450; Goldsworthy, *The Punic Wars*, p.112; Lazenby, *The First Punic War*, pp.88–96.
79. Examples of the trap: Hanno had beaten the Roman cavalry at the siege of Agrigentum in 262; in Africa in 256 the Roman army was encircled and destroyed in the Battle of the Bagradas Valley; the formation used by Hannibal in Cannae. Tipps, 'The battle of Ecnomus', pp.454–455, 460–461; Lazenby, *The First Punic War*, pp.94–96; Goldsworthy, *The Punic Wars*, pp.112–114.
80. *Fasti Triumphales*. Polybius, 1.29; Diodorus, 23.11. For the Roman campaign in Africa, see Goldsworthy, *The Punic Wars*, pp.84–92; Lazenby, *The First Punic War*, pp.97–110.
81. Polybius, 1.30–31.3; Orosius, 4.9.9.
82. Polybius, 1.31.4–8; Dio, 11.22–23. Lancel, *Carthage: A History*, pp.268–9, 367. Conditions: the Carthaginians were to retire from all Sicily and Sardinia, to release the Roman captives free of cost and to ransom their own, to make good all the expenses incurred by the Romans for the war and to pay more as tribute each year. They were to make neither war nor peace without the consent of the Romans, they were to keep for their own use not more than one warship, yet come to the aid of the Romans with fifty triremes as often as notice should be sent them. Translation, E. Cary and H.B. Foster.
83. Diodorus, 20.79.5; Justin, 22.8.15.
84. See Goldsworthy, *The Punic Wars*, pp.92, 149.
85. Polybius, 1.32–34.
86. Zonaras, 8.14. Cossyra could be used as a base where the fleet could concentrate before it landed in Africa. Rankov, 'A War of Phases: Strategies and Stalemates 264–241 BC', p.158.
87. Polybius, 1.36.5–12.
88. Polybius, 1.37.2. Translation, C. Habicht.
89. Diodorus, 23.18.1. Translation, F.R. Walton.
90. Eutropius, 2.22.3; Orosius, 4.9.8.
91. Polybius, 1.37. Walbank, *A Historical Commentary on Polybius*, I, pp.96–97.
92. Thiel, *Studies on the History of Roman Sea-Power in Republican Times*, p.444; Viereck, *Die Römische Flotte*, p.175; Scullard, 'Carthage and Rome', p.557; Goldsworthy, *The Punic Wars*, pp.115–116; Lazenby, *The First Punic War*, p.112. Wallinga, *The Boarding-Bridge of the Romans*, p.78.
93. Diodorus, 19.106.
94. Polybius, 1.38.5.

95. *Fasti Triumphales.* Livy, 42.20.1. S.B. Platner and T. Ashby, *A Topographical Dictionary of Ancient Rome* (Oxford, 1929), p.134.

96. Diodorus, 15.73.3–4.

97. Polybius, 1.38.1–5. Translation, C. Habicht. Diodorus, 23.18.2. Orosius and Eutropius place Hasdrubal's arrival to 251. See Lazenby, *The First Punic War*, pp.112–113; Rankov, 'A War of Phases: Strategies and Stalemates 264–241 BC', p.159.

98. *Fasti Triumphales.* Polybius, 1.38.6–10; Diodorus, 23.18.3–5. Dio, 11.29a; Zonaras, 8.14. Polybius wonders about the short building time. We must assume that there was an abundant supply of timber to make this possible.

99. Lazenby, *The First Punic War*, pp.114–115.

100. Zonaras, 8.14; Polybius, 1.39.1–5; Diodorus, 23.19; Eutropius, 2.23; Orosius, 4.9. Lazenby, *The First Punic War*, pp.116–117; Walbank, *A Historical Commentary on Polybius*, I, pp.99–100; Thiel, *A History of Roman Sea-Power before the Second Punic War*, pp.247–250.

101. *Fasti Triumphales.* Polybius, 1.39.6–7. Translation, C. Habicht. Diodorus, 23.19; Eutropius, 2.23; Orosius, 4.9. Zonaras, 8.14. Translation, E. Cary and H.B. Foster.

102. See Bleckmann, 'Roman Politics in the First Punic War', p.176.

103. *Fasti Triumphales.* Polybius, 1.39.13; Diodorus, 23.20; Zonaras, 8.14.

104. Polybius, 1.39.11–12. Goldsworthy, *The Punic Wars*, p.93; Lazenby, *The First Punic War*, pp.119–120 and Walbank, *A Historical Commentary on Polybius*, I, p.102.

105. *Fasti Triumphales.* Polybius, 1.40; Cicero, *On Government*, 1.1; Diodorus, 23.21; Livy, *Summary*, 19; Zonaras, 8.14. For the tradition of negotiations on Carthaginian initiative, see Livy, *Summary*, 18; Orosius, 4.10.1; Eutropius, 2.25; Florus, 1.18.23–6; Dio, 11.26; Zonaras, 8.15. Consul Regulus is supposed to have been present in Rome too but as the negotiations failed he returned voluntarily to Carthage and was tortured to death. There are no details of any proposed clauses for the peace treaty and Polybius and Diodorus have no information of negotiations at all, so perhaps we have to reject this information as unreliable. See Lazenby, *The First Punic War*, p.122.

106. Polybius, 1.41.1–2. Translation, C. Habicht.

107. Polybius, 1.39.15, 1.41.3; Diodorus, 24.1.1.

108. Diodorus, 24.1; Polybius, 1.42.7–11. See Lazenby, *The First Punic War*, p.124.

109. Diodorus, 14.47–53, 15.73.

110. Plutarch, *Pyrrhus*, 22–23; Diodorus, 22.10.

111. Goldsworthy, *The Punic Wars*, p.94.

112. For the siege of Rhodes, see Diodorus, 20.81–88, 20.91–99.

113. Polybius, 1.44.3–4. Translation, C. Habicht.

114. Diodorus, 24.1.3.

115. Polybius, 1.46.4–1.47.10.

116. Thiel, *A History of Roman Sea-Power before the Second Punic War*, pp.270–271.
117. Thiel, *A History of Roman Sea-Power before the Second Punic War*, p.268; Wallinga, *The Boarding-Bridge of the Romans*, pp.89–90.
118. Livy, 37.14.4–37.15.4.
119. See Murray, *The Age of Titans*, pp.226–227.
120. Polybius, 1.42.12–1.48; Diodorus, 24.2; Zonaras, 8.15.
121. Polybius, 1.49.1–3.
122. Diodorus, 24.1.5.
123. Polybius, 1.49.5. Translation, C. Habicht.
124. Polybius, 1.49.6–12.
125. Polybius, 1.50.2–3. Translation, C. Habicht.
126. Polybius, 1.50.4–1.51.12; Diodorus, 24.1.5. Lazenby, *The First Punic War*, p.133. Ship numbers for the Roman fleet: Orosius (4.10.3), of 120 vessels 30 escaped and 90 were captured or sunk; Eutropius (2.26.1), of 220 ships 30 escaped and 90 were captured; the rest were sunk.
127. Thiel, *A History of Roman Sea-Power before the Second Punic War*, pp.273–274.
128. Polybius, 1.52.1, 1.53.1–7; Diodorus, 24.1.6–7.
129. Diodorus states that the Carthaginians disabled 50 of the large freighters, sent to the bottom 17 warships and stove in and rendered useless 13 others. According to Polybius, the Romans anchored off a small town and defended themselves with the catapults and mangonels procured from the fortress; the Carthaginians carried off a few ships with provisions. See Thiel, *A History of Roman Sea-Power before the Second Punic War*, p.285; Walbank, *A Historical Commentary on Polybius*, I, p.117.
130. Diodorus, 24.1.7–11; Polybius, 1.52.5–8, 1.53.7–1.55.10; Zonaras, 8.15.
131. Roth, *The Logistics of the Roman Army at War (264 BC–AD 235)*, p.159.
132. Polybius, 1.52.2.
133. Diodorus, 24.3.
134. See Lazenby, *The First Punic War*, pp.136–137; Walbank, *A Historical Commentary on Polybius*, I, p.115; Scullard, 'Carthage and Rome', p.562; N. Rosenstein, *Imperatores Victi: Military Defeat and Aristocratic Competition in the Middle and Late Republic* (Berkeley, 1990), pp.78–79; Bleckmann, 'Roman politics in the First Punic War', pp.176–179.
135. Diodorus, 4.18.1, 24.10; Polybius, 1.73.1.
136. Hoyos, *The Carthaginians*, pp.188–189; Lancel, *Hannibal*, p.5; Lazenby, *The First Punic War*, p.143.
137. Polybius, 1.72.1–4. Translation, C. Habicht.
138. Lazenby, *The First Punic War*, p.143; Scullard, 'Carthage and Rome', p.563; Thiel, *A History of Roman Sea-Power before the Second Punic War*, pp.295–296; Hoyos, *The Carthaginians*, pp.187–189.
139. Zonaras, 8.16.
140. Polybius, 1.55.1–4.

141. Zonaras, 8.16; Orosius, 4.10.

142. Polybius, 1.56.1–3. Translation, C. Habicht. The nickname Barca means either 'lightning' or 'blessed' and comes from his raiding style and skill at fighting. See Hoyos, *The Carthaginians*, p.188.

143. Polybius, 1.56–58; Diodorus, 24.5.8, 24.6; Zonaras, 8.16. The sea battle recorded by Florus 1.18.30 is not credible. Thiel, *A History of Roman Sea-Power before the Second Punic War*, pp.298–301; Lazenby, *The First Punic War*, pp.146–148.

144. Velleius Paterculus, 1.14.8. See J.R. Patterson, 'Colonization and Historiography: The Roman Republic', *Greek and Roman Colonization*, p.192.

145. Zonaras, 8.16.

146. C. Howgego, *Ancient History from Coins* (Routledge, 1995), p.113.

147. P.A. Brunt, *Italian Manpower 225 BC–AD 14* (Oxford, 1971), pp.30–32; Scullard, 'Carthage and Rome', pp.563–564.

148. Polybius, 1.58.9–1.59.2; Appian, *Sicily*, 1.1.

149. Polybius, 1.59.6–8. Translation, C. Habicht.

150. Diodorus, 24.11.1.

151. See *OCD*.

152. Thiel, *A History of Roman Sea-Power before the Second Punic War*, pp.304–305; Wallinga, *The Boarding-Bridge of the Romans*, pp.89–90; Lazenby, *The First Punic War*, pp.150–151.

153. Polybius, 1.59.11–12. Translation, C. Habicht.

154. Polybius, 1.60.1–3. Translation, C. Habicht.

155. Diodorus, 24.11.1.

156. Walbank, *A Historical Commentary on Polybius*, I, pp.124–125.

157. Polybius, 1.61.1–4. Translation, C. Habicht.

158. Polybius, 1.61.5–8; Diodorus, 24.11. *Fasti Triumphales*. Eutropius 2.27.2 states that there were 32,000 Carthaginian prisoners and 13,000 were killed, 63 ships captured and 125 sunk. Orosius 4.10.7 gives the same information except for the number of killed which is 14,000. Thiel, *A History of Roman Sea-Power before the Second Punic War*, p.307; Scullard, 'Carthage and Rome', p.565 and Lazenby, *The First Punic War*, pp.153–154 discuss whether the Punic ships were undermanned. Yet this question is futile, considering that the crew on board was not the one intended for a full-scale sea battle. See Pietilä-Castrén, *Magnificentia Publica: The Victory Monuments of the Roman Generals in the Era of the Punic Wars*, pp.44–48.

159. Polybius, 1.62.1–2. Translation, C. Habicht.

160. Polybius, 1.62.7. Translation, C. Habicht. See A.M. Eckstein, *Moral Vision in The Histories of Polybius* (University of California Press, 1995), p.175.

161. Polybius, 1.62.8–1.63.3, 3.27.1–6. According to Zonaras (12.7) they also forbade them to sail past Italy or their allied territory abroad in ships of war, or to employ any mercenaries from such districts.

Chapter 4: A Short Period of Peace: The Contest for Sea Power Continues

1. H. Beck, 'The Reasons for the War', *A Companion to the Punic Wars*, pp.226–230.
2. Hoyos, *Hannibal's Dynasty*, pp.3, 62–63; Hoyos, *The Carthaginians*, p.195; J. Rich, 'The Origins of the Second Punic War', *The Second Punic War: A Reappraisal*, p.15.
3. Hoyos, *Hannibal's Dynasty*, pp.27–28.
4. Diodorus, 25.6; Livy, 21.2.1. Walbank, *A Historical Commentary on Polybius*, I, pp.148–149.
5. Polybius, 1.67.8–11. Translation, C. Habicht.
6. Polybius, 1.66–88.
7. Eckstein, *Moral Vision in the Histories of Polybius*, p.177.
8. Hoyos, *Hannibal's Dynasty*, p.36.
9. Diodorus, 14.77.
10. Polybius, 1.72.5–7.
11. Polybius, 1.71.2–6. Translation, C. Habicht.
12. Howgego, *Ancient History from Coins*, p.113.
13. Polybius, 1.73.1–2; Appian, *Punic Wars*, 5.
14. Polybius, 1.82.6. Walbank, *A Historical Commentary on Polybius*, I, p.145.
15. Polybius, 1.83.1–5. Hiero gave grain to the Romans at least twice in the inter-war period. In 237 he appeared in Rome in person with 200,000 modii of wheat. In 220, during the Celtic War he sent grain for the Roman armies, for which the Romans paid after the war.
16. See Hoyos, *Hannibal's Dynasty*, p.38; Goldsworthy, *The Punic Wars*, p.135.
17. Lancel, *Hannibal*, pp.14–16.
18. Polybius, 1.83.8–9. Translation, C. Habicht.
19. Polybius, 1.79.1–7, 1.83.11. See Lancel, *Hannibal*, pp.22–23; Walbank, *A Historical Commentary on Polybius*, I, p.144.
20. Hamilcar Barca possibly considered going to Sardinia himself or sending one of his supporters. Hoyos, *Hannibal's Dynasty*, p.48.
21. Polybius, 1.88.8–10. Translation, C. Habicht.
22. Orosius, 4.12.3; Polybius, 1.88.11–12.
23. For sources and discussion, see Walbank, *A Historical Commentary on Polybius*, I, pp.149–150; Lancel, *Hannibal*, pp.23–24.
24. Polybius, 3.28.1–2. Translation, C. Habicht.
25. G. Piccard, *Hannibal* (Paris, 1967), pp.74–76; Goldsworthy, *The Punic Wars*, p.136; Hoyos, *Hannibal's Dynasty*, pp.49–50; Harris, *War and Imperialism in Republican Rome*, pp.192–193.
26. Zonaras, 8.18; see Gellius, *Attic Nights*, 10.27.3–5.
27. Polybius, 2.12.7.
28. P. Derow, 'The Arrival of Rome: From the Illyrian Wars to the Fall of Macedon', *A Companion to the Hellenistic World*, pp.51–54.

29. L. Loreto, 'Roman Politics and Expansion, 241–219', *Companion to the Punic Wars*, p.188.
30. Polybius, 2.8; Appian, *Illyrian Wars*, 7. For the Illyrian piracy see Polybius 2.4.8–9. De Souza, *Piracy in the Graeco-Roman World*, pp.76–80.
31. Polybius, 2.9–12. *Fasti Triumphales*. For the nature of the alliances Rome made with Pharos, Issa, Epidamnos, Corcyra and Apollonia, see P. Derow, 'Pharos and Rome', *ZPE* 88 (1991), pp.261–270; Loreto, 'Roman Politics and Expansion, 241–219', pp.189–190. Derow, 'The Arrival of Rome: From the Illyrian Wars to the Fall of Macedon', p.53.
32. Polybius, 3.9.6–9, 3.10.4–6. Beck, 'The Reasons for the War', pp.230–231, 234–235. Hoyos, *Hannibal's Dynasty*, pp.98–99; P. Barceló, 'Punic Politics, Economy, and Alliances, 218–201', *A Companion to the Punic Wars*, pp.358–359.
33. Diodorus, 13.54, 19.106.
34. Diodorus, 25.10.1.
35. Cornelius Nepos, *Hamilcar*, 4.1.
36. Polybius, 2.1.9.
37. For Hamilcar's campaign, see Hoyos, *Hannibal's Dynasty*, pp.55–72; for Spain before 237, see p.246, n. 2.
38. Diodorus, 25.12; Cornelius Nepos, *Hannibal*, 3.1. There are other examples of calling a city *qart-hadasht* in Carthage's territories. Hoyos, *Hannibal's Dynasty*, pp.73–74, 79–80. For Polybius' description of New Carthage, see Polybius, 2.13.1, 10.8.1–3, 10.10. His account probably follows a literary source; he visited the city at some point but it cannot be established when. See F.W. Walbank, *A Historical Commentary on Polybius*, II (Oxford, 1967), pp.205–212.
39. Eckstein, *Mediterranean Anarchy, Interstate War, and the Rise of Rome*, p.170. Loreto states that Rome's international position had suffered during the First Punic War. Loreto, 'Roman Politics and Expansion, 241–219', pp.184–189.
40. Dio, 12, frg. 48. No other source has anything about this and the information has been doubted; see Hoyos, *Hannibal's Dynasty*, p.61. Accepting: Beck, 'The Reasons for the War', p.235; Loreto, 'Roman Politics and Expansion, 241–219', p.193; Eckstein, *Mediterranean Anarchy, Interstate War, and the Rise of Rome*, p.170.
41. Polybius, 2.13.7. Eckstein, *Mediterranean Anarchy, Interstate War, and the Rise of Rome*, pp.170–171. For the reciprocal interpretation, see Walbank, *A Historical Commentary on Polybius*, I, pp.168–172.
42. Loreto, 'Roman Politics and Expansion, 241–219', pp.194–195; Hoyos, *Hannibal's Dynasty*, pp.81–82. Hoyos dates the treaty to 225.
43. Polybius, 2.23–35. See Loreto, 'Roman Politics and Expansion, 241–219', p.197.
44. Livy, 27.22.8.

45. Crawford, *Roman Republican Coinage*, no. 35. E.S.G. Robinson, 'Punic coins of Spain and their bearing on the Roman republican series', *Essays in Roman Coinage Presented to Harold Mattingly*, eds R.A.G. Carson and C.H.V. Sutherland (Oxford, 1956), pp.34–53, coins 4a–c; www.sylloge-nummorum-graecorum.org coins SNGuk_0902_0091-93.
46. For Hasdrubal's campaign, see Hoyos, *Hannibal's Dynasty*, pp.73–86.
47. Polybius, 3.13.3–4. For a portrayal on Hannibal, see Polybius, 9.25; Livy, 21.4. Hoyos, *Hannibal's Dynasty*, pp.87–88.
48. Livy, 21.5.1–5.
49. Polybius, 3.15.5. Translation, C. Habicht.
50. Hoyos, *Hannibal's Dynasty*, pp.92–97. Polybius, 3.15; Livy's distorted version: 21.6.3–8, 21.9.3–21.11.2. The treaty with Saguntum: Polybius, 3.30.1.
51. Polybius, 3.17; *FRH* 1 F31; Beck, 'The Reasons for the War', pp.230–231.
52. Polybius, 3.20–21, 3.29–33.4.
53. See Beck, 'The Reasons for the War', p.231; Hoyos, *Hannibal's Dynasty*, p.98.
54. Polybius, 3.16, 3.18–19. For the discussion of motives of this operation and the level of Roman interest towards Illyria in the interwar period see Loreto, 'Roman Politics and Expansion', p.192; Eckstein, *Mediterranean Anarchy, Interstate War, and the Rise of Rome*, p.266; Derow, 'The Arrival of Rome: From the Illyrian Wars to the Fall of Macedon', pp.53–54.

Chapter 5: The Second Punic War, 218–201 BC: Roles Reversed
1. Barceló, 'Punic Politics, Economy, and Alliances, 218–201', p.365.
2. For the list of fleets, see Thiel, *Studies on the History of Roman Sea-Power in Republican Times*, pp.43–46; Steinby, *The Roman Republican Navy*, pp.140–141. However, due to gaps in our knowledge, the calculations cannot be precise.
3. J.J. Ferrer Maestro, 'El approvechamiento financiero de los Bárquidas en Hispania', in *Economia y finanzas del mundo fenicio-púnico de Occidente. XX Jornadas de arqueologia fenicio-púnica* (Ibiza, 2006), pp.107–126. *Non vidi*. Barceló, 'Punic Politics, Economy, and Alliances, 218–201', p.364.
4. Barceló, 'Punic Politics, Economy, and Alliances, 218–201', pp.362–363.
5. Polybius, 3.48 lists earlier attempts by the Celts.
6. Polybius, 3.33.5–18; Livy, 21.22.1–5, 28.46.16. We do not know when Polybius had visited the temple. Walbank, *A Historical Commentary on Polybius*, I, pp.364–365.
7. Polybius 3.56.3; Livy, 21.38.1. G.V. Sumner, 'The Chronology of the Outbreak of the Second Punic War', *The Proceedings of the African Classical Associations* 9 (1966), p.28; Walbank, *A Historical Commentary on Polybius*, I, p.365; Lazenby, *Hannibal's War: A Military History of the Second Punic War* (Warminster, 1978), pp.275–277. Hannibal left Spain with 90,000 infantry, 12,000 cavalry and 37 elephants; 38,000 infantry and 8,000 cavalry crossed the Rhône. He arrived in Italy with 20,000 infantry and 6,000 cavalry and a few

elephants. The numbers on the departure have been questioned for being too high; they were probably between 60,000 and 70,000. The losses on the route over the Alps can be explained not only in casualties but many of the newly-recruited soldiers deserted. Polybius has taken the figures on the arrival from the inscription at Lacinia. Polybius, 3.35.1, 3.56.3–4; Appian, *Hannibal*, 1.4–2.5. See Hoyos, *Hannibal's Dynasty*, pp.103–107; Lancel, *Hannibal*, p.60; Barceló, 'Punic Politics, Economy, and Alliances, 218–201', p.364.

8. Polybius, 3.41.4–9; Livy, 21.26.3–5. Walbank, *A Historical Commentary on Polybius*, I, p.377.

9. Polybius, 3.49.1–4, 3.56.5. Livy states that Scipio returned to Genua and Pisa 21.32.1–5, 21.39.3; and Appian that he returned to Etruria. Appian, *Wars in Spain*, 3.14.

10. Livy, 21.60.1–3. Translation, B.O. Foster.

11. Livy, 21.61.2–4. Translation, B.O. Foster. With some adaptations by the author.

12. Polybius, 3.96.3. Translation, C. Habicht. In Panormus in 250, the fugitives from the Carthaginian army had rushed to ships to escape the Romans. Zonaras, 8.15.

13. Polybius, 3.95–96.6; Livy, 22.19–22.20.1–3. We do not know what source Polybius used for this. Livy's account contains both Polybian and non-Polybian material. He probably used Coelius, who used the same source as Polybius, possibly Silenus. The information given by Frontinus and Dio is suspect. See Thiel, *Studies on the History of Roman Sea-Power in Republican Times*, pp.50–51; Walbank, *A Historical Commentary on Polybius*, I, p.430.

14. Applied by Heracleides of Mylasa at Cape Artemision.

15. *FGrHist*, ed. F. Jacoby (Leiden, 1957–), 176 F1.

16. Livy, 22.20.4–12. See Pliny, *The Natural History* 19.26 for *spartum*.

17. Polybius, 3.97.1–2; Livy, 22.22.1–2, 23.26.1–2.

18. Livy, 23.26.2–5, 23.27.9–23.28.3.

19. Thiel, *Studies on the History of Roman Sea-Power in Republican Times*, p.51.

20. Livy, 21.49.1–5.

21. Livy, 21.49.10–13. Translation, B.O. Foster.

22. Livy, 21.50.1–6. Thiel rejected the authenticity of this battle because it did not fit with his calculations of Roman ship numbers in 218. Thiel, *Studies on the History of Roman Sea-Power in Republican Times*, pp.44–45.

23. Livy, 21.50.6–11.

24. Livy, 21.51.1–5.

25. Livy, 21.51.6–7.

26. Polybius, 3.96.8–14; Livy, 22.11.6–9, 22.31.

27. Polybius, 3.68.9–15; Livy, 21.51.7. See Lazenby, *Hannibal's War*, pp.55–56.

28. Hoyos, *Hannibal's Dynasty*, pp.114–115.

29. Polybius, 3.86.8, 3.87.4–5.

30. Hoyos sees the failure of the Punic fleet to link up with Hannibal at Pisa as a lost opportunity to blockade Rome by land and sea. Walbank and Goldsworthy find the attack implausible. Hoyos, *Hannibal's Dynasty*, p.116; Walbank, *A Historical Commentary on Polybius*, I, p.421; Goldsworthy, *The Punic Wars*, pp.215–216.

31. Livy, 22.11.4. Translation, B.O. Foster.

32. Appian, *Hannibalic War*, 17.

33. Livy, 23.21.1–6, 23.32.9.

34. Livy, 22.37.

35. Garnsey, *Famine and Food Supply in the Graeco-Roman World*, p.185.

36. Polybius, 3.107–117; Livy, 22.40.5–22.50. For the Battle of Cannae, see Goldsworthy, *The Punic Wars*, pp.198–214; Walbank, *A Historical Commentary on Polybius*, I, pp.435–441; Hoyos, *Hannibal's Dynasty*, pp.118–119; Lazenby, *Hannibal's War*, pp.77–85.

37. Livy, 22.58.2. The clauses of the treaty Hannibal made with Philip in 215 indicate Hannibal's limited war aims. Walbank, *A Historical Commentary on Polybius*, II, p.44; Lancel, *Hannibal*, p.118; Barceló, 'Punic Politics, Economy, and Alliances, 218–201', p.368.

38. Goldsworthy, *The Punic Wars* (London, 2000), p.217.

39. Livy, 22.58.

40. Livy, 22.57.5, 23.11.1–6.

41. Livy, 22.57.12. Translation, B.O. Foster.

42. Barceló, 'Punic Politics, Economy, and Alliances, 218–201', p.367.

43. Livy, 23.7.1–2. Translation, Frank Gardner Moore.

44. Livy, 22.56.6–8.

45. Livy, 23.11.7–23.13.

46. Livy, 23.32.8–10.

47. Livy, 23.32.12, 23.34.10–17, 23.40–41.8–9.

48. Livy, 23.30.8, 24.1.

49. Livy, 24.1.13. Translation, Frank Gardner Moore.

50. Livy, 23.41.10–12.

51. Livy, 23.32.16–18.

52. Livy, 23.28.7–23.29, 23.32.5–7.

53. This is the same temple where Polybius found the inscription concerning Carthaginian troops. We do not know whether these three men had been with Hannibal from the beginning or whether they had arrived to participate in negotiations. See Lancel, *Hannibal*, p.117.

54. Livy, 23.33–34.9, 23.38.1–5.

55. Polybius, 7.9. Livy's text is not credible. Livy, 23.33.10–12. Lancel, *Hannibal*, p.117.

56. Polybius, 7.9.12–14. Translation, W.R. Paton.

57. Walbank, *A Historical Commentary on Polybius*, II, p.44. See Thiel, *Studies on the History of Roman Sea-Power in Republican Times*, p.68; M. Holleaux, *Rome, La Grèce et les monarchies Hellénistiques au IIIe siècle avant J.-C (273–205)*, p.186; Errington, 'Rome and Greece to 205 BC', *CAH* VIII, pp.96–97; E. Gruen, *The Hellenistic World and the Coming of Rome*, vol. II (Berkeley, 1984), p.376; Badian, *Foreign Clientelae (264–70 BC)*, p.56; Barceló, 'Punic Politics, Economy, and Alliances, 218–201', pp.367–368.

58. N.G.L. Hammond and F.W. Walbank, *A History of Macedonia*, vol. III (Oxford, 1988), p.394.

59. Morton, *The Role of the Physical Environment in Ancient Greek Seafaring*, pp.171–172.

60. Livy, 23.38.7–10.

61. Polybius, 7.2–5, 7.7–8; Livy, 23.30.10–12, 24.4–6. Walbank, *A Historical Commentary on Polybius*, II, pp.31–36; Lancel, *Hannibal*, p.118.

62. P. Erdkamp, *Hunger and the Sword: Warfare and Food Supply in Roman Republican Wars 264–30 BC* (Amsterdam, 1998), pp.166–168. Hiero had sent 200,000 modii of wheat and 100,000 modii of barley in 215. Livy, 23.38.13.

63. Polybius, 8.3–7; Livy, 24.11.6–9, 24.34–39; Plutarch, *Marcellus*, 15–17.

64. Polybius, 8.37; Livy, 25.23–24.

65. Livy, 25.25.11–13. Translation, Frank Gardner Moore.

66. Livy, 25.26.

67. Livy, 25.27.6–8. Translation, Frank Gardner Moore.

68. Livy, 25.27.11–12. Translation, Frank Gardner Moore.

69. Livy, 25.31.13–15.

70. Thiel, *Studies on the History of Roman Sea-Power in Republican Times*, p.85.

71. Livy, 26.20.7–9. Translation, Frank Gardner Moore.

72. Polybius, 9.9.11. Translation, W.R. Paton. See Walbank, *A Historical Commentary on Polybius*, II, pp.133–134.

73. Livy, 25.40–41.8, 26.21, 26.40.

74. Livy, 26.21.10–14, 27.5.7–8.

75. Livy, 26.21.7–9. Translation, Frank Gardner Moore.

76. M. McDonnell, 'Roman aesthetics and the spoils of Syracuse', *Representations of War in Ancient Rome*, eds S. Dillon and K.E. Welch (Cambridge, 2006), pp.69–90; Pietilä-Castrén, *Magnificentia Publica: The Victory Monuments of the Roman Generals in the Era of the Punic Wars*, pp.56–58.

77. See Crawford, *Roman Republican Coinage*, pp.33, 634–635.

78. For a full discussion of events at sea, see Thiel, *Studies on the History of Roman Sea-Power in Republican Times*, pp.100–104, 115–116, 128–130, 135–139; Morrison and Coates, *Greek and Roman Oared Warships 399–30 BC*, pp.68–73; Steinby, *The Roman Republican Navy*, pp.143–156.

79. Polybius, 5.109.1–4.

80. Polybius, 5.109.2. Translation, W.R. Paton.

81. Polybius, 5.109.5–5.110.11.
82. Livy, 24.40.
83. Polybius, 8.13–14. Hammond and Walbank, *A History of Macedonia*, pp.398–399.
84. Livy, 26.24. For the nature of Aetolian sea power, see De Souza, *Piracy in the Graeco-Roman World*, pp.70–76. Conquered territory and buildings would belong to the Aetolians; all the rest of the booty would go to the Roman people.
85. See Livy, 31.45.6–7, 31.46.16.
86. Livy, 27.15.7. Hammond sees this cooperation as Livy's fantasy. Hammond and Walbank, *A History of Macedonia*, p.403. Thiel and Walbank take it as real. Thiel, *Studies on the History of Roman Sea-Power in Republican Times*, pp.121–122; F.W. Walbank, *Polybius, Rome and the Hellenistic World: Essays and Reflections* (Cambridge, 2002), pp.118–119.
87. Livy, 28.7.17–18, 28.8.8.
88. Livy, 28.8.14.
89. The peace treaty: parties to the agreement on the Roman side: the Ilians near the Hellespont, Attalus of Pergamum, Pleuratos of Illyria, Nabis of Sparta and the people of Elis, Messenia and Athens. On the side of Philip: Prusias of Bithynia, the Achaeans, the Boeotians, the Thessalians, the Acarnanians and the Epirots. Livy, 29.12.8–16.
90. Livy, 29.11.1–8.
91. Livy, 23.48.4–5.
92. Livy, 23.48.8–23.49.4.
93. Livy, 25.3.7–25.4.
94. Livy, 25.3.10–11. Translation, Frank Gardner Moore.
95. Appian, *Wars in Spain*, 15.
96. Livy, 25.32–36. Masinissa commanded the Numidian cavalry against Publius Cornelius Scipio.
97. Livy, 26.17.1–2. Beaching ships after a voyage was a standard procedure needed to preserve the ships in good condition; it was not a sign of the Roman 'land-lubberist' character, as Thiel sees it. See Thiel, *Studies on the History of Roman Sea-Power in Republican Times*, pp.70, 107.
98. Livy, 26.18.1–19.10. Goldsworthy, *The Punic Wars*, p.271.
99. See Eckstein, *Moral Vision in the Histories of Polybius*, pp.178–181.
100. Polybius, 10.11–17; Livy, 26.41–47. The Roman cruelty was not exceptional; Polybius writes about similar scenes elsewhere and committed by other states but what took his attention was the highly-organized manner in which the looting took place, a Roman characteristic that gave them advantage in interstate competition. See Eckstein, *Mediterranean Anarchy, Interstate War, and the Rise of Rome*, pp.203–205.
101. Livy, 26.48.5–14.
102. Polybius, 10.20.
103. Polybius, 10.38.7–39.9.

104. For the Battle of Ilipa, see Lazenby, *Hannibal's War*, pp.145–150; Goldsworthy, *The Punic Wars*, pp.279–284.
105. Polybius, 11.20–33; Livy, 28.12–16, 28.24.2–28.29, 28.35.
106. Livy, 28.23.6–8, 28.30.4–12.
107. Livy, 28.36.
108. Livy, 27.5.11–13. Translation, Frank Gardner Moore.
109. Livy, 27.5.
110. Livy, 27.6.13–14.
111. Livy, 26.39.
112. Livy, 26.39.4–7. Translation, Frank Gardner Moore.
113. Livy, 27.15.5–7. Translation, Frank Gardner Moore. See also Livy, 27.30.16.
114. Livy, 27.15.9–27.16.16.
115. Livy, 27.9–10. The following colonies refused to supply troops: Ardea, Nepete, Sutrium, Alba, Carseoli, Sora, Suessa, Circeii, Setia, Cales, Narnia, Interamna. The following colonies kept supporting the war effort: Signia, Norba, Saticulum, Brundisium, Fregellae, Luceria, Venusia, Hadria, Firma, Ariminum, Pontia, Paestum and Cosa; and in the inland parts, Beneventum, Aesernia, Spoletum, Placentia and Cremona. For discussion, see Bispham, '*Coloniam deducere*: How Roman was Roman colonization during the middle republic?', pp.82–83.
116. Livy, 27.22.8–12.
117. Livy, 27.29.7–8. Translation, Frank Gardner Moore.
118. Thiel, *Studies on the History of Roman Sea-Power in Republican Times*, pp.131, 135; Briscoe, 'The Second Punic War', p.67.
119. Livy, 28.4.5–7.
120. Livy, 27.43.
121. Lazenby, *Hannibal's War*, pp.184–186; Hoyos, *Hannibal's Dynasty*, pp.147–148.
122. Livy, 27.38.6–7. Translation, Frank Gardner Moore.
123. Livy, 27.38.
124. For the Battle of Metaurus, see Lazenby, *Hannibal's War*, pp.182–190; Goldsworthy, *The Punic Wars*, pp.238–243.
125. Livy, 28.38.5–6.
126. Livy, 28.40–42.
127. Livy, 28.39.1, 28.45.8–12; Appian, *The Punic Wars*, 7.
128. Lazenby, *Hannibal's War*, pp.194–195.
129. Livy, 28.46.7–10.
130. Livy, 28.46.14.
131. Appian, *Hannibalic War*, 8.54.
132. This authorization is almost identical to that given to Marcus Valerius Laevinus in 208.
133. See Crawford, *Roman Republican Coinage*, p.33.
134. Livy, 28.45.15–21. Translation, Frank Gardner Moore.

135. Thiel, *Studies on the History of Roman Sea-Power in Republican Times*, p.147.
136. Livy, 28.10.4–5.
137. Livy, 29.36.9–12. See also Livy, 27.24, 30.26.12.
138. Livy, 29.1.1–14, 29.3.7–8.
139. Livy, 29.4.4–6; Appian, *Punic Wars*, 9.
140. Livy, 29.16.4–29.22.
141. Livy, 29.25.1–2; Appian, *Punic Wars*, 13. Lazenby, *Hannibal's War*, p.203; Goldsworthy, *The Punic Wars*, p.287.
142. Livy, 29.27.6–15.
143. Livy, 29.28–33.
144. Lazenby, *Hannibal's War*, p.206; Goldsworthy, *The Punic Wars*, p.294.
145. Polybius, 14.2.1–14.6.5; Livy, 29.34–36.1–3, 30.3–6; Appian, *Punic Wars*, 16–23.
146. Livy, 30.2.1–5.
147. Polybius, 14.10; Livy, 30.9.7–30.10.
148. Livy, 30.11.1–30.15.14, 30.17.12.
149. Polybius, 15.1.2–4; Livy, 30.16.3–14, 30.21.11–30.23.8.
150. Livy, 30.20.5–6, 30.25.11–12; Appian, *Punic Wars*, 31, *Hannibalic War*, 58. Thiel, *Studies on the History of Roman Sea-Power in Republican Times*, pp.170–171; Lazenby, *Hannibal's War*, p.215.
151. Livy, 30.19.1–6.
152. Livy, 30.24.5–12.
153. The Roman quinquereme was attacked by three Carthaginian triremes. Polybius, 15.1–2. Livy, 30.25.1–8 speaks of three Carthaginian quadriremes. Diodorus, 27.11–12; Appian, *Punic Wars*, 34.
154. Polybius, 15.9–14. For the Battle of Zama, see Lazenby, *Hannibal's War*, pp.219–225; Goldsworthy, *The Punic Wars*, pp.300–307.
155. Polybius, 15.18. Translation, W.R. Paton (with some adaptations by the author). See Appian, *Punic Wars*, 59. Walbank, *A Historical Commentary on Polybius*, II, pp.466–471.
156. Livy, 30.43.11–12. Translation, Frank Gardner Moore. The figure probably included transport ships.

Chapter 6: Rome and Carthage after the Second Punic War: The Last Fifty Years of the Punic State

1. See R.M. Errington, 'Rome against Philip and Antiochus', *CAH* VIII, pp.252–255; J. Ma, *Antiochus III and the Cities of Western Asia Minor* (Oxford, 1999), pp.74–76; Eckstein, *Mediterranean Anarchy, Interstate War, and the Rise of Rome*, pp.181–186, 259–261.
2. For a full discussion of events at sea, see Thiel, *Studies on the History of Roman Sea-Power in Republican Times*, pp.202–255; Morrison and Coates, *Greek and*

Roman Oared Warships 399–30 BC, pp.87–91; Steinby, *The Roman Republican Navy*, pp.156–170.

3. Polybius, 16.27. See Derow, 'The Arrival of Rome: from the Illyrian Wars to the Fall of Macedon', pp.59–60.

4. These were Euromus, Pedasa, Bargylia, Iasus, Abydus, Thasos, Myrina and Perinthus. Polybius, 18.44–48; Livy, 33.30.

5. See R.M. Errington, 'Rome against Philip and Antiochus', *CAH* VIII, p.273.

6. Livy, 34.35. For the tendency in Roman historiography to use the charge of piracy to discredit Nabis, see De Souza, *Piracy in the Graeco-Roman World*, pp.84–86.

7. For a full discussion of events at sea, see Thiel, *Studies on the History of Roman Sea-Power in Republican Times*, pp.255–372; Morrison and Coates, *Greek and Roman Oared Warships 399–30 BC*, pp.93–109; Steinby, *The Roman Republican Navy*, pp.171–196.

8. See Livy 37.23–24 for the Battle of Side where the Rhodians defeated Hannibal.

9. Livy, 37.30; Appian, *Syrian Wars*, 27. *Fasti Triumphales*. For Aemilius's triumph and temple-building, see Pietilä-Castrén, *Magnificentia Publica*, pp.91–94.

10. Polybius, 21.42; Livy, 38.38. Both texts are faulty on the naval clause and have been amended. Walbank, *A Historical Commentary on Polybius*, III, pp.159–160.

11. Goldsworthy, *The Punic Wars*, p.319.

12. See Derow, 'The Arrival of Rome: From the Illyrian Wars to the Fall of Macedon', pp.66–67; P. Derow, 'Polybius and the Embassy of Kallikrates', *Essays Presented to C.M. Bowra* (Oxford, 1970), pp.12–23.

13. For a full discussion of events at sea, see Thiel, *Studies on the History of Roman Sea-Power in Republican Times*, pp.372–415; Morrison and Coates, *Greek and Roman Oared Warships 399–30 BC*, pp.109–112; Steinby, *The Roman Republican Navy*, pp.197–206.

14. There were 2 Carthaginian quinqueremes, 2 triremes from Heraclea Pontica, 4 triremes from Chalcedon, 4 triremes from Samos and 5 quadriremes from Rhodes. Livy, 42.56.6–7.

15. Livy, 45.29.4–14.

16. *Fasti Triumphales*. The fleet participated in the Battle of Pydna that ended the war. See Pietilä-Castrén, *Magnificentia Publica*, pp.118–123. See Dart and Vervaet, for the timing of Octavius's triumph a day after the three-day triumph of his supreme commander Paullus. 'The Significance of the Naval Triumph in Roman History (260–29 BCE)', p.275.

17. Livy, 45.33.5–6. Translation, Rev. Canon Roberts.

18. Livy, 45.35.3. Translation, Rev. Canon Roberts.

19. Livy, 45.40.1. Crawford, *Roman Republican Coinage*, p.635.

20. See Pietilä-Castrén, *Magnificentia Publica*, pp.139–144.

21. Livy, 37.9.2–3, 37.19.1–6.
22. Livy, 43.4.6–13, 43.7.5–11.
23. Goldsworthy, *The Punic Wars*, p.320.
24. Livy, 44.20.
25. Hoyos, *Hannibal's Dynasty*, p.185; C. Kunze, 'Carthage and Numidia, 210–149 BC', *A Companion to the Punic Wars*, pp.400–403.
26. Livy, 31.11.4–18. Quote Livy, 31.11.12. Translation, E.T. Sage.
27. See Hoyos, *Hannibal's Dynasty*, pp.181–182.
28. Livy, 33.46.9.
29. Livy, 33.47.1–2. Translation, E.T. Sage.
30. Livy, 33.47.3–33.49.7.
31. Hoyos, *Hannibal's Dynasty*, p.189.
32. After the peace of Apamea, Hannibal fled to Crete and then to Prusias. Titus Quinctius Flamininus persuaded Prusias to surrender Hannibal in 183 or 182. Hannibal took poison to avoid being taken to Rome.
33. Livy, 31.19.2, 36.4.4, 36.44–45.4, 42.56.6–7.
34. Hoyos, *The Carthaginians*, pp.212–213. For the arbitration favouring Masinissa, see Walbank, *A Historical Commentary on Polybius*, III, pp.653–654.
35. Appian, *Punic Wars*, 69–73.
36. Polybius, 36.2. Translation, W.R. Paton. Appian, *Punic Wars*, 74.
37. Livy, 35.22.2.
38. Polybius, 36.3–6; Appian, *Punic Wars*, 69, 134; Plutarch, *Life of Cato the Elder*, 27. For the chronology of the events leading up to the war, see A.E. Astin, *Scipio Aemilianus* (Oxford, 1967), pp.270–272.
39. Morrison and Coates, *Greek and Roman Oared Warships 399–30 BC*, p.112.
40. H. Hurst, 'Exceptions rather than the rule: the shipshed complexes of Carthage (mainly) and Athens', *Ricoveri per navi militari nei porti del Mediterraneo antico e medievale, Atti del Workshop, Ravello, 4–5 novembre 2005*. Eds D.J. Blackman and M.C. Lentini (Bari, 2010), pp.27–29.
41. Livy, *Summary*, 47.15.
42. Y. Le Bohec, 'The "Third Punic War": The Siege of Carthage (149–146 BC)', *A Companion to the Punic Wars*, pp.431–435.
43. Le Bohec, 'The "Third Punic War": The Siege of Carthage (149–146 BC)', p.430.
44. Polybius, 36.3–6; Appian, *Punic Wars*, 75–92.
45. Appian, *Punic Wars*, 93. Translation, H. White.
46. Appian, *Punic Wars*, 94. To avoid the war, the Carthaginians had condemned to death Hasdrubal and other commanders who had conducted the campaign against Masinissa, putting the whole blame for the war upon them. Hasdrubal had then assembled a rebel army. Appian, *Punic Wars*, 74.
47. Appian, *Punic Wars*, 110.
48. Appian, *Punic Wars*, 115.

49. Appian, *Punic Wars*, 120.
50. Appian, *Punic Wars*, 96. Translation, H. White.
51. H. Hurst, 'The War Harbour of Carthage', *Atti del I Congresso di studi Fenici a Punici*, vol. II (Rome, 1983), pp.603–610; Lancel, *Carthage: A History*, pp.180–182.
52. Appian, *Punic Wars*, 121–123.
53. Appian, *Punic Wars*, 117–135; Polybius, 38.19–22. See Pietilä-Castrén, *Magnificentia Publica: The Victory Monuments of the Roman Generals in the Era of the Punic Wars*, pp.134–138.

Bibliography

Translations of the ancient texts are available in Loeb and Penguin series.

Abbreviations
CAH = *The Cambridge Ancient History*
CIL = *Corpus Inscriptionum Latinarum* (Berlin, 1863–)
CQ = *Classical Quarterly*
FGrHist = *Die Fragmente der Griechischen Historiker*, ed. Jacoby, E. (Leiden, 1957–)
FRH = *Die Frühen Römischen Historiker*
IG = *Inscriptiones Graecae*
Ined. Vat. = *Ineditum Vaticanum*
Inscr. Ital. = *Inscriptiones Italiae*
JAOS = *Journal of the American Oriental Society*
JHS = *Journal of Hellenic Studies*
JRS = *Journal of Roman Studies*
LTUR = *Lexicon Topographicum Urbis Romae*, ed. Steinby, E.M. vols. I-VI (Rome, 1993–2000)
MEFR = *Mélanges d'archéologie et d'histoire de l'École Française de Rome*
OCD = *The Oxford Classical Dictionary*, 3rd ed. (Oxford, 1996)
RIN = *Rivista Italiana di Numismatica*
SEG = *Supplementum Epigraphicum Graecum* (Leiden, 1923–)
TAPA = *Transactions and Proceedings of the American Philological Association*
ZPE = *Zeitschrift für Papyrologie und Epigraphik*

Acquaro, E., 'Sardegna', in *I Fenici*, ed. Moscati, S. (Milan, 1988)
Andrewes, A., 'The peace of Nicias and the Sicilian expedition', *CAH* V, 2nd ed. (Cambridge, 1992)
Asheri, D., 'Carthaginians and Greeks', *CAH* IV, 2nd ed. (Cambridge, 1988)
Asheri, D., 'Sicily, 478–431', *CAH* V, 2nd ed. (Cambridge, 1992)
Astin, A.E., *Scipio Aemilianus* (Oxford, 1967)
Aubet, M., *The Phoenicians and the West: Politics, Colonies and Trade*, 2nd ed. (Cambridge, 2001)
Badian, E., *Foreign Clientelae (264–70 BC)* (Oxford, 1958)
Barceló, P., 'Punic Politics, Economy, and Alliances, 218–201', *A Companion to the Punic Wars*, ed. Hoyos, D. (Blackwell, 2011)

Beaumont, R.L., 'The date of the first treaty between Rome and Carthage', *JRS* 29 (1939)

Beck, H., 'The Reasons for the War', *A Companion to the Punic Wars*, ed. Hoyos, D. (Blackwell, 2011)

Beloch, J., 'Zur Geschichte des pyrrhischen Krieges', *Klio* 1 (1901)

Bispham, E., '*Coloniam deducere*: How Roman was Roman colonization during the middle republic?', *Greek and Roman Colonization*, eds Bradley, G. and Wilson, J-P. (Cardiff, 2006)

Bleckmann, B., 'Roman Politics in the First Punic War', *A Companion to the Punic Wars*, ed. Hoyos, D. (Blackwell, 2011)

Bresson, A., 'Grain from Cyrene', *The Economies of Hellenistic Societies, Third to First Centuries BC*, eds Archibald, Z.H., Davies, J.K. and Gabrielsen, V. (Oxford, 2011)

Briscoe, J., 'The Second Punic War', *CAH* VIII, 2nd ed. (Cambridge, 1989)

Brunt, P.A., *Italian Manpower 225 BC–AD 14* (Oxford, 1971)

Buccellato, C., and Tusa, S., 'Il Rostro', *Il Museo Regionale 'A. Pepoli' di Trapani, Le collezioni archeologiche*, ed. Famá, F.L. (Bari, 2009)

Cary, M., 'The early treaties with Tarentum and Rhodes', *Journal of Philology* 35 (1920)

Càssola, F., *I gruppi politici Romani nel III secolo A.C.* (Trieste, 1962)

Casson, L., *Ships and Seamanship in the Ancient World* (New Jersey, 1971)

Casson, L., *The Ancient Mariners*, 2nd ed. (Princeton, New Jersey, 1991)

Casson L., and Linder, E., 'The evolution in shape of the ancient ram', *The Athlit Ram*, eds Casson, L. and Steffy, J.R. (Texas University Press, 1991)

Caven, B., *The Punic Wars* (New York, 1980)

Clemente, G., *Guida alla storia Romana* (Mondadori, 1977)

Coarelli, F., *Il Foro Boario* (Rome, 1988)

Coarelli, F., *Il Campo Marzio dalle origini alla fine della Repubblica* (Rome, 1997)

Cornell, T.J., 'Rome and Latium to 390 BC', *CAH* VII 2, 2nd ed. (Cambridge, 1989)

Cornell, T.J., *The Beginnings of Rome: Italy and Rome from the Bronze Age to the Punic Wars (c. 1000–26 BC)* (London, 1995)

Crawford, M., *Roman Republican Coinage*, vols. I-II (Cambridge, 1974)

Cristofani, M., *Gli Etruschi del Mare* (Milan, 1983)

Dart, C.J., and Vervaet, F.J., 'The Significance of the Naval Triumph in Roman History (260–29 BCE)', *ZPE* 176 (2011)

Davies, J.K., 'Cultural, social and economic features of the Hellenistic world', *CAH* VII, part 1 (Cambridge, 1984)

Derow, P., 'Polybius and the Embassy of Kallikrates', *Essays Presented to C.M. Bowra* (Oxford, 1970)

Derow, P, 'Pharos and Rome', *ZPE* 88 (1991)

Derow, P., 'The Arrival of Rome: From the Illyrian Wars to the Fall of Macedon', *A Companion to the Hellenistic World*, ed. Erskine, A. (Oxford, 2003)

Dietler, M., 'The iron age in the western Mediterranean', *The Cambridge Economic History of the Greco-Roman World*, eds Scheidel, W., Morris, I. and Saller, R. (Cambridge, 2007)

Eckstein, A.M., *Senate and General: Individual Decision-Making and Roman Foreign Relations, 264–194 B.C.* (Berkeley, University of California Press, 1987)

Eckstein, A.M., *Moral Vision in The Histories of Polybius* (University of California Press, 1995)

Eckstein, A.M., *Mediterranean Anarchy, Interstate War, and the Rise of Rome* (University of California Press, 2006)

Erdkamp, P., *Hunger and the Sword: Warfare and Food Supply in Roman Republican Wars 264–30 BC* (Amsterdam, 1998)

Errington, R.M., 'Rome against Philip and Antiochus', *CAH* VIII, 2nd ed. (Cambridge, 1989)

Errington, R.M., 'Rome and Greece to 205 BC', *CAH* VIII 2nd ed. (Cambridge, 1989)

Feeney, D., *Caesar's Calendar, Ancient Time and the Beginnings of History* (University of California Press, 2007)

Ferrer Maestro, J.J., 'El approvechamiento financiero de los Bárquidas en Hispania', *Economia y finanzas del mundo fenicio-púnico de Occidente. XX Jornadas de arqueologia fenicio-púnica* (Ibiza, 2006)

Forsythe, G., 'The Army and Centuriate Organization in Early Rome', *A Companion to the Roman Army*, ed. Erdkamp, P. (Blackwell Publishing, 2007)

Frank, T., *An Economic Survey of Ancient Rome*, vol. I (New Jersey, 1959)

Franke, P.R., 'Pyrrhus', *CAH* VII 2, 2nd ed. (Cambridge, 1989)

Frederiksen, M., *Campania* (Rome, 1984)

Gabrielsen, V., *Financing the Athenian Fleet, Public Taxation and Social Relations* (London, 1994)

Gabrielsen, V., 'Piracy and the Slave-Trade', *A Companion to the Hellenistic World*, ed. Erskine, A. (Oxford, 2003)

Garbini, G., 'The Phoenicians in the Western Mediterranean (through to the Fifth Century BC)', *The Western Greeks: Classical Civilization in the Western Mediterranean*, ed. Pugliese Carratelli, G. (London, 1996)

Garnsey, P., *Famine and Food Supply in the Graeco-Roman World: Responses to Risk and Crisis* (Cambridge, 1988)

Goldsworthy, A., *The Punic Wars* (London, 2000)

Green, P., *Armada from Athens* (London, 1971)

Gruen, E., *The Hellenistic World and the Coming of Rome*, vol. II (Berkeley, 1984)

Günther, L-M., 'Die karthagische Aristokratie und ihre Überseepolitik im 6. und 5. Jh. v. Chr.', *Klio* 75 (1993)

Hammond, N.G.L. and Walbank, F.W., *A History of Macedonia*, vol. III (Oxford, 1988)

Harris, W.V., 'The Development of the Quaestorship, 267–81 BC', *CQ* 26 (1976)

Harris, W.V., *War and Imperialism in Republican Rome 327–70 BC* (Oxford, 1979)

Harris, W.V., 'Quando e come l'Italia divenne per la prima volta Italia? Un saggio sulla politica dell'identità', *Studi Storici* 48 (2007)

Heurgon, J., *The Rise of Rome to 264 BC*, translated by Willis, J. (London, 1973)

Holleaux, M., *Rome, la Grèce et les monarchies hellenistiques au IIIe siècle avant J.-C. (273–205)* (Paris, 1921)

Holloway, R.R., *The Archaeology of Early Rome and Latium* (London, 1994)

Horden, P. and Purcell, N., *The Corrupting Sea: A Study of Mediterranean History* (Oxford, 2000)

Howgego, C., *Ancient History from Coins* (Routledge, 1995)

Hoyos, B.D., *Unplanned Wars: The Origins of the First and Second Punic Wars* (Berlin, 1998)

Hoyos, D., *Hannibal's Dynasty, Power and Politics in the Western Mediterranean, 247–183 BC* (Routledge, 2003)

Hoyos, D., *The Carthaginians* (Routledge, 2010)

Humphreys, S.C., *Anthropology and the Greeks* (London, 1978)

Hurst, H., 'The War Harbour of Carthage', *Atti del I Congresso di studi Fenici a Punici*, vol. II (Rome, 1983)

Hurst, H., 'Exceptions rather than the rule: the shipshed complexes of Carthage (mainly) and Athens', *Ricoveri per navi militari nei porti del Mediterraneo antico e medievale, Atti del Workshop, Ravello, 4–5 novembre 2005*. Eds Blackman, D.J. and Lentini, M.C. (Bari, 2010)

Huss, W., *Geschichte der Karthager* (Munich, 1985)

Jordan, B., *The Athenian Navy in the Classical Period: A Study of Athenian Naval Administration and Military Organization in the Fifth and Fourth Centuries BC* (Berkeley, University of California Press, University of California Publications, Classical studies), vol. 13 (1975)

Kagan, D., *The Peace of Nicias and the Sicilian Expedition* (Cornell University Press, 1981)

Kondratieff, E., 'The Column and Coinage of C. Duilius: Innovations in Iconography in Large and Small Media in the Middle Republic', *Scripta Israelica Classica*, vol. XXIII (2004)

Kontorini, V., 'Rome et Rhodes au tournant du IIIe siècle av. J.-C. d'après une inscription inédite de Rhodes', *JRS* 103 (1983)

Kunze, C., 'Carthage and Numidia, 210–149 BC', *A Companion to the Punic Wars*

Lancel, S., *Carthage: A History*, translated by Nevill, A. (Oxford, 1995)

Lancel, S., *Hannibal*, translated by Nevill, A. (Oxford, 1998)

Lazenby, J.F., *Hannibal's War: A Military History of the Second Punic War* (Warminster, 1978)

Lazenby, J.F., *The First Punic War* (London, 1996)

Le Bohec, Y., 'The "Third Punic War": The Siege of Carthage (149–146 BC)', *A Companion to the Punic Wars*

Lejeune, M., Pouilloux, J. and Solier, Y., 'Étrusque et ionien archaïques sur un plomb de Pech Maho (Aude)', in *Revue Archéologique de Narbonnaise* 21 (1988)

Lepore, E., *Storia di Napoli* (Naples, 1967)

Loreto, L., 'Roman Politics and Expansion, 241–219', *A Companion to the Punic Wars*, ed. Hoyos, D. (Blackwell, 2011)

Ma, J., *Antiochus III and the Cities of Western Asia Minor* (Oxford, 1999)

Mazzarino, S., *Il pensiero storico classico*, vol. I (Bari, 1966)

McDonnell, M., 'Roman aesthetics and the spoils of Syracuse', *Representations of War in Ancient Rome*, eds Dillon, S. and Welch, K.E. (Cambridge, 2006)

Meiggs, R., *Trees and Timber in the Ancient Mediterranean World* (Oxford, 1982)

Meiggs, R., *Roman Ostia*, 2nd ed. (Oxford, 1997)

Van De Mieroop, M., *A History of the Ancient Near East ca. 3000–323 BC*, 2nd ed. (Blackwell, 2007)

Mitchell, R.E., 'Roman-Carthaginian treaties: 306 and 279/8 BC', *Historia* 20 (1971)

Momigliano, A., 'Terra Marique', *JRS* 32 (1942)

Morel, J-P., 'L'atelier des petites estampilles', *MEFR* 81 (1969)

Morel, J-P., 'La Ceramica di Roma nei secoli IV e III a.C.', *Roma medio repubblicana, Aspetti culturali di Roma e del Lazio nei secoli IV e III a.C.* (Rome, 1973)

Morel, J-P., 'The Transformation of Italy, 300–133 BC, The Evidence of Archaeology', *CAH* VIII, 2nd ed. (Cambridge, 1989)

Morel, J-P., 'Early Rome and Italy', *The Cambridge Economic History of the Greco-Roman World*, eds Scheidel, W., Morris, I. and Saller, R. (Cambridge, 2007)

Moret, P., 'Mastia Tarseion y el problema geográfico del segundo tratado entre Cartago y Roma', *Mainake* 24 (2002)

Morrison, J.S. and Williams, R.T., *Greek Oared Ships 900–322 BC* (Cambridge, 1968)

Morrison, J.S. and Coates, J.F., *Greek and Roman Oared Warships 399–30 BC* (Oxford, 1996)

Morrison, J.S., Coates, J.F. and Rankov, N.B., *The Athenian Trireme*, 2nd ed. (Cambridge, 2000)

Morton, J., *The Role of the Physical Environment in Ancient Greek Seafaring, Mnemosyne Supplementum* (Leiden, 2001)

Moscati, S., 'La colonizzazione mediterranea', *I Fenici* (Milan, 1988)

Neatby, L.H., 'Romano-Egyptian Relations During the Third Century BC', *TAPA* 81 (1950)

Ogilvie, R.M., *A Commentary on Livy, books 1–5* (Oxford, 1965)

Ogilvie, R.M., *Early Rome and the Etruscans* (London, 1983)

Pallottino, M., *A History of Earliest Italy*, translated by Ryle, M. and Soper, K. (London, 1991)

Patterson, J.R., 'Colonization and Historiography: The Roman Republic', *Greek and Roman Colonization*, eds Bradley, G. and Wilson, J-P. (Cardiff, 2006)

Piccard, G., *Hannibal* (Paris, 1967)

Pietilä-Castrén, L., *Magnificentia Publica: The Victory Monuments of the Roman Generals in the Era of the Punic Wars* (Helsinki, 1987)

Pitassi, M., *The Navies of Rome* (Boydell Press, 2009)

Platner, S.B. and Ashby, T., *A Topographical Dictionary of Ancient Rome* (Oxford, 1929)

Pugliese Carratelli, G., 'An Outline of the Political History of the Greeks in the West', in *The Western Greeks: Classical Civilization in the Western Mediterranean*, ed. Pugliese Carratelli, G. (London, 1996)

Purcell, N., 'South Italy in the fourth century BC', in *CAH* VI, 2nd ed. (Cambridge, 1994)

Rankov, B., 'The Second Punic War at Sea', *The Second Punic War: A Reappraisal*, eds Cornell, T., Rankov, B. and Sabin, P. (London, 1996)

Rankov, B., 'A War of Phases: Strategies and Stalemates 264–241 BC', *A Companion to the Punic Wars*, ed. Hoyos, D. (Blackwell, 2011)

Rhodes, P.J. and Osborne, R., *Greek Historical Inscriptions 404–323 BC* (Oxford, 2003)

Rich, J., 'The Origins of the Second Punic War', *The Second Punic War: A Reappraisal*, eds Cornell, T., Rankov, B. and Sabin, P. (London, 1996)

Richardson Jr, L., *Pompeii: An Architectural History* (Baltimore and London, 1988)

Ridgway, D., 'Relations between Cyprus and the West in the Precolonial Period', *The Western Greeks: Classical Civilization in the Western Mediterranean*, ed. Pugliese Carratelli, G. (London, 1996)

Robinson, E.S.G., 'Punic coins of Spain and their bearing on the Roman republican series', *Essays in Roman Coinage Presented to Harold Mattingly*, eds Carson, R.A.G. and Sutherland, C.H.V. (Oxford, 1956)

Roselaar, S.T., *Public Land in the Roman Republic: A Social and Economic History of Ager Publicus in Italy, 396–89 BC* (Oxford, 2010)

Rosenstein, N., *Imperatores Victi: Military Defeat and Aristocratic Competition in the Middle and Late Republic* (Berkeley, 1990)

Roth, J.P., *The Logistics of the Roman Army at War (264 BC–AD 235)* (Leiden, 1999)

Russo, F., 'Rodi e Roma tra IV e III secolo a.C.', *Considerazioni di storia ed archeologia* (2010)

Sage, M.M., *The Republican Roman Army: A Sourcebook* (Routledge, 2008)

de Sanctis, G., *Storia dei Romani*, vol. III (Rome, 1916)

Scardigli, B., *I trattati Romano-Cartaginesi* (Pisa, 1991)

Schmitt, H.H., *Rom und Rhodos* (Munich, 1957)

Schmitt, H.H., *Die Staatsverträge des Altertums*, vol. III (Munich, 1969)

Schmitz, P.C., 'The Phoenician text from the Etruscan sanctuary at Pyrgi', *JAOS* 115 (1995).

Scullard, H.H., 'Carthage and Rome', *CAH* VII 2, 2nd ed. (Cambridge, 1989)

de Souza, P., *Piracy in the Greco-Roman World* (Cambridge, 1999)

de Souza, P., 'Naval battles and sieges', *The Cambridge History of Greek and Roman Warfare*, eds Sabin, P., van Wees, H. and Whitby, M. (Cambridge, 2007) de Souza, P., 'Rome's contribution to the development of piracy', *The Maritime World of Ancient Rome*, ed. Hohlfelder, R.L. (Ann Arbor, Michigan, 2008)

Staveley, E.S., 'Rome and Italy in the early third century', *CAH* VII 2, 2nd ed. (Cambridge, 1989)

Steinby, C., 'Early Roman coins with naval types', *RIN* 106 (2005)

Steinby, C., *The Roman Republican Navy, From the Sixth Century to 167 BC* (Helsinki, 2007)

Sumner, G.V., 'The Chronology of the Outbreak of the Second Punic War', *The Proceedings of the African Classical Associations*, 9 (1966)

Tarn, W.W., 'The Fleets of the First Punic War', *JHS* 27 (1907)

Tarn, W.W., *Hellenistic Military and Naval Developments* (Cambridge, 1930)

Thiel, J.H., *Studies on the History of Roman Sea-Power in Republican Times* (Amsterdam, 1946)

Thiel, J.H., *A History of Roman Sea-Power before the Second Punic War* (Amsterdam, 1954)

Tipps, G.K., 'The battle of Ecnomus', *Historia* 34/4 (1985)

Torelli, M., 'Colonizazzioni etrusche e latine di età archaica', *Gli Etruschi e Roma* (Rome, 1981)

Torelli, M., 'Archaic Rome between Latium and Etruria', *CAH* VII part 2, 2nd ed. (Cambridge, 1989)

Tucci, P.L., '*Navalia*', *Archaeologia Classica* 57, n.s. 7 (2006)

Tusa, V., 'Sicilia', *I Fenici*, ed. Moscati, S. (Milan, 1988)

Vagnetti, L., 'The First Contacts between the Minoan-Mycenaean and the Western Mediterranean Worlds', *The Western Greeks: Classical Civilization in the Western Mediterranean*, ed. Pugliese Carratelli, G. (London, 1996)

Viereck, H.D.L., *Die Römische Flotte* (Herford, 1975)

Walbank, F.W., *A Historical Commentary on Polybius*, vols. I–III (Oxford, 1957–79)

Walbank, F.W., *Polybius, Rome and the Hellenistic World: Essays and Reflections* (Cambridge, 2002)

Wallinga, H.T., *The Boarding-Bridge of the Romans: Its Construction and its Function in the Naval Tactics of the First Punic War* (Groningen, 1956)

van Wees, H., '"Those who sail are to receive a wage": Naval warfare and finance in Archaic Eretria', *New Perspectives on Ancient Warfare*, eds Fagan, G.G. and Trundle, M. (Brill, 2010)

Williams, J.H.C. and Burnett, A., 'Alexander the Great and the Coinages of Western Greece', *Studies in Greek Numismatics in Memory of Martin Jessop Price* (London, 1998)

Zanker, P., *Augustus und die Macht der Bilder*, 2nd ed. (Munich, 1990)

Zevi, F., in *Roma medio repubblicana, Aspetti culturali di Roma e del Lazio nei secoli IV e III a.C* (Rome, 1973)

Zevi, F., 'Appunti per una storia di Ostia repubblicana', *MEFR* 114.1 (2002)

www.sylloge-nummorum-graecorum.org

Index

(Entries that appear *passim*, such as Rome, Carthage, Italy, Sicily, Syracuse, Polybius and Livy, have been omitted.)